Turning to Jesus

Turning to Jesus

The Sociology
of Conversion in the Gospels

Scot McKnight

Westminster John Knox Press
LOUISVILLE • LONDON

Scripture quotations from the New Revised Standard Version of the Bible are copyright © 1989 by the Division of Christian Education of the National Council of the Churches of Christ in the U.S.A. and are used by permission.

Book design by Sharon Adams
Cover design by Jennifer K. Cox

First edition
Published by Westminster John Knox Press
Louisville, Kentucky

This book is printed on acid-free paper that meets the American National Standards Institute Z39.48 standard. ⊛

PRINTED IN THE UNITED STATES OF AMERICA

02 03 04 05 06 07 08 09 10 11 — 10 9 8 7 6 5 4 3 2 1

Library of Congress Cataloging-in-Publication Data is on file at the Library of Congress, Washington, D.C.

ISBN 0-664-22514-4

For my father and mother
Alex and Lois McKnight
In appreciation

Contents

Stories

Preface

I have written this book because I think the orientations to conversion in the evangelical, the Roman Catholic, and the mainline Protestant churches force each person to "tell the same story." But each person doesn't have the same story to tell. Stories of God's grace differ from person to person, so there is no reason for any church to make each person tell the same story. One example: C. S. Lewis. Claimed by evangelicals as a patron saint (we don't use that term), by Roman Catholics as close to Catholicism, and by mainline Christians as a theologian with a tolerant twist of charity, Lewis's own letters don't show that his conversion experience was what any of these three lay out as the standard and expected form of conversion. If a person chooses to sit down for a summer and read "stories of Christians," one finds the same: no two tell quite the same story. But each orientation to conversion found in these different Christian groups shuffles all oddities to the side and sanctifies only a certain ordered experience. If you are troubled by this tragic closed-mindedness, this book is for you.

To study conversion is to study stories, and to study stories is to participate in community. I wish here to record my debt to those whom I can see from my coign of vantage, my community, who have read parts or the whole of the various stages of this book. I am grateful to the encouragement and helpful discussions I have had with Sonia Bodi, Klyne Snodgrass, Jim Nelson, and David Horner, president of North Park University, and Kate Maver. Former students who asked me questions and led me to rethink statements are Matthew C. Williams and Garry Poole (and his close associate Mark Ashton). A former student, Bruce Fisk, also invited me to give the Erasmus Lecture at Westmont College, and there I was able to present a few ideas of this book. I am grateful to Bruce for the congenial discussions that took place after the lecture and over dinner that evening with faculty members. A friend, Rainder Van Til, who may be the only theological book editor who also writes baseball books, read through the manuscript and made suggestions.

I received encouragement from scholars who have also worked on this topic, including especially Ben Witherup, Beverly Gaventa, and Marc Borg. None of these can be asked to shoulder any of the weight of my thoughts, though I am indebted to them. I owe an especial thanks to students of my Ethics of Jesus classes who, over the years, have asked me questions about conversion and who are given the option of writing a paper on their conversion stories. Three students went out of their way, as students can do, to call into question some of my thoughts, and I owe to them special appreciation: Elanor Leskiw, Tor Erickson, and Jarek Klodzinski. Carey Newman called to inform me that the manuscript would be accepted by Westminster John Knox the day after I returned from the hospital following shoulder surgery. What was otherwise a bleak and dreary day became for a few moments a joyous occasion. I am grateful to him for his expert handling of this study. I remain grateful to editors like Daniel Braden who saved me from disasters by looking after this manuscript.

Finally I wish to express my appreciation to my family and especially my love to my wife, Kristen, whose own work in psychology energizes my studies. In our daily walks around Butler Lake, she offers comments and evaluations of my ideas. Some of her ideas have found their way into this book (without proper footnotes!). My father and mother, Alex and Lois McKnight, each read the manuscript, and my father's preretirement vocation as a high school English teacher was resurrected with red pen in hand. Because they taught me the Christian faith, I dedicate this book to them. After one has read this book, the reader should know why I do so.

Introduction

Conversion in the Church Today

The thicker of the walls between Christians is experience, not creed. *Belief in* conversion unites all Christians; the *experience* of conversion, however, divides the same Christians into a myriad of groups. There are ample stories of conversion to tell; sadly, the *telling* of those stories fragments the church into groups of listeners that prefer one way of telling the story over all the other tellings of the same story of God's grace.

Conversion, the formation of self-identity in accordance with the central features of a faith,[1] characterizes Christianity from the days of Jesus to the church of the twenty-first century. Perhaps more than other religions, Christianity emphasizes conversion and triumphs in its stories of conversion. Indeed, some of its denominations and parachurch groups find their central identity in conversion storytelling and the active evangelization of those outside that (sometimes overly articulated) faith. If some make conversion storytelling more central, conversion remains at the very core of all of Christianity. It is the *approach* to conversion that differs among the major movements of the Christian faith, and these approaches divide the church.[2]

Three Orientations to Conversion

In abstract terms there are three orientations to conversion: socialization, liturgical acts, and personal decision. Each is aligned with a major component of the church, and each appears to be allergic to the others. Evangelicals worry about Roman Catholic conversion; Roman Catholics are uneasy with evangelical conversion; mainline denominations are uncomfortable with both; on the rebound, evangelicals and Roman Catholics lift their eyebrows at mainline Christianity. (We could, of course, substitute other names—Lutherans, Eastern Orthodox, charismatics, housechurches, etc.) Each group fosters a specific approach to conversion,

1

regardless of the variety of persons within each group. And these groups squabble and feud with one another, usually politely but sometimes polemically, for those within their walls. But, as Vladimir Nabokov says of a battle-scene painting in his boyhood estate, this is a battle "in which the episodic and the allegoric are the real adversaries."[3] Individuals are the ones who suffer; groups allegorize the individual and then "win."

Each group shapes its story for conversion, its orientation, and expects each person inside its walls to find that story true to life. But the demand for similarity of conversion experience in each of these orientations stretches the circle of coincidence too far and leads some to jettison one group for another (or for none at all). A close examination of the experience of conversion in each group, in fact, reveals that what is for some a circle of love is for others a confining wall. Like tormented pets in a zoo, persons in each group may go mad running just inside that circle if someone does not open the gate to freedom. What are we to make of the stories of so many who have crossed boundaries from one of these orientations to the other? Are we to write off each as a form of legitimating our own orientation, or will we listen more carefully to hear in the undertones that each orientation is too restrictive for the nature of Christian conversion?

Accordingly, what none of these orientations explains is why people convert to the other orientations to Christian faith. And not always behind closed doors, each contemns the transition of a person from "our" group (read "superior") to "their" group (read "inferior"). Evangelicals are befuddled why some have headed for Rome[4] or hit the Canterbury trail because evangelicals consider Roman and Anglican rites more obsolete than covered wagons. Roman Catholics are baffled why so many parishioners turn evangelical or join some small church group, while they also find the Protestant denominational splintering offensive to the unity of the church proclaimed by the New Testament. Protestant mainliners aren't bedazzled by the attraction of their sort of Christian to either liturgical churches or to low-church Protestant denominations, even if their measured courtesy keeps that opinion at the level of a whisper. Someone who didn't keep her voice at a whisper was Flannery O'Connor, and her short story "Parker's Back" is no small indictment of (how she perceived) the treatment of Roman Catholic conversions in the South.[5] This swelter of options in America's hothouse of Christian faith is the context of this book—and this book is *a plea for understanding and appreciation*. I am asking each of us to pause long enough to hear the stories of *all* Christians and not just those who frame their stories as do we.

But this book is not to be read as a plea for toleration of other viewpoints; instead, it is a call to profound appreciation of the variety of conversion experiences within the Christian family, the holy catholic church. The difference between toleration and appreciation is immense. Toleration accepts without personal responsibility; appreciation understands with a commitment to others. Toleration leads to indifference; appreciation to concrete acts of relationship. Ultimately, tolerance emerges from utility; appreciation from love. Conversion is a complex phenomenon—unusually adaptable, affecting multitudes, and expressing itself in all contexts. The urgent appeal of this book is that the various sectors of Christianity not arm wrestle one another for power but instead marvel at the manifold grace of God.

Let me clarify: contending for understanding and appreciation of one another's conversions is not the same as contending mindlessly for toleration. A conscious stance of "toleration" makes for bad theology; Christians are asked to "love" one another, not "tolerate" one another. I tolerate my neighbor cutting down his big, shady trees that have for over a decade tossed morning shade onto my favorite perch; I don't appreciate his doing so, even as I try to love him. The terms here are important. Contending for a variety of conversion experiences is not a plea to tolerate other conversions but to appreciate them for what God does in persons other than ourselves. To be sure, some conversions are genuine and some are forgeries. This book concerns genuine conversions. But conversion is a process, and we should recognize that what one person might think of as less-than-a-full-conversion may be an early dimension in the process of conversion. To adapt the language of Jesus, we should take care not to rip out wheat in our desire to remove weeds. Speaking personally, I have never shared the ecstasy of the charismatics or the liturgically ordered worship of the Orthodox or the socialized education of the Lutherans, but I can say that I have grown to appreciate each—for what these experiences do to people and for the glory they bring to the immensity of God's ways with his people. This unsettled reality—that each of us might have avenues of grace to teach each other—is like a dim light at the end of the hallway, beckoning us forward. Once we arrive, we find light among all but probably not overly concentrated on any one group. Asking any one of these orientations to change is like asking the desert to cool off—it's just plain silly. Instead, because each orientation discussed herein reflects a deep need in the human heart, the aim of this book is conscious appreciation. If the request is answered, the church will be more salubrious, a fountain of healing.

But neither is the dream of this book the old ecumenical dream, for that movement sought too resolutely a lowest common denominator and, as a result of that reduction, lost its power and then its steam and then its push. Instead, I believe we need to appreciate the diversity of Christian experience and theology and see that diversity as human expressions of the divine reality among us. Incomplete expressions, each of them, to be sure. But still expressions that teach us about God's grace and goodness. By listening to one another, we can see what God is doing in different ways among different groups in order to grasp what God is doing in the fullness of grace. We have no reason to ban any group from our study—neither Orthodox nor fundamentalists, neither Episcopalians nor Pentecostals, neither Methodists nor Amish. Each deserves a hearing, and each is worthy of appreciation. Toleration grants a muted hearing and a token appreciation. True appreciation extends a warm hand to each, listens to the manifold grace of God, and goes away with a larger vision of God's work on earth through his people.

In what follows, I will argue that conversion is a process, sometimes more sudden than others. At its core, conversion is a process of identity formation in which a person comes to see himself or herself in accordance with the gospel of Jesus Christ. The I who is I is an I related to Jesus after conversion. Humans share commonalities, but each of us embodies humanity in a unique whole. As well, the sheer complexity of Christian identity and experience throws up an early caution to imposing one form of conversion on all people. So we need both understanding (we need to comprehend the experience of others) and appreciation (God and humans are big enough to create a patchwork diversity in conversion experiences).

When we are tempted to provincialism or limited by parochialism, we need to remember that there are erudite speakers for each orientation. Whatever we might think of the following, each brings to expression the experience of a large number of Christians, and their stories are still read with profit by scores: St. Augustine, St. Francis, Teresa of Ávila, Martin Luther, John Calvin, John Wesley, John Henry Newman (1st, 2nd, and 3rd John!), Sojourner Truth, Leo Tolstoy, Billy Sunday, Simone Weil, Dietrich Bonhoeffer, Martin Luther King Jr., C. S. Lewis, Dorothy Day, Billy Graham, Oral Roberts, Jesse Jackson, Desmond Tutu, Gustavo Gutierrez, John R. W. Stott , Charles Colson, Parker Palmer, Mike Singletary, Payne Stewart, Kathleen Norris, and Anne Lamott. The church is catholic enough for all, but local parishes themselves are provincial. This book will tell the stories of many, especially the stories of students, because stories are the primary form for Christians to express the experience of conversion.

It might be asked of me (an evangelical) what the (late) Stoic Seneca asked himself when he imagined what others might ask when he asserted something that sounded like his Epicurean opponents: "Why," he imagined them asking, "in the very headquarters of Zeno [the Stoic] do you preach the doctrines of Epicurus?" (*On Leisure* 1.4). Is my appeal to appreciation of a broader understanding of conversion a denial of a central evangelical tenet (personal decision)? Or, as I prefer to think, is my case for a larger appreciation of the church and its biblical foundations in Jesus? Seneca went on: "For if a man always follows the opinion of one person, his place is not in the senate, but in a faction" (3.1). If I ask for the boundaries to be broadened, it is only because I believe a truer appreciation of the faith suggests so. Again from Seneca: "For I am wont to cross over even into the enemy's camp,—not as a deserter, but as a scout" (*Epistles* 2.5). To scout out the camps of others, that is, their orientations to conversion, we need to describe each.

Socialization

How, then, has conversion been understood in the church? First, for many Christians *conversion is a process of socialization*, which is to say that many Christians "become Christians" by being nurtured under the sacred umbrella of a particular church. Their mother and father were members of a church; they were baptized into the church as infants; they went through a process called "catechism" and then were "confirmed," after which they began participating publicly in the Eucharist; and they continued to attend church—with various degrees of regularity. These grow up in the faith and often do the same with their children. This sacred umbrella was the primary force shaping their Christian conversion, and many have no comprehension of a time and date on which they *became* a Christian. The process of becoming a Christian for such persons is imperceptible yet palpable, like the soft-step dance of evening shadows. They have been puttering about in the church for some time and intend to stay because it is "who and what they are." These conversions involve a series of gentle nods of the soul. They have experienced religiously what Joseph Epstein, America's best essayist, called a happy childhood and a "happy childhood is not easy to overcome."[6] And they find no reason to overcome it. Selah!

Mix into this special brew an *ethnic identity*, and you have the conversion realities that many Christians experience. Ethnic identity doesn't make a person a Christian, but in the experience of many, the two, that is, ethnic identity and church association, are closely related. I have students who are Irish, Polish, and Italian Roman Catholics, as well as Serbian, Russian, and Greek Orthodox, along with Swedish Covenant and Dutch Reformed, sitting next to Messianic Jews, Southern Baptists, and African Methodist Episcopal Christians. Most, I think, would say that being Irish, Polish, Italian, Serbian, Russian, Greek, Swedish, Dutch, Jewish, Southern, or African American does not necessarily make them Christian in their particular variety, but they do not know how to experience it in any other way. Neither do many of them want to surrender that ethnic heritage for a generic form of the Christian faith. For them, to be truly Irish is to be Roman Catholic, to be faithfully Serbian is to be Orthodox, etc. There are no neutral territories or buffer zones. We are all ethnically particular; we are not just "human beings." Is not the normal American Christian expression at the same time very American? If you don't think so, you need to visit Christianity in another country, say South Africa, Germany, England, or Canada. My own understanding of the holy catholic church was revolutionized when I spent a summer in Austria. Experience tells us that ethnic and cultural patterns wrap themselves tightly into religious expression. Humans can't be otherwise—they are cultural and ethnic beings. Conversion will be experienced within that ethnic and cultural framework.

Socialized converts never remember when they weren't Christians and the questions "When did you become a Christian?" or "Are you born again?" or "When were you saved?" make no sense to them. Neither do those questions conform to their Christian experience. In fact, many who were socialized into the Christian faith find the aggressiveness on the part of Christians who were converted according to a different orientation an open blister on their soft hands of faith. Further, the apparent triumphalism and cocksure convictions of these others is to them a religious turnoff, so they shut down any hope of unity within the catholic faith of the church. "How," they might ask, "can those who have a different experience of faith claim I have no faith and, worse yet, force me to start it all over again so I can have *their experience*?" It is sad, in fact a tragedy, that the more aggressive types don't realize how offensive and divisive their approach can be.

Of course, we are all aware of some persons who leave such a religious tradition for another religious tradition, more often than not because it affords a different experience that conforms to that person's expectations and needs. (These experiences stoke the fires of those other orientations.)

We are also aware of those who, over time, return to that original religious tradition after all the commotion has settled down. I don't see the movement back and forth as inconsistent with biblical evidence, and I certainly don't think we ought to see such a pilgrimage as the steps of an insecure person. Individuals, different histories, new phases of life, different religious settings—each in its own way contributes to the ongoing story of conversion.

Liturgical Process

Alongside this first approach, and perhaps a dimension within it, is a second orientation where a convert's primary moments emerge from a *liturgical process*. Socialization into the faith can focus itself for some on key moments and sacramental rituals that are performed by ordained priests empowered to dispense grace. Here an emphasis is on what the priest is authorized to accomplish for the benefit of the parishioner. If the "liturgical convert" and the "socialized convert" share a similar growth process, they diverge when it comes to the value laid on the rites performed by priests. Thus, baptism assures a purification from original sin and entrance by proxy into the church; catechism is official enlightenment into the special teaching of the church; confirmation is an authorized and divinely anointed blessing from God securing that convert's passage into God's kingdom; the Eucharist profoundly enables the grace of God to be received with all its glories and blessings; and continued participation in the church secures, maintains, and promises eternal blessing.[7] This emphasis on rite has a long history, both excellent and tawdry. But an emphasis on rituals emerges from the biblical evidence about covenant rituals of ancient Israel as given final expression by Jesus, so rituals should not be minimized. Liturgical converts might ask the socialized convert why liturgy and rite are not given a more prominent role in their religious expression, while a socialized convert might ask, in turn, why so much attention is given to baptism, the Eucharist, and official rites of passage. The personal-decision orientation is uneasy with both, in spite of their long history and biblical foundations.

The socialization or liturgical orientations share not only a similar process of conversion but also a common understanding of how faith develops in the lives of those who are nurtured within the walls of a specific faith. From the cradle to adulthood a person's religious life evolves no less developmentally than does one's body, one's emotions, one's psyche, and one's relationships with others. There will be ups and downs,

swings left and swings right, just as there will be progressive, nearly undetectable development. Since one's religious development for those who
are nurtured into a faith accompanies one's development of a self-identity,
it follows that a church's program of socializing and liturgizing persons
into the faith respects the other dimensions of self-development. Flannery O'Connor, who learned the hard way what it meant to be a Catholic
in the South, once wrote in a letter, ". . . what one has as a born Catholic
is something given and accepted before it is experienced. I am only slowly
coming to experience things that I have all along accepted."[8]

However, not all under these sacred umbrellas are socialized into the
faith successfully, and neither are all who are placed in such a framework
always receptive to its designs. Their unease frequently emerges from
personal needs not met by those orientations. Nonetheless, these two orientations have a distinct advantage in taking on board the importance of
human development, as traced in the modern theories of psychosocial and
religious development.[9]

For a specific reason I have chosen for both of these descriptions to
minimize personal faith but not because it is absent. The third orientation to conversion, discussed below, too often trumpets this accusation
unfairly and inaccurately, so I need to make the presence of faith in these
two orientations clear. There is no more reason to believe that "socialized
converts" or "liturgical converts" have no faith than to believe that those
who are raised with a focus on personal decision possess a genuine faith.
Faith can't be forced, guaranteed, or controlled—it comes in mysterious
ways and through diverse channels. My experience shows that it is present
in each of the orientations. Thus, children whose parents socialize them
into the faith can learn to believe, sometimes as a result of a traumatic crisis and othertimes with a gentle nod of the soul, and children who are
indebted to a liturgical orientation can also learn to see the value of these
"sacraments" as a form of generating and encouraging faith, but they may
also have a sudden or dramatic "conversion" experience in adolescence or
later. Concretely, Christian Methodist Episcopal, Presbyterian,
Methodist, Covenant, the Church of God in Christ, Lutheran, Episcopal,
Eastern Orthodox, and Roman Catholic—within each there are on display the marvels of faith. The particular orientation in which one is raised
can be challenged as to its success, but it cannot be *tout ensemble* accused
of mismanaging its affairs. Conversions take place in different environments and under diverging orientations. Conversions occur socially and
liturgically because humans have liturgical and social needs.

Personal Decision

This leads to a third orientation, the *decision orientation*, which emphasizes the importance of *personal faith* (in contrast to a socialized and implied [therefore impersonal] faith) on the part of a converting individual. Some call this "born again Christianity." Conversion, as personal decision, is often understood as crisis and release, and the experiences of the apostle Paul, St. Augustine, and Martin Luther are paradigmatic for this orientation. A commonly invoked example today is Charles Colson, former "hatchet man" for Richard Nixon who told his story in the book *Born Again*.[10] If these stories themselves reveal a more remarkable variety of beliefs and experience than what they are used to illustrate, each emphasizes personal decision. These "decision converts" may or may not have been raised in a church, may even have been baptized as infants, perhaps were exposed to the doctrines of the church through "catechism" or an "instruction class," but were not considered an acceptable Christian until they "made their decision for Christ." And neither did they consider themselves Christians (at all) until they made that decision. In fact, these "decision converts" can undergo a "dual decision" frequently enough to make it a matter of official record. Many of these converts make some kind of decision to "receive Jesus" or "accept Jesus into their heart" (their language) when they are young—at four, five, six, or seven. Human nature being what it is, and fidelity difficult to achieve when undergoing those difficult years of early and late adolescence for most, it is only as teenagers, or even twenty-somethings, that a "rededication" takes place when that faith is more completely integrated into the person's life and starts to make a steady, growing impact.

Part of the backwash for the personal-decision orientation, sadly, is a denigration of the socialized convert or the liturgical convert, in part because of ignorance, in part because personal-decision converts suppose incorrectly that liturgy or socialization implies *im*personal involvement, and in part because of the all-too-human desire for each of us to make others undergo our personal experience. On the positive side, and not to be minimized, are the emphases given by this orientation to *personal* decision. This orientation concentrates on individual responsibility before God as well as a thorough integration of faith into all the complexities of a person's life. The witness of thousands of converts from a socialized or liturgized background makes me think their emphasis is important.

In each of these orientations, "creeds," "official tenets," and "statements of faith" come into focus in a variety of ways: for the socialized convert, *what* must be believed is shaped more directly by the church community through catechism, but we can be sure there are specific tenets each is to believe. For the liturgical convert, there is more emphasis on "official church doctrines" in catechism that are less open to personal opinion and debate, but they are present. For the decision convert, catechism may have been present, though in this case these tenets seem to be given a particular emphasis and centrality so that the term "orthodoxy" (right thinking) shoulders a heavier burden in genuine faith. Tenets are part of conversion. Certain tenets need to be affirmed for a religious conversion to qualify as "Christian," things especially about God, Jesus, the cross, etc.—notable attempts being the Apostle's Creed or the Chalcedonian Creed. But tenets are frequently overrated, like the poetry of e.e. cummings. Most notably, the twentieth-century phenomenon of "packaging the gospel" for (what amounts to little more than) marketing strategies has undoubtedly domesticated what deserves to be given freedom.[11] Turning to Jesus is more than signing a statement of faith, and it is more than affirming certain doctrines; it is a deeply personal engagement with God that transcends, though it includes, subscription to certain articles of faith.[12] Turning to Jesus is also more than being nice and working for justice. Conversion is transformation of identity, involving both affirmations and behaviors.

Some bold boundaries have been declared; I now need to call in a couple sentries of nuance for protection. I do not want to suggest that any of the three orientations completely lacks what is emphasized in the others. Only caricatures present such a picture, as one sees of the church in the film *Chocolat*. The socialized convert experiences faith with some liturgy and some kind of personal decision, just as the liturgical convert has had a rich history of socialized religious presence as well as a call to personal faith, and the decision convert has had a socialization process as well as some liturgy. I am speaking here in general terms and of the emphasis within separate religious traditions of the Christian faith. However, these three orientations are generally accurate for how conversion is experienced in the holy catholic church. Further, each of these orientations tends to substitute convictions for its conventions. A truly Christian perspective—one that takes into consideration what Jesus says about conversion and one that balances the biblical evidence with realistic descriptions of how conversion happens today—permits each of us to appreciate the other's orientation to conversion.

These orientations to conversion have interested me for a long time, at least as far back as my teenage years. I was raised smack dab in the middle of the third orientation, buttoned and zippered all the way to the top, and so the above description is in part my personal story of coming to faith (*nulla salus extra evangelicaliam*). But interest in this topic as a theological and personal issue has led me to think that the name-callings, dart throwings, and division makings in the squabbles between the orientations have done more damage than good. For me, the process of conversion has to be unbuttoned and unzipped. I am a Christian. I am not a denominationalist as if to say that one denomination has it mostly, or even completely, right and the others less so. When I confess to be a Christian, I embrace the wholeness of the holy catholic church and all the experiences of conversion Christians have to tell.

Allow me to use another image: the basic Christian creed, that of catholic Christianity, is a like an acoustic, six-string guitar. That is, catholic Christianity affirms the Godhead (Father, Son, Holy Spirit), the holy catholic church, the communion of the saints, the forgiveness of sins, the resurrection of the body, and the life everlasting. My evangelical heritage, to name but one variation on the six-fold theme, adds strings and makes the instrument a twelve-string guitar. Sometimes the additional tones speak my music, but not always. I am committed to the six-string sound; I enjoy the others. But I am not bold enough to think that the entire evangelical, twelve-string sound is the only viable sound of the Christian gospel. Some people prefer a different six- or twelve-string guitar. Some like them electric or folk. I have learned to enjoy their music as well, itself a variation on the basic six-string theme. The above-mentioned orientations, unfortunately, are often more related to the additional strings than to the basic six, and it is my hope that we reconsider our music in light of the holy catholic faith. To extend the metaphor: when each group is playing its twelve strings, the harmony is noticeable as are the distinct tones. We need to appreciate the music of the entirety.

Perhaps no scholar has appreciated this entirety more or influenced American evangelicalism as much as C. S. Lewis, but he was no prude when it came to the experience of conversion. And he comes to the heart of our concern when he was writing to a certain Mrs. Ashton in February of 1955:[13]

> It is right and inevitable that we shd [*sic*] be much concerned about the salvation of those we love. But we must be careful not to expect or demand that their salvation shd [*sic*] conform to some ready-made pattern of our own. Some Protestant sects have gone very wrong

about this. They have a whole programme of conversion etc. marked out, the same for everyone, and will not believe that anyone can be saved who doesn't go through it "just so." But (see the last chapter of my *Problem of Pain*) God has His own way with each soul. There is no evidence that St John underwent the same kind of "conversion" as St Paul.

There is, however, evidence that each orientation has its own inherent potential problems, and they deserve to be mentioned. Each has its blind spots: for the socialized and liturgical converts, that not enough personal integration occurs or that too much responsibility is given to the churches (vicarious faith or impersonal faith or disintegrated faith); for the decision convert, that not enough attention is given to either liturgy, sacrament, or church, or that the emphasis on personal conversion can lead too easily to individualism (Henry David Thoreau Christianity), or to the worship of the moment of conversion ("Date it or do it!"), or to a *Nunc dimittis* saturation ("I can now die because my soul is satisfied!"), or to what Eric Gritsch called the "Nicodemus factor."[14]

More important, theologically, each of these views unambiguously affirms that God loves each person and that God meets each person wherever he or she is. Paradoxically, however, each orientation betrays the love of God by institutionalizing an orientation to conversion that favors some and excludes others. The person who does not fit into the orientation will feel excluded, at the profound structural level, by that Christian group, while the person who was nurtured into that orientation will feel privileged. All the while, the Sunday sermons and the message of that same group is that God loves you, regardless of who you are, where you are from, and what you have done.

And, for each of the orientations, the ongoing process of conversion throughout one's religious life can be short-circuited because for each a single moment can be seen as settling the issue too decisively, once for all (baptism, confirmation, testimony, etc.). Others have hurled invectives over the walls for this emphasis among Christians on a one-time experience as the "be-all and end-all" of acceptance with God. For instance, the eloquent and former president of my present institution, Karl A. Olsson (whose named chair I occupy), once said,

If it is a heresy in the church that man can achieve salvation in his own strength and that he need not concern himself with a justifying encounter, it is equally heretical to believe that it is a one-time expe-

rience. *Nothing* in this life saves permanently: not baptism or confirmation or decision-making or even ministerial ordination. To con-
front grace is to be plunged into a dynamic experience which ebbs
and flows, waxes and wanes.[15]

One of the most vocal critics of this emphasis within evangelicalism has
been Jim Wallis, who can neither live without or with his evangelical heritage. He is the founder of the influential Sojourners Community in
Washington, D.C., as well as the leading voice in the recent Call to
Renewal movement. Wallis, not alone, calls the church to an activist
expression of its faith and contends that such activism is the only legiti-
mate manifestation of a biblical faith. His words:

> Perhaps the greatest heresy of twentieth-century American religion
> was to make faith into a purely personal matter and a private affair,
> which went neatly with the rise of consumer society. . . . But in the
> Bible, faith is not something you possess but rather something you
> practice.[16]

Wallis is right; the emphasis on personal decision can lead to private
Christianity. And the latent emphasis on a one-time decision settling for
all time the issues is also worthy of criticism. As we will see in what follows, Jesus gives absolutely no attention to "the big decision" or to a single-event conversion. Instead, he continues to call the same group of
followers to renew their commitment to following him in love, service,
and obedience. Whether one is socialized into the faith, is liturgized into
the faith, or makes a decision later in life does not matter: at the end is the
challenge from Jesus to follow an unknown path of surrendering to him,
of loving God and others, and of experiencing joy in the journey. He did
not permit then, and his followers should not permit now, an over-
emphasis on a single moment as an event so big everything about day-to-
day faith shrinks to the trivial or unnecessary. Nor did he inculcate
individualism or privatized personal experiences as the fundamental shape
of what discipleship entailed.

But each orientation also has its upside: the liturgical orientation generates rituals, symbols, and worship in a profoundly evocative manner; in
general, the liturgical convert has come to appreciate the centrality of the
cross and the importance of worship. The absence of liturgy for many
prohibits those converts from what is humanly normal: rites are a part of
the human need to express faith in physical form. The process of

socialization integrates the child naturally into the faith of his or her parents while it also seems frequently to align that same child with a cultural expression of Christianity—and few can contest the impact a cultural expression of Christianity has. The emphasis in socialization conversion on family and community cannot be eliminated without doing damage to the corporate form of Christianity. And the decision orientation focuses its energies on personal responsibility as the framework in which all true religious expression takes place. One cannot evade this emphasis in the marvelous preaching of the prophets or their threnodies over Israel's exile. Once again, each has something to offer to the others.

I have chosen in this book to focus less on the problems each of these orientations generates and more on the grandeur of what God has done and continues to do and will do through a great message about Jesus Christ and God's love for us. The gentle nod of the soul that occurs for children raised lovingly and positively by parents who love them and who love God and God's people is, for me, the ideal form of conversion. But no one has perfect parents, so all are in need of a conversion that will have to occur in less than ideal conditions. I am willing to say tentatively at this point that one's psychological condition has much to do with how one is converted. In other words, the experience of conversion correlates absolutely with one's context. Consequently, each person deserves respect to work out conversion in her or his own way. Forcing the issue endangers spiritual fulfillment. America's premier church historian, Jaroslav Pelikan, once said, "For, as Augustine says, God does not rape; God woos, and therefore God will take his chances on winning or losing and will finally prefer to let someone be lost rather than to interfere with the sacredness of the human being."[17] Such respect, when shown within each orientation, will enable the faith of each person to develop in accordance with that person's integrity.

After teaching for eleven years at a prominent evangelical seminary, I joined a faculty at a liberal arts college, North Park University, and what I found there far transcended my expectations. College students are yearning for spiritual realities—I see this yearning daily in my classes; I hear more about it in collegial discussions; and I find it true in my office with students when they share with me their stories of faith. Sometimes this yearning is clumsy or callow groping, but other times it is profound quest and discovery. Our present college students want authenticity from their parents, their leaders, their peers, and their faith. When it is absent, their God-made radar detects it, and they are "out of there." As Jim Wallis has recently said, "Many people today are hungry for spirituality but have no appetite for religion."[18] My experience in listening to the stories of students reveals massive variety in the orientations of converting to Jesus but a powerful desire for spiritual realities. In this book, I will record, with their approval, some of their stories.

If the thickest wall between Christians is that of experience, I will appeal to America's (perhaps) most-recognized poet, Robert Frost, who speaks of his neighbor's wall that needs spring mending:[19]

> Before I built a wall I'd ask to know
> What I was walling in or walling out,
> And to whom I was like to give offense.
> Something there is that doesn't love a wall,
> That wants it down. . . .
> . . . .
> He will not go behind his father's saying,
> And he likes having thought of it so well
> He says again, "Good fences make good neighbors."

Our creedal distinctions sometimes make us good neighbors by keeping us in our own gardens, but our experience of the grace of God ought not to be a wall. Instead, it ought to be what unites us; we are united by *life* not *light*. The walls in our orientations need to come down, even after we learn that our creeds vary. Put prayerfully, may the hands that broke the bread break these walls.

Conversion Then

But isn't the biblical evidence clear enough to give more value to one orientation or another? A further question puts the assumed answer to the chase: Which biblical evidence should we take as normative? I agree that Christian faith is established in the Bible, and so to it we should (and will) go. However, in affirming the importance of the scripture principle, we need to let it say what it says and we shouldn't make it say what it doesn't say. Can we go to it to understand conversion? Yes. But how to proceed? If we settle ourselves into ancient Jewish history, we would have to settle for either the socialization or the liturgical orientation. Ancient Jews were raised into the faith; they underwent various rituals in life's development, but it was an ethnic identity and a faith heritage that shaped faith development. If we proceed through the biblical texts, one standard approach for the Christian is to examine the apostle Paul—and whether from the angle of his biographer or himself matters[20]—who was converted from a form of Pharisaism to faith in Jesus Christ on a trip to Damascus for the purpose of persecuting early converts to Jesus.[21] Paul, so the story in Acts goes, saw a blinding light and a vision of Jesus, did a double take, and his life was revolutionized famously from a persecutor to a preacher of Jesus. Or should we take Peter? If we take a full account from the pages of the New Testament,[22] we begin with Peter being led to converse with Jesus by his brother (John 1:35–42), and then, after his return to Galilee, we find Peter embarrassingly converted by learning from a nonfisherman, Jesus, how to fish and be wildly successful (Luke 5:1–11)—Peter confesses his sinfulness, drops his nets, and follows Jesus. But Peter's faith was not all smooth sailing: only later does he confess Jesus as Messiah (Mark 8:27–30), but he does so with less than a clear understanding of who Jesus is. In fact, here we see Peter squaring off with Jesus, looking him straight in the eyes, and asking to be taught by the master—but with his ears corked! Later he abandons Jesus in his most important hour (Mark 14:66–72). He is eventually restored to his ministry (John 21:15–20), and experiences the charismatic power of God's Spirit at Pentecost (Acts 2) and a new openness to Gentiles (Acts 10). Or, more briefly, we might take Zacchaeus (Luke 19:1–10)—who, though powerful and moneygrubbing, gained insight into Jesus, pledged allegiance, and then gave away bags of his money. Or, more known for what he got Jesus to say than for his own story, Nicodemus illustrates the need to be "born from above" (John 3:1–21), the need to experience the awakening and regenerating grace of God. He stands between Jesus and the Jewish leaders in the tapestry of John's narrative (7:45–53) but later sides with those who attend to Jesus after his death (19:38–42).

We could take other stories of conversion but these just described lead us to ask at least the following questions: For Paul, can an experience like this serve as a model for the ordinary Christian convert?[23] Anyway, is this Paul's conversion, or is it his "call to apostleship"? Scholars are divided on that one. Or does this scholarly nicety take a complex experience and separate it rigidly into drawers: here conversion, there calling? More important, is this really all that happened to Paul? In other words, is it fair to equate this narrative of Paul's conversion with all that happened? Should we assume, for instance, that Paul's previous contacts with Christians (though not mentioned by Paul) were of such a nature that he was in fact on a teeter-totter with respect to Jesus? Another set of questions emerge from Paul's experience: Isn't it fair to ask if Paul's experience was not somewhat unique? Do all, or even many, see blinding lights? Is not Paul's experience of the traumatic and dramatic sort in fact an unusual kind of conversion?

For Peter, we might ask, When was he converted? Was it when he thought about Jesus because his brother led him into a conversation with Jesus; or was it when he learned what fishing was all about (Luke 5); or was it when he confessed Jesus as Messiah (Mark 8) after which Jesus had to answer Peter to his beard; or was it when he was restored (John 21); or was it at Pentecost (Acts 2)? Just when was Peter converted? *That* we can't be sure might tell us a lot. Was Peter converted several times? Or, in modern jargon: Did Peter pass through several phases of religious development? Maybe the Pauline experience of a traumatic moment is less normative, and the Petrine experience of a growing conversion is more normative.

Zacchaeus, about whom we know both less than about Paul and Peter but enough to make us, economically speaking, terrorizingly uncomfortable, presents another issue: Do we really want a model of conversion drawn from a man who gives away everything? How would that sell in the Western world, in the most affluent country ever?

What about Nicodemus, who suddenly appears on the stage of John's narrative and also quietly succumbs to the shadows cast by John's irony-laden records of other things, who seems to be a seeker for divine realities, who casts doubts on the pushings and shovings of those opposed to Jesus, and who willingly exposes himself to danger and betrayal by participating in Jesus' preparation for burial? Has he converted to Jesus? One could infer his interest in Jesus from John 3 and his courage from John 7 and 19, but how are we to read his actions? That he had moved from "night" actions to "day" actions, from darkness to the light? More important, if this shadowy figure is to represent what "born from above/again" means, when was he "born from above?" Is "born from above" a one-act performance or an ongoing performance? It is more likely that Nicodemus illustrates precisely what John intends: that divine birth is as detectable as the drifts of wind and as subtle as the manifest presence of God's Spirit.[24]

Which example shall we choose? Or, do we need to make a choice? Does conversion perhaps occur differently for different people? Or, as Richard Peace has argued, is it just one conversion pattern that is experienced by Paul and the Twelve differently? As he says it, "The main difference is what was an *event* for St. Paul is described by Mark as a *process* for the Twelve. . . . If Paul's turning took place in a flash, theirs took place in fits and starts over the course of their years with Jesus."[25] Or does this oversimplify the evidence and stretch the explanatory skin too tightly? Too tightly, we think.

So, yes, we need to go to the Bible, but in so doing we need to check our own ideas at the door to see if they are intruding so much on our study of the sacred text that we are no longer seeing anything but our own orientations or experience. Put differently, we need to develop courage in our lack of convictions. In examining conversion stories, we find what we are looking for: we find socialization, we find liturgy, and we find decision. And we confess that the text is normative and fundamental to our beliefs. What if it doesn't tell us all we are looking for? Is there a better way of transcending our personal orientation so we can discover what the Bible really says and implies about conversion? The issues are even more complex. Not only does the biblical data only whisper to us some insightful thoughts, but it leaves unspoken many other ideas. Complicating this is that we are twenty centuries removed and light years away in cultural instincts.

What About Today?

Another set of questions: If we consider these conversion stories as the parameters for discovering what conversion is, have we restricted our evidence too much? Have we not cut off the experience of many others? In other words, is there a difference between conversion in the first century and conversion in the twentieth century? Is their story, at least what is told of it, supposed to shape our stories? The Gospel stories are about Jewish men. But, assuming that males and females have similar, though surely (full emphasis given) not identical, experiences to tell, what about the difference between ancient Jewish converts to Jesus and their counterparts among modern Europeans, or Americans, or Canadians, or South Americans, or Africans, or Koreans, or Chinese, or Latin Americans, or Australians? There is a real question here: Are the conversion stories in the Gospels the experience of only one ethnic dimension of humanity? Further, our stories in the Gospels are mostly about Jewish men turning to Jesus. Why so few women? Do men and women have the same needs? Do they convert in the same way? Do women and men experience God without variation?[26] And what of one's psychological health? William James claimed sudden conversions are more typical of specific psychological conditions than others.[27] Is Paul's experience different than Peter's perhaps because their psychological histories varied? There are, in other words, some serious questions to ask in using the biblical evidence simply to construct a theory of conversion. There are obstacles. I have mentioned only three: ethnicity, sexuality, and psychological health. Consequently, in light of this cornucopia of human variation, is it theologically and pastorally sound to expect most to have a similar experience? The answer is firmly and resolutely "no." Accordingly, the present emphasis in education and society on diversity of persons should lead us to think of conversion in different categories. And the orientations we saw previously assume most people in a given body will convert in a similar manner. If conversion weren't so serious, we would have to wonder about divine mirth. Instead, we worry about our intelligence! An old saw has it that God meets us where we are—as he did the Woman at the Well, the Good Samaritan, the Rich Young Ruler, as well as Simon Peter. God met each differently; history tells the same story. But do the churches institute what they so frequently preach? The answer to that question is just as resolute and firm.

Another obstacle pertains to the *Zeitgeist*—whether of a majority or a minority culture, whether of a particular or broader culture—that each of us breathes. Is there a difference between someone converting in an agrarian society and a capitalistic empire? Between the conversion of the homeless and a senator? Between the religious experience of a factory worker and a royal family member? Do adults convert differently than teenagers? And what about Westerners who were raised, as was Henry Adams, either in the transition to the modern secular world or in that secular world itself. Adams writes his autobiography in the third person: "But neither to him nor to his brothers or sisters was religion real" and, when he came of age, the "Church was gone, and Duty was dim, but Will should take its place, founded deeply in interest and law."[28] Adams is not like Peter or Paul. Surely the biblical call to conversion strikes such persons as from another world. Thus, Scott Russell Sanders, one of the Midwest's most sensitive writers, once said,

> Ruth [his wife] and I have known since childhood who he [Jesus] is, this dangling man, for we both spent nearly all of our childhood Sundays in Methodist churches, singing hymns, memorizing Bible verses, listening to sermons, learning that Jesus saves. Although Ruth still sings regularly in a church choir and I sit in a pew on the occasional Sunday morning with a Bible in my lap, neither of us any longer feels confident that the man on the cross will preserve us from annihilation, nor that he will reunite us with our loved ones in heaven. The only meetings we count on are those we make in the flesh. The only time we're sure about is right now.[29]

How do such people respond to the call of Jesus to conversion? Can we expect them to convert just as did Zacchaeus, or Paul, or Peter? Ancient texts and ancient figures, modern context and modern people. The connections between the two are strained. Pretending otherwise is but a childhood game.

My goal in asking these questions is not to strip the authoritative Gospel texts from the church's message about conversion. Instead, I wish to strip us of our modern barnacle-like accretions, as when we think all must be like us or when we think all must be like Paul, so we can see the bedrock of Jesus' message in all its own historical significance. This, I believe, is the only hope we have of letting the Bible speak with its intended force. The biblical message about conversion has a simplicity within a complexity, the establishment of a relationship with God and the consequent reshaping of identity, while respecting the integrity of a human life.[30] When we force all to be like Paul or like us, we destroy the Bible's simplicity-in-complexity, destroy personal integrity and abort human stories in their myriad individuality.

Stepping back in time: in the pages of the Gospels we are not dealing with kids who grow up in the same faith as their parents or in a context where faith in Jesus has a rich history. In fact, we are dealing almost exhaustively with first-century Galilean Jews who are already Jews by faith and observance but who found something fresh and new in Jesus. And since Jesus' vision for his converts is a singular Jewish vision for Israel, it follows that we have here "Jews" converting to "Judaism." More particularly, we are not dealing with Galilean Jews who are leaving their religion to form a new religion but with Galilean Jews who are *intensifying their Judaism by shifting its focus onto Jesus' vision for Israel.* Many assume we can grab that information from the first century and apply it without transfer to kids who grow up in the Methodist Church, or to Arabs who want to convert to Christianity, or to adult, secular Americans who find conversion to Christianity is what they need but with significant problems[31]—this assumption is not to be taken for granted and neither is its application that simple. No, in fact, it is more than a little bit of a hermeneutical struggle to move from Jesus' world into our own world and to transfer in the process the message about conversion. Therefore, we need to understand Jesus in his own terms and what is implied in his own world. Only then can we even begin to address our particular world of faith. However, letting Jesus be Jesus gives us hope of finding his relevance (to activate once again an overused word) to our religious contexts.

We are still not done. Complicating the entire process is that the modern concept of the "self" or "selfhood," especially as fashioned in the capitalistic West, differs dramatically from that of the ancient Jewish world as well as of parts of the Orient today. Our own view of the self leads to, but also impedes, our understanding of the Gospel stories about conversion. We might say that the personal-decision orientation previously discussed is the most out of tune, at the social level, with first-century conversions. It is more out of step than the socialization or liturgical orientations because for these the self is conceived more corporately while the former, because it radically fashions "self-hood" individually, constructs the conversion process in a highly individualized, even privatized, form.[32] The "socialization" orientation develops the conversion process within a social framework but, in so doing, it is asking highly individualized people to conform—once again, something not in harmony with first-century Judaism. Recent sociological, anthropological, and psychological studies of the self then may provide insights into the conversion process.

But use of the social sciences for religious and historical questions and for ancient evidence has its own questions as well. Does such an approach trap what is transcendental into the ephemeral, what is spiritual into what is material, what is "from God" into what is "from humans"? Are we attempting to measure a mountain with a yardstick? Sometimes, but not always. In fact, if we are honest with our examination of conversion, we will admit that Christian conversion takes place largely within the parameters of physical, social and psychological experience[33] though some converts experience levels of transcendence outside the lens of the sociologist's or psychologist's eye. And what remains within those lenses is worthy of study with social-scientific tools. In so doing, however, the sociologists or theologians who use social-scientific tools need to remind themselves that studying spiritual experiences opens the door to potential wonders and mysteries, to places where angels dwell. In what follows we shall examine the complexity of turning to Jesus—with the door to the spiritual world open.

Strategy

My research on conversion intersects rather frequently with my special field of study, the historical Jesus of Nazareth and how the evangelists present him in the Gospels. What I intend to do in this book, therefore, is look at how Jesus understands conversion. Unfortunately, he does not

sit down with his disciples and explain his "theory of conversion."
Fortunately, because he does not do this, we have a challenge before us:
we have to piece together various bits and bobs of evidence to frame a
model or general pattern of conversion that reflects how he goes about it,
and this is where the sociology of conversion enters. My expertise in Jesus
studies restricts this study to the Gospels with only an occasional escape
into the larger world of the New Testament. But this is why this study has
significance: I believe the foundation for all Christian belief should begin
with Jesus. I am surprised at the number of recent studies about conversion that fail to examine the conversion stories of the Gospels. In any
Christian study of conversion, we must first of all see what Jesus says
before we move into the wider fields of theological inquiry.[34] I called this
(in another context) the "hermeneutic of confessing Jesus as Lord."[35] But
even this restriction of evidence won't give us all the information we
would like, as we have previously pointed out. Hence, a second grouping
of evidence deserves to be mentioned.

Nearly a dozen years ago, when I was involved in historical research
about Jewish missionary activity, I began to read in the field of the sociology of conversion. After publishing the results of that study,[36] I continued
reading studies about conversion as a hobby with no particular goal in
mind until I encountered Lewis R. Rambo, Professor of Psychology and
Religion at San Francisco Theological Seminary, San Anselmo, and at the
Graduate Theological Union, Berkeley. Rambo has written a monograph,
with the title *Understanding Religious Conversion* (Yale University Press,
1993). What I found in Rambo's process theory of conversion was that his
theory fit nicely with the evidence I had been attempting to put into a reasonable whole from the Jesus traditions.[37] Furthermore, Rambo, unlike
some social-scientific approaches to biblical evidence, doesn't sew on the
fox's skin when the lion's won't stretch far enough. Rambo is the Alexis de
Tocqueville of the sociological landscape of conversion. He describes and
doesn't force the evidence.

Three recent studies of the biblical evidence justify another look at
conversion through the lens of sociology.[38] First, fifteen years ago Beverly
Gaventa explored the New Testament idea of conversion in light of recent
social-scientific study on conversion.[39] Her study appeared before the
consensus report of Rambo had been reached, and she also restricted her
study of evidence to Luke–Acts and the (largely) Johannine language of
conversion. Nonetheless, hers is an important study that remains foundational to my own analysis. Not only did Gaventa throw sand in the eyes
of those who overdo the stereotyped, traditional view of Paul's conver-

sion, but she also established the value of sociological theory for digging deeper into the New Testament evidence.

A second, recent study of conversion, with emphasis on ritual, confirms the value of social-scientific scholarship for the study of ancient conversions: Thomas M. Finn, *From Death to Rebirth: Ritual and Conversion in Antiquity* (New York: Paulist Press, 1997). The author adopts and adapts Rambo's model to a cross-section of evidence about conversion, including evidence about Greco-Roman paganism, ancient Judaism, and early Christianity.[40] His conclusion is nearly identical to the categories laid out by Rambo.[41] Finn's study, however, because it focuses so one-sidedly on ritual, fails to take note of precisely the evidence our book explores: the stories of conversion in the pages of the Gospels. It is this evidence, I believe, that forms the solid foundation on which Christian theology needs to construct a theory of conversion.[42]

Third, Richard Peace, in his study, *Conversion in the New Testament: Paul and the Twelve* (Grand Rapids: Wm. B. Eerdmans Publishing Co., 1999), constructs a theory of conversion anchored quite forcefully in Paul's own experience of conversion, involving three elements: insight, turning, and transformation. Further, he argues that Mark's Gospel is constructed in such a manner that it is all about conversion itself. In his study of Mark, Peace hides his theory in front of the biblical evidence. It is highly unlikely that this is what Mark's Gospel is about. If Peace's work represents the foil of my study, it is only because the conversion of Paul (and those with experiences like Paul's) has influenced the Christian perception of conversion so powerfully. In addition, our study broadens the playing field by looking more directly both at evidence for conversion in the Gospels as well as how modern sociological theory can enable our own study of these important biblical texts. Thus, to adapt the words of Flannery O'Connor, I would say to each of these three scholars: "You are right, you just arn't right enough."[43]

So if the first dimension is the Gospel evidence about Jesus, the second is a model of conversion as drawn from contemporary sociologists, a model broad enough to encompass a wide variety of conversion experiences but one that also respects the reality of religious experience. In looking for a model of conversion, however, we need to be sensitive to the evidence as well as to experience. In the words of G. K. Chesterton, "What we want is not the universality that is outside all normal sentiments; we want the universality that is inside all normal sentiments."[44]

Consequently, this study of converting to Jesus is an interdisciplinary study that integrates study of Jesus with study of conversion in the modern world. I should caution the reader that this book is not a complete examination of the biblical evidence for Christian conversion. It concerns one segment of the Christian faith, the evidence of the Gospels, and it examines those teachings in light of the modern theory of religious conversion. I am reasonably confident, however, that the evidence we find there is an adequate basis on which to build broader conclusions. Furthermore, I use this study to speak to the three modern orientations to conversion (as previously discussed). In short, we are ultimately concerned with pastoral theology.

Because some have questioned the viability of using modern studies of conversion to analyze biblical evidence, we need to pause one more time to consider the question, Is it fair to use the social sciences in the field of biblical studies? I believe so. Far too often biblical scholars have (to adapt an expression or two from James Thurber) looked down their noses at the social scientists as active volcanoes spewing forth cotton balls, or at least we biblical scholars carried on our debate with them with our argumentative index fingers pointing at their inexact sciences. Today, however, the growth of knowledge in the social sciences has led to its penetration into, and dramatic influence of, biblical studies. Integrating the two no longer needs serious defense.[45] At one time biblical scholars protested the presence of sociologists at dinner; we assigned them to a different house. Then we began to peer through their windows. Then we asked them to stand at our windows and listen in on our conversations. But today they frequently host our banquets. More important, theologians have long spoken of conversion with flash and spark but with little knowledge of what was inside the fireworks. At times, sociologists explain the chemical reaction; it is left to the biblical theologians to announce the spark and declare the boom. Today the discussion unites around a common table of interests.

The study of modern conversions is an industry today, and it takes lots of reading to get a handle on its complexities. But, for the reader who wishes a nice anthology of Christian conversion stories, I recommend H. T. Kerr and J. M. Mulder, *Famous Conversions: The Christian Experience* (Grand Rapids: Wm. B. Eerdmans Publishing Co., 1994),[46] since it collects the kinds of stories useful for the one who wants to understand the variety of experiences gathered under the rubric "conversion." The problem with anecdotal stories of conversion, of course, is that their authors are famous decorators and the ornaments express the theology of the decorator. A good storyteller can tell a good story, sometimes leaving out lots of contrary information. We need to keep this in mind in examining the accounts told in the following pages. But one observation should be before our eyes immediately: even a cursory scan of the stories of conversion reveals an impressive array of stories. So much so, in fact, that one is led to think that conversion is as varied as persons are diverse. Even when the major orientations claim certain persons as "prototypes" of conversion (the major ones being Martin Luther, John Henry Newman, G. K. Chesterton, Karl Barth, and C. S. Lewis), a closer look at those individuals reveals that each of them has a story that is far from typical of the "garden-variety type" of Christian within that orientation. Garden-variety converts may find inspiration in the stories of these "heroes of the faith" but will find parallel stories in more garden-variety conversion stories.

In the sections on modern conversion that follow, I shall draw from the stories of famous converts but also from those of some of my (not yet famous) college students at North Park who provide a more "normal" type of conversion. These stories are used with their permission and are reprinted here as they wrote them, with only rare and minor revision. For each, however, I have changed the name. I asked them to retell their own stories in light of modern theories of conversion but told them they had complete freedom to tell their stories in their own way. Some followed Rambo's theory more exactly than others, but each does have a story to tell. I remain grateful to them for their permission—even more, for sharing their stories with me.

Having called attention to modern experiences of conversion, it needs to be understood that this book is not another study of moderns converting to the Christian faith, and my primary goal is certainly not to adjudicate between the "orientations"previously described. Instead, this book attempts to describe Jesus' understanding of conversion as it can be seen through his actions and teachings and through the records of his followers—all in light of a modern sociological model. And the drift of my study is that conversion is complex enough to permit each of the orientations a major seat at the table. It is my hope that the practitioners of the various orientations will share this table, enjoying the story of God as it is has been told by his children.

Chapter One

Jesus and Conversion

A First Look

T o study Christian conversion properly we need to begin with Jesus, and this chapter will be a first look at the Gospels to see what they say on the surface about conversion. The orientations sketched in the Introduction revealed select emphases in the process of conversion: the community's influence (socialization), the priest's role (liturgy), and the individual's responsibility (personal decision). There we argued that to grasp a Christian understanding of conversion, we would have to examine the Bible. But where should we begin? I contend that we should begin with Jesus, but to do so we need to understand his message of conversion in its Jewish context, especially its relationship to Israel's prophets.

The place to begin is with the term "repentance" (Greek: *metanoia*; Hebrew: *shuv*). But repentance, the primary term used in the Gospels to describe the fundamental act of conversion, draws different images for modern Christians. Modern spectacles shape the vision of our inquiring eyes. For some, repentance *is a change in life and morals*, usually described as the abandonment of a path of sinful behaviors for a new path of love, justice and peace. Some think of the moral revolution in the life of St. Francis, or Billy Sunday, or Charles Colson.[1] For others, repentance is more of *a theological revolution*, as is the case with Menno Simons, John Henry Newman, C. S. Lewis, and Karl Barth. And yet others see repentance as *a deep probing of conscience, a painful journey inward, an introspection revealing all the turmoils, lusts, and attitudes of the subconscious with its accompanying tears*, as most have understood the conversions of St. Augustine, Teresa of Ávila, Martin Luther , even John Wesley and Jonathan Edwards. Alongside such interiority, but in more modern categories, some see repentance *as a remaking of the personality, a biographical rewriting of one's life story*. I think here especially of Charles Spurgeon, the Baptist Puritan of the nineteenth century whose own autobiography tells us more about his later perspective than about the events he describes.[2] But all conversions involve this reshaping of our personal histories. What else can conversion mean? For others it is more of *a commitment to social, national, or international action,* as is the case with William Wilberforce,[3] George Fox, Peter Cartwright, Sojourner Truth, Albert Schweitzer, Dorothy Day, and Martin Luther King Jr.. What then is repentance? Is it moral? Theological? Psycho-emotional? Personal biography? Social? To discover what conversion is, we will need to study the conversion stories of the Gospels.

Oddly, but we should not be surprised, each orientation discussed previously can find a way to include each of the above Christian heroes into their scheme of understanding conversion. Perhaps this is an overstatement. If one or more of the above happen not to fit into a particular orientation or scheme for conversion, some within an orientation might (and do) say that so-called convert was not in fact a genuine Christian. Illustrations need not be given—to protect the guilty. But can we really explain Luther's conversion as a moral revolution? Or Lewis's as a journey inward? Conversion means something personal to each convert, and its manifestations vary according to the personality with its history and needs.

If we but look at the above list of "famous" Christians, we say that conversion can mean many things and can happen in a variety of ways. Is there a core to what conversion is? Can we reduce each of the above experiences to a basic mass? Perhaps. How? I suggest we ask the following first: what did conversion mean to Jesus when he called his fellow Jews to conversion? In the Introduction we saw that recent studies about conversion have two major weaknesses: either they overemphasize the evidence about Paul's conversion, or they fail to embrace a large enough understanding of conversion as made known to us through studies of conversion in the social sciences. In addition, recent scholarship has also neglected a tree loaded with fruit: conversion to Jesus in the Gospels.

We begin with this then: Just *what did Jesus mean* when he called his nation to *repentance*? How does this information enable us to understand conversion? We begin here not only because these stories about conversion are substantively what we are looking for but also because it is the natural impulse of those who claim to follow Jesus to begin a theological quest by looking at his teachings.

Conversion in Israel's Prophets

Since Jesus climbed onto public places in the Galilee[4] as a prophet, it will do us good to pause for a moment to consider the theme of repentance among Israel's prophets. Six features of the prophet's call to conversion surface.⁵ Not only does Jesus appear on the stage as a prophet, his message vigorously reexpresses their message and vision. So, what Jesus said was immediately grasped by his first hearers as a renewal of the prophet's challenge to Israel.

First, they are a rather gloomy and pessimistic lot, these prophets of Israel and Judah. One can certainly sympathize with those who accused them of bad manners and negative attitudes. Thus Amos, an early prophet of Israel from the eighth century B.C.E., says,

> I gave you cleanness of teeth in all your cities,
>   and lack of bread in all your places,
> yet you did not return to me,
> says the LORD.
> And I also withheld the rain from you
>   when there were still three months to the harvest;
> I would send rain on one city,
>   and send no rain on another city;
> one field would be rained upon,
>   and the field on which it did not rain withered;
> so two or three towns wandered to one town
>   to drink water, and were not satisfied;
> yet you did not return to me,
> says the LORD.
>
> I struck you with blight and mildew;
>   I laid waste your gardens and your vineyards;
>   the locust devoured your fig trees and your olive trees;
> yet you did not return to me,
> says the LORD.
>
> I sent among you a pestilence after the manner of Egypt;
>   I killed your young men with the sword;
> I carried away your horses;
>   and I made the stench of your camp go up into your nostrils;
> yet you did not return to me,
> says the LORD.
>
> I overthrew some of you,
>   as when God overthrew Sodom and Gomorrah,
>   and you were like a brand snatched from the fire;
> yet you did not return to me,
> says the LORD. (Amos 4:6–11)⁶

No matter what YHWH did, says Amos, speaking for God, Israel did not respond: God took away their food, sent them a spotty rain, gobbled up their sustenance, withered them through pestilence, captured their soldiers and horses—but Israel still would "not return" (read: convert) to YHWH and the covenant.

Incidentally, we find here the three dimensions of repentance in the prophets: (1) a turning one's back on one's present behaviors, (2) a turning back to the way things were at the beginning, and (3) a national orientation. That is, Amos's message is not directed so much to individuals, although repentance came down to individual Israelites changing their course of behavior, as it is directed to the nation. Jesus' focus was on the salvation of the whole nation. He was not satisfied with just a couple of budding converts; he wanted the nation to respond and turn from its ways. Had Jesus been nothing but a revivalist, he would have stayed his course in the Galilee. Instead, he set out for Jerusalem, a trip that proved fatal and a trip that revealed what he was all about.

Amos was pessimistic about his chances for success with his people. He was not alone. The same pessimism can be found, for example, in Jeremiah 3:1–2 or 8:4–7, to name two other such occasions. While it was the prophetic vocation to announce a coming judgment, it was also that same vocation to urge the people to escape the coming judgment by repentance. Experience taught the prophets that their message too often fell on craven, cold and callused hearts since the message did not pierce enough hearts to make a difference.[7] Such is life for Israel's prophets.

Pessimism seems to derive from *prophetic pathos*, a second feature of a prophet. A. J. Heschel, the brilliant Jewish theologian and social activist who rose to national leadership to speak of major moral issues during the 1960s, wrote his dissertation out of deep personal involvement in the issues facing Jews of central Europe early in the twentieth century.[8] His topic: prophets and what a prophet is. It was Heschel who used the concept of pathos to describe the prophetic mission. Scholarship unanimously agrees that he had his hat on straight in this insight into prophetic pathos. The expression, as he used it, is too deep and active to permit neat and tidy definition. But, as I understand him, the term describes the prophet's identification—personally, emotionally, spiritually, totally—with his people in their situation and his identification with God as he discloses to them a message from God about their past, their present, and their future. He mediates between God and the people by absorbing, in his own person, the divine message about them and for them. If the prophet seems to be overdoing it, he must, for he has absorbed the word of God for Israel and Judah, and his burden is to unburden himself on them. Jesus is noted by the same pathos: he carries the burdens of the nations on his shoulders, knows his message for them is from God, and, more significantly, senses that Israel's response to him is its response to God. Such a view can only emerge from a prophetic pathos.

A third feature of the prophetic concept of repentance is that YHWH promises forgiveness to those who do repent. None of the prophets expresses this any more beautifully than does Jeremiah, at 15:19–21:

> Therefore thus says the LORD: If you turn back, I will take you back, and you shall stand before me. If you utter what is precious, and not what is worthless, you shall serve as my mouth. It is they who will turn to you, not you who will turn to them. And I will make you to this people a fortified wall of bronze; they will fight against you, but they shall not prevail over you, for I am with you to save you and deliver you, says the LORD. I will deliver you out of the hand of the wicked, and redeem you from the grasp of the ruthless.

A distinguishing feature of the classical prophets is what might be called *fundamental contingency*: for the prophets, the doom and gloom expressed by pessimism gives way to hope for renewal—the judgment can be averted by simply returning to the old days. These prophets don't go to bed with a deterministic history or a deterministic God. God's plan can change and Israel's history can change—if Israel repents. If the nation turns away from its sinful course, then God will change the plans and the people's history will chart a new path into paradise. Jeremiah (as previously quoted) probably sees his own experience as the experience of Judah: YHWH's call for him to repent mirrors what Judah is also to do. And if it does . . . reacceptance, restitution to ministry, strength for the task. Or, we can turn to Joel 2:12–13:

> Yet even now, says the LORD,
>   return to me with all your heart,
> with fasting, with weeping, and with mourning;
>   rend your hearts and not your clothing.
> Return to the LORD, your God,
>   for he is gracious and merciful,
> slow to anger, and abounding in steadfast love,
>   and relents from punishing.

Repentance on the part of the people brings a wholesale restoration of the nation.

The famous British writer Charles Lamb once discovered the joy of retirement so intense that he claimed that if he had a little son, he would name him "NOTHING-TO-DO" so the child could embody Lamb's delightful experience.[9] This practice of naming children after one's vocation owes something to Israel's greatest prophet, Isaiah, and sets up a fourth point about prophets. So critical was repentance to the prophet Isaiah that he named his son *Shear-Yashuv*, "a remnant will return/repent" after judgment (Isa. 7:3). Imagine growing up with that as your handle! Scholars differ on whether this is a hope: "be assured, a remnant will return/repent," or a thin promise: "only a remnant will return/repent" from the captivity. Either way the same message gets across: repentance is necessary to escape an awful future. Isaiah's action of naming is among the notoriously interesting prophetic actions of the prophets. Hosea also embodied his message in the names of his kids (Hosea 1). Jesus did the same: he called Simon "Peter," setting him out as a sign to his people, and he called the Zebedee boys "sons of thunder." Naming is a part of the prophetic mission.

A fifth point is somewhat indirect: there is acceptable and unacceptable prayer for conversion. In the pages of the prophets there are some prayers of repentance, but they only rarely appear to be acceptable to YHWH.[10] We think, for instance, of Hosea 6:1–3 or Jeremiah 14:19–22, both serious prayers that appear to be unacceptable to YHWH (see Hos. 6:5; Jer. 15:2). But, the prayer of the exiles of the Northern Kingdom in Jeremiah 3:22–25 is acceptable. Here are its words:

> Return, O faithless children,
>   I will heal your faithlessness.
> "Here we come to you;
>   for you are the LORD our God.
> Truly the hills are a delusion,
>   the orgies on the mountains.
> Truly in the LORD our God
>   is the salvation of Israel.

"But from our youth the shameful thing has devoured all for which our ancestors had labored, their flocks and their herds, their sons and their daughters. Let us lie down in our shame, and let our dishonor cover us; for we have sinned against the LORD our God, we and our ancestors, from our youth even to this day; and we have not obeyed the voice of the LORD our God."

This is followed up in Jeremiah 4:1–3 where YHWH's response by way of promise is clear: if you repent, I will heal and forgive and restore your name among the nations. What makes this prayer acceptable is the change of behavior that flows from a "personal and profound relationship to Yahweh."[11] Prayer for forgiveness, with its claims of repentance, will be acceptable to God only if the supplicant turns from sin.

Finally, the *ideal of repentance* can be seen in both the message of Deuteronomy and in the actions of Josiah, Ezra, and Nehemiah. For instance, Deuteronomy 30:1–14 promises at least the following for the exiled nation if it repents with all its heart and obeys God, both adults and children. God will (1) restore the nation's fortunes, (2) return to the people in compassion, (3) regather the scattered people from the diaspora so they can (4) reconvene in the Land of Israel, where they will enjoy the following blessings: (5) prosperity and national growth, (6) a circumcised heart producing love for God and long life, and (7) vindication against its enemies. This is a list full of good things that come to those who repent, and it is the ideal goal of repentance. Accordingly, we find these very items when we read the stories of the repentance of the nation under Josiah (2 Kings 22–23; 2 Chronicles 34–35), Ezra, and Nehemiah (Ezra 9; Nehemiah 9).

Jesus and Conversion

The six points about conversion outlined in the preceding section are the context of Jesus' call to repentance, his call for his people to convert before the onrushing of God's judgment against his sinful people. His message and his mission are both deeply connected to Israel's past and to its prophets. In this context, we can appreciate the major emphases of his message of conversion.

The Call to Conversion

Jesus declared that it was time for God's kingdom to arrive and by that he also meant the ideals of the Deuteronomic tradition sketched above: restoring Israel's national fortunes, compassion, the twelve tribes being regathered, etc.[12] An important observation needs to be made: Jesus' message is anchored in a specific historical period for a specific people. He is called to awaken Israel from its spiritual slumber and to rise into a new life of covenant obedience. So it is not surprising that an important note in Jesus' message of repentance is that it is primarily national and not narrowed simply to the salvation of individuals. His heart was for his people, not for small conventicles of spiritual development. Modern Westerners usually miss this because of their inherent individualism. The order, in the ancient world, was this: I am an Israelite; my name is Reuben. Not: my name is Reuben; I do this and that, and (by the way) I am an Israelite. Corporate solidarity shaped personal identity and gave to it a significance that transcends contemporary individualism. I emphasize here, as I will do in other places, that this order does not eliminate individual responsibility; still, the ancient world was not as individualistic as our cultures are. In what follows I will explain Jesus' message from the angle of this larger, national mission, but I do not mean in this to excuse his contemporaries from individual response. A call to the nation meant that individuals would have to take up the challenge, but it was not a call to individuals, regardless of what the nation chose to do.

Thus, the regional and corporate nature of repentance can be seen in Matthew 12:38–42 (italics added):

> Then some of the scribes and Pharisees said to him, "Teacher, we wish to see a sign from you." But he answered them, "An evil and adulterous generation asks for a sign, but no sign will be given to it except the sign of the prophet Jonah. For just as Jonah was three days and three nights in the belly of the sea monster, so for three days and three nights the Son of Man will be in the heart of the earth. The people of Nineveh will rise up at the judgment with this generation and condemn it, *because they repented* at the proclamation of Jonah, and see, something greater than Jonah is here! The queen of the South will rise up at the judgment with this generation and condemn it, because she came from the ends of the earth *to listen* to the wisdom of Solomon, and see, something greater than Solomon is here!

One of Jesus' terms for his contemporary Galilean and Judean Jews was "this generation." When that term appears, as it does here, a disk crash is on its way. To say that Ninevites and the queen of the South will find more acceptance with God on the day of judgment (than will Israelites) is a plucky condemnation of contemporary Judaism. Israel's current condition, Jesus says, is rooted in its unwillingness to repent, to turn back to things as they once were when the covenant ruled Israel. The same message is found in Luke 13:1–5 (italics added):

> At that very time there were some present who told him about the
> Galileans whose blood Pilate had mingled with their sacrifices. He
> asked them, "Do you think that because these Galileans suffered in
> this way they were worse sinners than all other Galileans? No, I tell
> you; *but unless you repent, you will all perish as they did.* Or those eigh-
> teen who were killed when the tower of Siloam fell on them—do you
> think that they were worse offenders than all the others living in Jeru-
> salem? No, I tell you; *but unless you repent, you will all perish just as they
> did.*"

An unfortunate tragedy, like the collapse of a building in a sleepy southern city, becomes for Jesus an opportunity to inform his contemporaries
about the need to convert. For Jesus, *all* need to repent; in the opinion of
most Jews, only the "wicked" (*reshaim*) need to repent, those who intentionally and unremorsefully disregard Jewish laws. His is a call to national
survival in its last hour, a call for the whole nation to turn back to the old
ways to find its fortunes restored. There is no time to wait. If the entire
nation doesn't convert, disaster will come.

At times Jesus says his contemporaries must turn from their sins, as he
does in Luke 5:32; 13:1–5; and 15:7, 10—but it is not always clear just
what sins are in view. If the primary aim of repentance is the national
restoration, then it follows that its sins are primarily "the present course
of the nation." Some have suggestively related this to an overly ambitious
reliance on a growing sense of violence, as becomes so clear in the behavior of the Zealots of the Great Jewish War against Rome in 66–73 C.E.
Others have seen in the call to repentance a plea for a "politics of compassion" to replace the current "politics of holiness."[13] In both of these,
the behavior of violence is given too great an emphasis. The evidence is
not broad enough for us to focus Jesus' message on a context of escalat-
ing rabid violence. So we may tone this approach down to hear Jesus' mission as follows: Israel's problem is a lack of holiness *and* compassion, as
well as a mistaken sense of priorities. Haggai, that great prophet whose
short sermons spoke of the need to get priorities straight, becomes a pro-
totype for Jesus. Jesus, in other words, is less concerned with Rome's permanent threat to provoke Israelite violence than with Israel's permanent
acquiescence in infidelity. Jesus thinks Israel has jumped its tracks, tracks
laid by the Torah and God's ways with Abraham, Moses, and the prophets.
Israel's problem is infidelity to the covenant.

Jesus calls all his followers to a regular confession of sins. Embedded in
the Lord's Prayer is a small petition, so familiar that its original context is

comfortably shoved to the side, which asks God daily to forgive sins (Luke 11:4; Matt. 6:12).[14] In light of both the above context of how prophets understood repentance as well as the Jewish context of the *Qaddish* and *Shemoneh Esreh*, two characteristic prayers in the air at the time of Jesus, we have to say that while Jesus expected his followers to request forgiveness from God for their "indebtedness to him," that is, sins, we need to learn to see the request in its proper context. This request is a representative prayer: the individual Israelite seeks God for forgiveness just as God's kingdom is petitioned. In other words, the follower of Jesus is standing for his people in asking God to forgive Israel and restore the fortunes of Israel. I do not mean to suggest that forgiveness is not also an individual matter, but I do think it is much less concerned with asking God for forgiveness for routine sins and much more about a social issue—persistent disobedience. Jesus knew this because he could infer it by reading the Torah and noting the absence of the blessings God had promised to the nation. The prayer says "forgive *us*" and not "forgive *me*." The prayer, by nature, is corporate. It was the individual followers of Jesus, who were Israelites, pleading with God to save their nation—much the way Americans might do on the National Day of Prayer or when a foreign country undergoes a national crisis or disaster. I offer a concrete analogy: Jesus' prayer for forgiveness can be likened to how persons from the Balkans were praying for the war to stop, for the nation to find peace, and for the senselessness to halt. In so doing, the pious Balkan might enter the presence of God and utter, "Father, forgive us!" Forgiveness would in that context be known by peace.

Jesus imagines a repentance that leads to a social restitution for those formerly wronged. When offering at the Temple, the follower of Jesus is counseled to drop the offering if a case of unforgiveness exists with another (Matt. 5:23–26). Dropping a sacrifice at Temple, occurring only on High Holy Days, leads us to think that this matter of restitution is fundamental to Jesus. Moreover, Zacchaeus's own conversion is a telling story of what Jesus expected of his followers (Luke 19:1–10). He transcends expectations in an overflowing abundance of repentance and restitution as he attempts to rectify in society what he has distorted. In other words, the prayer of repentance (as with the older prophets) is effective only if the people's behavior changes.

Life in the Community of Jesus

In short, Jesus unburdens himself with a message of conversion for his nation: Israel, if it wishes to avert the disaster of Jerusalem's destruction, must turn from its waywardness and accept God's offer of the kingdom. This message, so far outlined, however, is pessimistic even if incomplete: if the converts to Jesus were to repent, that is turn back to the things as they once were, what would this new life in Israel look like? Jesus envisioned a social reality to his message of conversion, showing once more that Jesus' entire mission had a socially creative goal. Eventually this "social vision" would become the church. At least three features of the practical life of a convert to Jesus can be mentioned here.

Jesus *called for a moral core of love for his followers.* Recall that Jews at the time of Jesus prayed the *Shema,* now found in Deuteronomy 6:4–9, perhaps several times daily. Recall also that Christians consider the essence of Jesus' moral teachings to be "love God" and "love others as yourself" (Mark 12:28–34). If Christians think their distinct note is love and that it differs from Jesus' Jewish roots, they will be surprised to learn that Jesus' teachings in Mark 12:28–34 are identical to the *Shema.* The love taught there (back in the OT!) was to be their moral compass: *love God and love others.* Nothing new here, but something, nevertheless, very important. Deductive logic from these two premises leads Jesus to a complete moral guidance. Love is for Jesus the greatest and primary commandment. It seems highly likely to me that Jesus saw the *Shema* as a summary of the two tables of the Ten Commandments,[15] and this may also be seen in the response of Jesus to the rich young ruler (Mark 10:17–31). Setting out the Ten Commandments as particular manifestations of loving God and loving others clearly places Jesus within Judaism as a prophet and gives wonderful guidance to his followers who were not trained to follow all the intricacies of scribal, oral tradition.

Jesus expected his converts, who were committed to loving God and one another, *to live as a community of peace.*[16] Once again, we need to push ourselves outside the mold of understanding peace as "inner tranquility" (another feature of individualism) and see it as Jesus understood it—as a social, communal, and interpersonal moral condition. A first-century Jew would think of peace in terms of Isaiah's great visions: Isaiah 9:5–6; 11:6–9. Here peace is national well-being and covenantal contentment, the condition of living within the blessings of Deuteronomy 28. Jesus opposed what was on the nation's horizon: national strife (Matt. 5:9) and the option of violence (Luke 9:51–56; 22:38). The parable of the Weeds and Wheat is a parable about the peaceful coexistence of followers of Jesus with nonfollowers of Jesus, within the broader umbrella of Judaism—the "world" as Jews knew it. Further, this parable calls for a placid, patient hope for God to make the decisions of "who is who" in God's kingdom

(Matt. 13:24–30, 36–43).[17] That Jesus' followers were looking for "peace" can be gleaned from the unintentional but revealing comments of the crowds at his entry into Jerusalem: they want peace (Luke 19:38, 39–42). A community of love, a community of peace. Two important traits of Jesus' converts to the kingdom.

In addition, Jesus wanted his followers to *be marked by another moral marker: righteousness.*[18] This term, so important to the piety of Jesus' day, described in a variety of ways how Israelites conformed to God's will as expressed in the Torah, Prophets, and Writings (the Jewish terms for the Christian Old Testament, though in a different order). Jesus expects his followers to live with an abundant righteousness (Matt. 5:17–20), a righteousness that contrasted with the Pharisees not because the option was "merit" versus "imputed" righteousness, but because he called for a righteousness whose standard was shaped by living according to Jesus' new kingdom ethics (cf. Matthew 5:21–48; 6:1–18; 7:12). Jesus' eyes, as any reader knows, had blades, sharp and active, darting here and there. His fundamental complaint against his nation was not so much that people were disobeying the Torah. No, they were not loving God and not loving others as he understood that love. The good life Jesus called for was a life of "righteousness," and righteousness is living within the rubrics of loving God and loving others, of living for peace.

To summarize: Jesus' concrete expectations emerging out of this national repentance were to live lovingly, peacefully, and righteously. His conception of the moral life then is derived from Torah but is shaped now in light of his kingdom mission for Israel. For Jesus, this call to love, peace, and righteousness had a special angle: economic justice. From John (Luke 3:10–14), his relative, Jesus learned that those who repented must abandon their luxurious indulgences, their pursuit of a material existence, and their hoarding of goods at the expense of others. Jesus blesses especially the poor (Luke 6:20); he calls his followers to pay the cost, no matter what;[19] and he gives special kudos to anyone abandoning wealth and possessions (Luke 12:32–34; 14:33; 19:1–10). This economic responsibility for one another had a special manifestation in the earliest churches of Jerusalem (Acts 4:32–35)—a community that attempted to live out the vision of Jesus.

We now have on the table a general summary of Jesus' understanding of repentance or conversion. This is our first look at the evidence. We know the "basics of conversion" for Jesus—but what we know, however important, is abstract and general. We know people need to repent; we know people need to follow Jesus; and we know they need to associate themselves with one another in love, peace, and righteousness. But what are the specifics of conversion? More important, how did conversion take place when those people did convert to Jesus?

At this point a more specific context needs to be given a first look to see if we can find more about the process of conversion. To accomplish this, I will now offer a brief survey of the "conversion" stories of the Gospels. These stories will flesh out somewhat those basics of conversion we have learned from Jesus' message and mission.

The Gospel Stories of Conversion

Even before we begin looking at the Gospel stories involving a conversion we have a problem: which stories do we study to find information about specific examples of conversion? Once again, one orientation to conversion, discussed in the Introduction, leads us to certain traditions while a different orientation might lead us to other Gospel traditions. For instance, the "socialization orientation" finds absolutely no evidence for conversion to Jesus—for good reason: the evidence is not about those who were raised to believe in Jesus.[20] The "liturgical orientation" will focus on John the Baptist calling people to baptism in the Jordan (Luke 3:1–22), on Jesus' probable baptism of others (cf. John 3:22), or on the "first eucharist" (Mark 14:12–26). But there is no record of any follower of Jesus being baptized (even if it probably happened) or of a convert expressing faith and then going to "first eucharist." There are analogies for the " personal-decision orientation" in the Gospel stories though the experience varies so much from one person to another and the specific language of "receiving" or "believing" is so infrequent that we are best led to enter this issue from another angle.

Furthermore, we can clear the stubble out of this forest even more: the Gospel stories that we do have are not so much conversions from apathy and unbelief to faith, but from a faith *within* Judaism to another kind of faith within Judaism, a new kind of faith—kingdom faith. This means we are dealing with a revitalization of one's faith or a conversion to a new form (the Jesus movement kind of Judaism) of an old faith (a Pharisee or an Essene or a Zealot kind of Judaism).

Another issue also confronts us: If we are looking at conversions as altered belief and behavior within Judaism, which stories do we examine? Do we just look at the stories about Peter, Levi, and Zacchaeus, or do we look also at those who were healed and who then began to follow Jesus? Previous study of conversion in the Jesus traditions focuses too much on the nonhealing stories, those dealing with Peter, Levi, and Zacchaeus. I don't want to deny their importance, but modern sociology of conversion reveals that people convert for a variety of reasons and not all of them are religious and spiritual. Certainly, many convert without the foggiest notion that they are seeking release from sinfulness. This means that previous study has had a theory of conversion, that being purely and solely religious in motivation, shaping how it has addressed the Jesus traditions. I shall in what follows then take a cue from sociological theory and ask if the healing tradition might also be worth looking at when it comes to the issue of conversion in the ministry of Jesus.

The following survey of the evidence, no doubt at times reflecting the special editing of the evangelists themselves, will give us a second context of conversion in the Jesus material. This first look focuses on how little these stories actually tell us. The same traditions will be examined later when new tools have been added to the workshop.

The Conversion of Simon Peter (and Three Others)

I begin with the stories of the first four converts: Simon and Andrew, James and John, sons of Zebedee (Mark 1:16–20). Our author uses densely formulated prose, and in the account we read the following:

> As Jesus passed along the Sea of Galilee, he saw Simon and his brother Andrew casting a net into the sea—for they were fishermen. And Jesus said to them, "Follow me and I will make you fish for people." And immediately they left their nets and followed him. As he went a little farther, he saw James son of Zebedee and his brother John, who were in their boat mending the nets. Immediately he called them; and they left their father Zebedee in the boat with the hired men, and followed him.

In this account we learn (1) that Jesus calls these four men and (2) that they followed him immediately. We could infer from this, as many have done, that conversion is an intrusive call and an immediate response. But is it? Does this simple story of no more than seven lines intend to tell us about *how conversion takes place?* Or does the account intend simply to give us a stylized account of the first four converts to Jesus? The latter seems more likely. For us to understand the nature and process of conversion, we would need more.

In fact, the evidence about Peter from another Gospel widens the scope of this story considerably. Luke's Gospel records a fuller account of Peter's conversion. It is too bad for us that we don't have more information about the other three. Luke 5:1–11 says,

> Once while Jesus was standing beside the lake of Gennesaret, and the crowd was pressing in on him to hear the word of God, he saw two boats there at the shore of the lake; the fishermen had gone out of them and were washing their nets. He got into one of the boats, the one belonging to Simon, and asked him to put out a little way from the shore. Then he sat down and taught the crowds from the boat. When he had finished speaking, he said to Simon, "Put out into the deep water and let down your nets for a catch." Simon answered, "Master, we have worked all night long but have caught nothing. Yet if you say so, I will let down the nets." When they had done this, they caught so many fish that their nets were beginning to break. So they signaled their partners in the other boat to come and help them. And they came and filled both boats, so that they began to sink. But when Simon Peter saw it, he fell down at Jesus' knees, saying, "Go away from me, Lord, for I am a sinful man!" For he and all who were with him were amazed at the catch of fish that they had taken; and so also were James and John, sons of Zebedee, who were partners with Simon. Then Jesus said to Simon, "Do not be afraid; from now on you will be catching people." When they had brought their boats to shore, they left everything and followed him.

Here we get more of what we want if we are looking at how conversion actually occurred at the time of Jesus: Jesus enters Simon's real-world life, fishing, and asks him to cast the nets on the other side—why we don't know. After some (reasonable, it seems) hesitations, Peter waives his rights to fish as he knows best and casts the nets on the other side of the boat where he finds wild success. So much so that Peter falls to his knees and confesses—of all things!—his sinfulness. We learn that the other three also were at the scene and, for whatever reasons, after this incident with Peter began to follow Jesus in fishing for people. But we have some questions: Why did Jesus invade Simon Peter's life? Why not the others? Why did Jesus suggest casting the nets on the other side? Was it because he knew more about fishing? Why did the other three begin following Jesus?

Here's the bigger question: Why did a net full of fish lead Simon (and perhaps the others) to a confession of sinfulness? How could such an action lead to such a response? One suspects we are not getting the whole story. After all, if you have spent any time on the docks, there is no connection between fishing, even when wildly successful, and confessing sins! We are driven by the evidence to a first conclusion: *these are not complete stories of conversion.* The evangelists give us what interests them and their audiences—the basics of the call of these four. The basics are the call and the response. A few details are tossed in to give the body some life. But we dare not infer from the reports here that we know a full account of how these conversions took place. In fact, if the Johannine story is taken into account, this was no Uncle Sam's "I Want You!" event; instead, it is the climax of an already-existing relationship with Jesus (cf. John 1:35–51). We are on safer ground if we learn to admit that the texts tell us only part of the story. We might be tempted to speculate, but more important, we ought not be tempted to think we know all the details.

The Conversion of Levi/Matthew

We can turn, with less comment, to other stories. Levi, who in the Gospel of Matthew is called "Matthew," has the following story told of him:

> Jesus went out again beside the sea; the whole crowd gathered around him, and he taught them. As he was walking along, he saw Levi son of Alphaeus sitting at the tax booth, and he said to him, "Follow me." And he got up and followed him.
>
> And as he sat at dinner in Levi's house, many tax collectors and sinners were also sitting with Jesus and his disciples—for there were many who followed him. When the scribes of the Pharisees saw that he was eating with sinners and tax collectors, they said to his disciples, "Why does he eat with tax collectors and sinners?" When Jesus heard this, he said to them, "Those who are well have no need of a physician, but those who are sick; I have come to call not the righteous but sinners." (Mark 2:13–17; cf. Matt. 9:913)

Why Levi? We don't know. Did he know Jesus before this incident? We don't know. If we presume for Levi what we learned about the first four, we might speculate that Jesus knew Levi already. Or, should we imagine Jesus showing up at a toll station, looking a man dead in the eye, and, as a result of some magical charisma, issuing a call to follow him? If so, should we think Levi abandons the station to get out of work? Or should we imagine that he had already heard plenty about Jesus and that this is but the climax to a relationship with Jesus? It makes far more sense to think realistically—that Levi had heard about Jesus and this was (possibly) his crisis point of decision or at least a significant moment in his conversion. What happened to Levi after his evening with Jesus? We really don't know. If Levi is the same as Matthew, as seems the case in Matthew's Gospel, and if this Matthew is the apostle, then we know that this tax collector became a serious follower of Jesus and was chosen to be sent forth by Jesus to proclaim his message. To be honest, though, the Gospel records don't seem to care much about Matthew or Levi. They tell us almost nothing about the man, and so the full story of his conversion is left in a shroud of mystery and unanswerable questions.

The Conversion of Zacchaeus

We think next of the account of a conversion in the story of Zacchaeus: Luke 19:1–10.

> He entered Jericho and was passing through it. A man was there named Zacchaeus; he was a chief tax collector and was rich. He was trying to see who Jesus was, but on account of the crowd he could not, because he was short in stature. So he ran ahead and climbed a sycamore tree to see him, because he was going to pass that way. When Jesus came to the place, he looked up and said to him, "Zacchaeus, hurry and come down; for I must stay at your house today." So he hurried down and was happy to welcome him. All who saw it began to grumble and said, "He has gone to be the guest of one who is a sinner." Zacchaeus stood there and said to the Lord, "Look, half of my possessions, Lord, I will give to the poor; and if I have defrauded anyone of anything, I will pay back four times as much." Then Jesus said to him, "Today salvation has come to this house, because he too is a son of Abraham. For the Son of Man came to seek out and to save the lost."[21]

Again, should we assume that Zacchaeus already knew about Jesus? Probably so, since he does run ahead to see Jesus, and that makes best sense if the tax collector knows who is coming and something about him. Why did Jesus single him out? We don't really know. Why would Zacchaeus respond so quickly to Jesus' message and give up all his money and make such daring restitution? Was it because of what Jesus said at his table later? Was there a previous encounter? Or was it just a shrewd, lucky insight on

Zacchaeus's part to think of restitution? Probably it was because Jesus told him all about his vision for economic justice. So many questions, but not as much evidence as we would like about conversion. Once again, we see the basics of conversion: enter Jesus, enter repentance, enter discipleship. But we see little about *the process of conversion*. How then did it take place?

Other Details in the Gospels

We know more: we know that Jesus called crowds to deny themselves and follow him (Mark 8:34–9:1); we know that Jesus gave at times stiff conditions for would-be followers (Luke 9:57–62); we know that Jesus sometimes invaded a person's life and turned it inside out (John 4:1–42; cf. 7:53–8:11). And we know that sometimes people just stiffed Jesus (Mark 10:17–31). This information needs to be put in yet another context: the same demand to follow Jesus as the focus of God's new work in the Galilee for Israel continues to be urged for the same group of people. For instance, it is to "disciples" that Jesus gives the call to come to him and take his yoke (Matt. 11:28–30). The calls to discipleship, then, are probably not "evangelization" so much as the continued call to previously known people to commit themselves to the vision of Jesus for his people. That is, it is a call to join his social group that is characterized by love, peace, and righteousness. Is this perhaps what Jesus meant by "evangelism"?

The Conversion of a Leper

Healing stories also give us some clues about converting to Jesus since some of those who began to follow Jesus did so because they found in him a healing power. Three stories will suffice here. I begin with a purified leper in Mark 1:40–45:

> A leper came to him begging him, and kneeling he said to him, "If you choose, you can make me clean." Moved with pity, Jesus stretched out his hand and touched him, and said to him, "I do choose. Be made clean!" Immediately the leprosy left him, and he was made clean. After sternly warning him he sent him away at once, saying to him, "See that you say nothing to anyone; but go, show yourself to the priest, and offer for your cleansing what Moses commanded, as a testimony to them." But he went out and began to proclaim it freely, and to spread the word, so that Jesus could no longer

go into a town openly, but stayed out in the country; and people came
to him from every quarter.

Here we find a similar pattern noted previously: enter Jesus, enter
response, enter obedience. There is no reason to exclude those healed by
Jesus from the evidence about conversion. With supernatural experiences
on the rise in modern consciousness, we find an avenue to them easier,
more tolerable, and worthy of more careful consideration for what they
might also say about conversion. But, again, we are left with some questions: Did the leper's experience stick? Did he flesh it out with obedience
as a permanent condition? We have no reason to doubt that he did, but
we also have no way to know if he did. Did he know about Jesus' message
of the kingdom? About his vision for Israel? He knew Jesus did not
exclude lepers from his new community of followers and that was at least
something different. How did he know about Jesus? We don't know. Had
he heard of Jesus before? Did he know more about Jesus than that he was
a healer? Again, we don't know. Did he disregard Jesus' instruction to go
to the Temple to undergo a proper ritual to be reestablished as a pure
Israelite? We don't know. I'd like to think he did. Did he consider his
cleansing as a salvation experience? The texts don't tell us. What was the
leper telling everyone? That Jesus was ushering in the kingdom—which
is how Jesus understood his miracles (cf. Matt. 11:2–6; 12:28)? Or that
Jesus was a healer and could really do big things? Again, we don't know
what he was telling people. We know so little; therefore, we need to be
more careful in what we infer from this story.

The Conversion of Blind Bartimaeus

A similar kind of story occurs in Mark 10:46–52, where we find the story
of Blind Bartimaeus:

> They came to Jericho. As he and his disciples and a large crowd were
> leaving Jericho, Bartimaeus son of Timaeus, a blind beggar, was sit-
> ting by the roadside. When he heard that it was Jesus of Nazareth,
> he began to shout out and say, "Jesus, Son of David, have mercy on
> me!" Many sternly ordered him to be quiet, but he cried out even
> more loudly, "Son of David, have mercy on me!" Jesus stood still and
> said, "Call him here." And they called the blind man, saying to him,
> "Take heart; get up, he is calling you." So throwing off his cloak, he
> sprang up and came to Jesus. Then Jesus said to him, "What do you

want me to do for you?" The blind man said to him, "My teacher, let me see again." Jesus said to him, "Go; your faith has made you well." Immediately he regained his sight and followed him on the way.

We have here a quester, one who was "looking" for Jesus to come his way so he might find healing; we find Jesus entering into this man's blind world to turn on his lights; we find a man who responds in simple faith; we find the man then following Jesus on the way—surely an expression for discipleship. But, again, we have questions: Why did he call Jesus "Son of David"? We can only assume he had heard of Jesus and that this term, which is not the normal term used by Jews for a healer, expressed what he thought of Jesus. Did his request of "mercy" involve some idea of salvation? Was he thinking at all of sinfulness? Perhaps; that would be Jewish. It is more likely, however, that he was thinking of his eyesight. It says Bartimaeus had "faith"? In what? In Jesus as healer? as restorer of Israel? as Messiah? as King of Israel? as Kingdom bringer? as forgiver of sins? We can't be completely sure, but we are on safe grounds thinking that Jesus as a healer was uppermost in his mind. And what does "followed him on the way" mean? How far? A mile? Two miles? All the way to Jerusalem? Or, is the expression more metaphorical, and does it mean that he followed him as a disciple? That he followed Jesus literally and then came back home and began living for Jesus and his kingdom? Again, we have lots of questions and few solid answers.

The Conversion of "Some Women"

Soon afterwards he went on through cities and villages, proclaiming and bringing the good news of the kingdom of God. The twelve were with him, as well as some women who had been cured of evil spirits and infirmities: Mary, called Magdalene, from whom seven demons and gone out, and Joanna, the wife of Herod's steward Chuza, and Susanna, and many others who provided for them out of their resources. (Luke 8:1–3)

If healing is considered a motive for conversion, then the account of these women needs to be considered in a study of converting to Jesus. In fact, the women who frequent the pages of the Jesus traditions are not irregularly neglected in studies of conversion mostly, it seems, because the term "disciple" is not used for them (but cf. Mark 15:41 where *akoloutheo* is used). In fact, the witness to women following Jesus is abundant, implying that conversions by women are taking place for a variety of motives (cf. Matt. 8:14–15; Mark 5:21–43; Luke 7:36–50; 10:38–42; 13:11–17; John 4; 7:53–8:11; 11). Like other followers of Jesus, we learn very little about their conversions. We can infer that their conversions took place prior to this "mission tour" (Luke 8:1), but we know only the following: that there were many women who followed Jesus (8:3), that they had been healed, and that their coming to Jesus was probably rooted in their needs of healing and health. But there is so much we don't know: Why did a woman from the circle of Herodian power, Joanna, convert to Jesus? Why is nothing else in the entire Jesus tradition said about Susanna? Is it the case that Joanna and Susanna felt compelled by Jesus' charisma to provide financially for his ministry? Were these women accepted alongside the other disciples by society as equals? As fellow-disciples? The text is tantalizing but lets us in on very few details about how conversion took place. More could be said about the conversion of women, but the stories of women tell us no more about conversion than the stories of men.

Conclusion: What Do We Learn about Conversion?

In summary, we find some features about conversion to Jesus but don't find all we want. We find, for instance, that people convert for different reasons; that people are questing for Jesus; that Jesus surely enters into the world of all sorts of people; that they respond to Jesus in faith and obedience; and that they follow him. But is this all there is: call, repentance, and discipleship? Early in our discussion, I am willing to say that these three features are surely the core of Jesus' call to conversion. But can we know more? Do we learn from these stories much about the process of conversion? How it took place? We have picked up stray bits of information here and there, but in the end, since the Gospel stories have other concerns, we do not learn here as much as we would like about how conversion took place.

Let me respond to some potential problems from what has been said. I am not saying the Gospel stories are wrong or that they distort the stories of conversion. What I am saying is that the evangelists had other things on their minds when they wrote such accounts. While they tell us some things about conversion, they don't hone in on the more fundamental details because that was not part of their purpose. They gave us the basics; that was enough for them. But, in the intervening years two issues have been raised: (1) Christians have used the stories as if the whole story of conversion is there, or they have neglected them entirely; and (2) we have gradually come to the point where we wonder what actually took place in conversions to Jesus in the first century. Is there a way for us to discover more? I think there is, even if we have to proceed cautiously.

We can now look at how modern sociologists look at conversion so that we can refocus our lens when we come back to the Gospel traditions. This approach will give us a clearer lens, a wider lens, and even a more telescopic lens, through which we can see dimensions of the text and its context that we did not previously observe. What the sociology-of-conversion approach implies is that the process of conversion can be investigated by the use of sociological models and that there is a fair degree of uniformity, with plenty of room for emphasis and diversity, in all conversion experience. If we can determine then a model of conversion that is adequate to human experience in general and Christian conversion in particular, we can look again at the Jesus traditions to see if more can be learned about conversion at the time of Jesus.

In using a sociological approach, however, I want to add that I do not think religious experience can be reduced to social determinism. What sensitive sociologists do when they look at religious experience is to explain the phenomenon in social categories, but in so doing they are simply living within the guidelines of their profession. I shall accept those guidelines in the next few chapters, though at times we shall step outside those lines to clarify matters from the perspective of faith.

Chapter Two

Conversion

From Context to Quest

The most complete study of conversion of the last century is that of Lewis R. Rambo, *Understanding Religious Conversion*.[1] His model shows the balance of a "consensus report," and thus provides an even more adequate basis for the integration of biblical and sociological study attempted in this book.[2] More important, Rambo has the courage to grab a sacred bag and examine its contents sociologically with such care that its contents remain sacred. Conversion is not reduced to social forces or psychological urges (though no one should deny the presence of either); nor does Rambo trample all over the faith of individuals, as is unfortunately the case in some sociological studies of conversion. He presents a "process" understanding of conversion, with which I agree, but I question his seven stages: context, crisis, quest, encounter, interaction, commitment, and consequences. Rambo claims that each stage is found in all conversions; the term "stage," however, leaves one with the feeling of a deterministic march from earth to heaven. In what follows, I propose that we call these *dimensions* of conversion. Some people begin to see "consequences" even before they have consciously made a commitment, and some are still "questing" and "interacting" even after the "commitment." Further, it is proposed that "context" is not so much a "stage" as the *necessary condition of human existence* out of which a person emerges individually and socially to interact with the world, sometimes leading to a conversion. If these modifications are proposed, it is not because I think Rambo's model is insensitive to human realities. Nothing could be further from the facts of his presentation.

In what follows, I propose the following model of six dimensions of conversion.[3] First, each person's *context* must be understood—a context that dialectically shapes the convert as well as the process of conversion. Second, for conversion to take place some kind of *crisis* emerges, though this crisis requires careful examination and sensitive handling. Not all crises are big; not all are like St. Augustine's and Martin Luther's, nor is each like the painful process of John Henry Newman. Some are volcanic; others are no more than gentle nods of the soul. It is here that sociological study must be sensitive to the realities of genuine spiritual formation. Third, a person *quests* for answers to needs. The quest might generate a crisis; it might follow it. Fourth, a person *encounters* an advocate for the Christian faith and interacts with that advocate. To emphasize again that these are not successive stages, the "encounter" with an advocate may take place prior to a crisis. In fact, the advocate for the faith may well be a part of the context in which a person is reared, and the converting person may be in an ongoing interaction with that advocate (which need not be limited to a person but can be the "truth" system itself). Fifth, the converting person *commits* to the religious persuasion. Again, while logically one does not "commit" until one has quested and encountered the Christian faith, the realities of the conversion may not be so simple. Some converts may say they never knew a time when they weren't committed to Jesus though they are quite open about crises, quests, encounters, and various commitments. Sixth, the *consequences* of conversion manifest themselves in a person's life in a variety of ways. In what follows, we will go through each of these dimensions and provide examples, both from stories in print and from stories given to me by my students.

One further modification: a recent study on the "politics of conversion" by Gauri Viswanathan will augment this model of conversion with insights into the sociopolitical implications of religious conversion.[4] Viswanathan demonstrates that conversions are themselves "political actions," either as dissent or assent to a governing belief system. Assent to one is often dissent to another. Her study at times throws fresh light on modern conversions as well as on those at the time of Jesus. After surveying this adapted model, we will then return to the Gospel stories to apply our insights and show that this model enables us to grasp a fuller historical understanding of how conversion took place at the time of Jesus. But before we can examine the model, we need to make just a few general observations about conversion as a group and individual dynamic as well as about different kinds of conversion.

Group/Individual Dynamics in Conversion

What is conversion? That is, what is it if we take into consideration nearly a century of intense biblical and sociological study of the phenomenon? Two definitions, the first from L. R. Rambo and the second from James

Fowler, reveal a range of emphases. After stating that the term "conversion" has a wide range of possible uses, Rambo says,

> Conversion is what a group or person *says* it is. The process of conversion is a product of the interactions among the convert's aspirations, needs, and orientations, the nature of the group into which she or he is being converted, and the particular social matrix in which these processes are taking place.[5]

It will surprise some to hear this: "Conversion is what a group or person *says* it is." Is conversion determined by a group and hence a form of social control, or is it shaped by some more objective form of spiritual reality, that is, by God's Spirit? All that needs to be remembered here is that religious conversion is almost never purely individual. Conversion involves incorporation; the person's "personal story" becomes part of the "group's story." Since conversion is in fact *social or corporate* by nature (all converts convert to a group),[6] then it follows that conversion is in some sense defined by the group and, in most cases (and surely in our case in this book), by the charismatic leader of that group (the advocate).[7] Rambo's social focus and interactionist approach then need to be appreciated. Further, Rambo contends that converts interact with the religious group to achieve some kind of integrated understanding. This, too, makes sense. The potential convert has a world out of which he or she comes; the group is its own world; until those worlds interact, no conversion takes place. There is always give and take both ways.

More commonly today, conversion is defined more individualistically—and both the individual and the corporate dimensions deserve attention. James Fowler, a notable proponent of understanding faith in accordance with human development, has written a book entitled *The Stages of Faith*, which has had a wide hearing. He defines conversion as follows:

> Conversion is *a significant recentering of one's previous conscious or unconscious images of value and power, and the conscious adoption of a new set of master stories in the commitment to reshape one's life in a new community of interpretation and action.*[8]

This kind of language, as one of my students put it, "boggles my goggles." His abstractions, with their little chests puffed out, however, have a morning shave and a cleaner appearance in another of Fowler's books. Here he shapes this understanding of conversion as follows:

Rather, by conversion I mean *an ongoing process*—with, of course, a series of important moments of perspective-altering convictions and illuminations—*through which people (or a group) gradually bring the lived story of their lives into congruence with the core story of the Christian faith.*[9]

For sociologists and psychologists, then, though coming from various angles, conversion involves the person and a group, the person's identity and behavior as well as the group's "story," and when the identity and behavior are absorbed into the group's story, conversion takes place. What these definitions try to do is balance both the individual's experience and the group's symbolic universe of meaning—balance the would-be convert to Jesus and the church (read: particular churches and advocates) already associated with Jesus.[10]

The following stories of Maggie and Angela give living examples of the interaction of the group on the individual and the individual's personal decision. They come from different worlds, with dissimilar families and divergent religious communities, so the distinctions of the stories are also striking. (I have italicized expressions illustrating the group and individual interaction. Omissions are for the sake of space or clarity.)

Maggie's Story

My spiritual journey is quite boring in its own right . . . I was born in 1979 into a strong Italian-Catholic family. All of my family, and most of my friends around me were and still are Catholic. *It was all around me; it was like I was encapsulated in it and that is what I knew was right.* I was baptized as a baby, had my first Communion in second grade, and made my confirmation when I was in eighth grade. That is all I knew. *I just knew that I had to make my first Communion and confirmation when it came the time to because that is what everyone did.* My cousins did it, my neighbors did it, and my friends did it too. It was just the acceptable thing to do, *and I did it really without knowing why I did it besides the fact that I was just supposed to do it. So, that just made me believe that it was just the normal thing to do as you became an adult.* As I was growing up, we went to church almost every week. Sometimes we went to mass on Saturday evenings, and sometimes we went to mass on Sunday mornings. I absolutely hated church back then. It was long and boring. *But, as I grew older, like after my Communion and before my confirmation, I started to realize the other meanings behind why I was doing all of this "church stuff." I started to realize the important things. . . . I started to realize the important aspects on my own, like the meaning of God and why He is so important to us.*

[Maggie then speaks of her "rough patch" in high school, during which time she questioned God's existence, and then of her return to faith.]

. . . But, things changed, and I got back on the right path. *I realized my selfishness,* that just because I had hit a rough patch, that didn't mean that God had abandoned me. He was still there, and that is why I am still here, because He was there right by my side. . . . I believe that things happen for a reason, and the reason that I went through my rough time in high school was to make me realize how important God was to me, and it made me appreciate Him more.

But, the main thing is that I didn't choose my spiritual path; I was just born into it and it worked for me and still works for me so that is where I stayed. You could say that my path of conversion was a process of socialization. . . . I didn't go to Catholicism; it came to me. It was like I was taken by the hand and led to it. Even though I grew up "into" the Catholic faith, I do feel that my spiritual journey, which I was led through as I grew up, was *the right path for me.* I am happy in my path.

Angela's Story

*G*rowing up in a Christian home, one does not consider the process of conversion to be important to the child (him or herself) until he or she reaches a certain age of discernment. This age for myself came when I was in sixth grade, when I experienced for the first time Rambo's second type of conversion—intensification. However, as easy as this sounds, my experience was slightly complicated in that I experienced what I call a pseudo-conversion preceding my actual conversion decision. . . .

I must begin by . . . explaining *my rather normal Christian* [i.e., evangelical] *kid experiences.* Prior to being 11, *I had grown up in a Christian home, attended Sunday School, and Christian camps.* My parents were actively involved in the church and, obviously, *encouraged us to do the same.* However, it was not until I entered middle school *that I actually began questioning inwardly* these actions that we did every Sunday and on other formal occasions. I began attending the Junior High Youth Group and began asking questions.

One day at church there was an announcement that both the Senior High and Junior High Youth Groups were to be going to a play at the First Community Church in [city name given]. The title of the play was "Heaven's Gate and Hell's Fate." As one can discern from the name, the play was a hellfire and brimstone type of message. Sitting there next to a friend, I most definitely heard the message. I was sad and fearful in that auditorium seat. *People about me were crying out and raising their hands. I felt as though I should do the same,* for I knew that I believed God existed and had known that from viewing the big oak trees and my family's unconditional love. However, it was strange for me to do so, and I could not get out of my head how maybe all of it was for show.

When the altar call came, my friend nudged me and said, "I'll go if you go." My response at first was "No, we should go alone." But I changed my mind when I saw how disappointed my friend was and decided that I did not want to be "left behind" either. Thus, *together,* holding hands we proceeded to go up to the front of the church where the entire gymnasium prayed, and cried, for us. Then, much to my surprise, we were herded into a back room where the clinched hands of my friend and I were broken apart by two separate strangers who wanted to pray with us. I think the name of the man who prayed for me was "Bob," but I spent no more than two minutes with him praying and going through the Romans Road to Salvation [e.g., the important passages about salvation in Paul's letter to the Romans]. . . . *After the prayer, we were congratulated* and—today I am unsure why—given a cookie, and *herded back to our youth pastors.*

The van ride back was quiet as I remember, but very loud inside of my own head. I could not understand why I did not feel happy and content. *It seemed as though the whole experience had made me feel more unsettled, and not content at all.* I did not quite understand what had happened. I knew that it could not have been bad, but I was concerned that it felt nothing like the feeling *I had always read about in Jannette Oak Books, or heard about on TV.*

I did not inform anyone of my decision. Although my pastor spoke a bit to me, he stopped when he saw that I was uninterested in speaking. A lady from my church wrote a very kind note to me, but besides these two I spoke of this to no one. I cannot give any clear reason why; I can simply say that it felt weird and unnatural to speak about it. *That night when I came home I opened my Bible* and began reading those passages that "Bob" had skimmed through for me. *I read the words that I had always known and found truth in them again. Then I prayed a second prayer alone on my floor at one o'clock in the morning. I asked God to always stay with me, because I knew that He already had been with me. I told Him through His son that I loved Him, and told Him that I would do whatever He wanted me to do, and I would take whatever He gave me.* Remembering something that my mother had said about her own faith in that she would believe even if heaven and hell did not exist, I also mentioned that I did not want to believe because it would give me security. I just wanted truth. Looking back, I believe this was my moment of conversion.

In the case of both Maggie and Angela, the group—for one a local Italian family in a Roman Catholic church and for the other a typical American family in an evangelical church—made a significant impact on the expectations for religious sentiments and conversion. Maggie went through the separate steps of liturgy, as she was expected to do, and over time came to embrace that faith on a personal basis. Angela experienced a normal group-shaped form of evangelism, so typical of evangelicalism, but found the pressure led her beyond where she felt comfortable. As a result, she resolved the tension by taking care of business personally in her own room, late at night, in a prayer of confession and commitment. For each, however, group expectations were present to shape, form, and guide how conversion was experienced.

Each of these persons experienced a heavy dose of group expectations though each also resolved it in a personal manner. In particular, notice how Angela was "congratulated" and "given a cookie" (forms of approval) and how, when she got back home, the word spread so that the pastor and a nice lady both expressed approval in their own way. From these Angela learned what was approved by a group. However, she did not feel at ease with group approval and sought out a more personal-divine approval in prayer. Both Angela and Maggie were socialized into the Christian faith; both experienced moments of crisis that led to a more integrated faith; and both, now as young adults, are seeking to live out their faith in their own way.

Kinds of Conversion

The examples of Maggie and Angela illustrate a special kind of conversion: both of these young women converted into a faith in which they were reared. That is, they affirmed the faith in which they were nurtured. Both were reared in a church that had a rite called "confirmation," which makes official the act of "confirming" what was given to them through infant baptism and through Christian nurture in the church. For both of them, however, that rite was not as personally important as a later decision to deal with spirituality as they experienced it. Some sociologists see this as an intensification form of conversion—an intensification of faith that was formerly present in the form of a seed that then blossoms into full flower. We need now to look at the various kinds of conversion.

There are least five kinds of conversion.[11] First, conversion involves an *apostasy or defection* from some group. Some conversions involve a repudiation of a former religious movement.[12] Apostasy, of course, is in the eyes of the judge, not the convert. The young Baptist man who becomes Roman Catholic may be called an "apostate" by his Baptist church, but the Roman Catholic parish would welcome him into the flock of God. Second, a common form of conversion is *intensification* of the Christian faith with which one is already associated to some degree. This occurs when a young adult steps up his or her commitment to the faith in which he or she was reared. Third, *affiliation* conversion takes place when a person moves from either a minimal or no association with the Christian faith to full commitment. Thus, affiliation takes place when a lethargic Presbyterian or an apathetic person becomes a fully activated Presbyterian. Fourth, crossing a larger chasm, *institutional transition* occurs when a person changes from one "denomination" to another "denomination" within the Christian faith. This is particularly noticeable when we find Roman Catholics becoming Episcopalians, or Orthodox becoming Mennonites, or evangelicals becoming Pentecostals. Finally, it is called *tradition transition* when a person jumps to the Christian faith from another religion. On October 14, 1956, Ambedkar moved from Hinduism to Buddhism and took 500,000 Untouchables with him! These conversions are not the same, though one could find each of the six dimensions of conversion (discussed previously) for each conversion.

The special dynamics of each kind of conversion deserves careful respect and is worthy of more serious attention as our world becomes more and more of a melting pot. The following example of Maria illustrates institutional transition as she and her family converted from an

Orthodox faith to an evangelical faith. In providing this example, however, I must add that I don't think Orthodox faith is inferior to evangelical faith. I record here the experience of one convert from the Orthodox Church. Examples can be found for those who have converted the other direction. My purpose is to illustrate how someone moves "within the larger Christian family" and not to make an evaluation of such a move.

Maria's Story

I came to understand the gift Jesus gave by dying on the cross when I was in fifth grade. I had grown up in an Orthodox Christian home, but my family and I did not fully understand what it meant to have a personal relationship with Jesus. I remember going to church with my parents when I was a little girl. As soon as we would enter the sanctuary, I could smell the incense that was being burned and was being carried around by a man who would walk around every aisle in the church swinging the holder back and forth. Everyone was encircled by the trails of smoke that it left. After accepting Communion, my family and I would walk into a small room, slip a few dollars in a tin box, and light candles. Afterwards, we would go home.

Living in Iran for the first five or six years of my life, I knew the importance of what it meant to be a Christian. Since Iran was an Islamic Republic, it was difficult being a Christian. I remember having to cover my hair with a scarf and having to wear a *manto*, which was a long coat that covered my body. I remember having to wear long-sleeved shirts and long pants under the *manto* during the blistering hot summers. It used to be absolutely horrible having to go to school dressed in heavy dark clothes and sweating all the way there. . . . I learned from my parents how important it was to stay true to your faith even if it meant you were going to be persecuted for it. . . .

Although God was important to my family, he seemed to be a distant, almighty being who was separate from human beings. I did not understand why my family members were Christians. I just knew that we were, and that was all that mattered. After living for a while in the United States, my family and I stopped going to church, and the sad part was that we didn't even miss going. A few years later when we lived in [city name given], we started going to a Covenant church because my parents realized I needed God in my life due to the bitter change in my personality. At first I hated having to go to Sunday School because I did not know anyone, but my parents did not give up. Soon I began to make friends and started learning about who God truly was. One day as I was sitting in my room, I felt a pang of sorrow in my stomach, and I knew that I did not want to be bitter anymore because it hurt. I remember crying uncontrollably and asking Jesus to forgive me in between sobs.

. . . I became a Christian to find pleasure and to avoid pain. I was tired of the way my heart always felt so heavy, and I was tired of my bitterness. I no longer wanted to carry my burdens, and Jesus came and asked to carry them for me. I just could not say "no" to such an offer. As a new believer I experienced a joy that I had never known. It was a lot better than anything that I had ever experienced.

Maria's experience touches on three types of conversion. She has *apostasized* from the Orthodox faith; she *intensified* the Christian faith of her childhood when, as a teenager, she integrated faith into her life and dropped her bitterness; and she experienced *institutional transition* when she moved from the Orthodox Church into the Covenant Church, that is, from one Christian denomination to another. Apostasy, of course, is a matter of perception: for a broad-minded Orthodox person, Maria's transition to the Covenant Church could be explained as the flowering of the faith; for a more closed-minded person, she may be seen as one who has left the faith. Maria's faith, however, is best understood as institutional transition. She experienced new faith, not just an old faith come alive. Notice in her first few lines: ". . . but my family and I did not fully understand what it meant to have a personal relationship with Jesus." Her perception of the Christian faith, now shaped as it is by a personal-decision orientation, led her to think of her former faith as really no faith at all or, at the least, as not good enough to do her much good. Notice how the new faith she found led her to revise her own autobiography and how it gave her a handle on the meaning of life. In contrast to Angela and Maggie, Maria's pilgrimage involved a switching of one's primary group (denomination) where the second group's perception of conversion overwhelms and rejects the other group's perception of conversion. She moved from a socialized orientation to a personal-decision orientation, though we have little doubt that Maria's faith was as much the result of some socialization forces as it was a one-time decision.

In these three stories, we have examined what conversion is to various people. We now need to look more closely at how conversion takes place and what the process is that converts experience. In suggesting there is a process, I do not intend to override the convert's conviction that it is God who is working in his or her life. Nor do I intend to wipe out the mystery of religious experience and spiritual awareness. We are looking at conversion from a different angle: What are the common dimensions of the convert's experience? The remainder of this chapter examines in detail the first three dimensions of conversion: context, crisis, and quest.

Dimension 1: Context

Converts are not isolated islands in the ocean of human experience. Instead, they are involved in a complex set of relationships we call a *context*. Each convert's context can be broken down into a macro- and micro-context. Thus, a potential convert to an American evangelical, nondenominational church has a macrocontext (e.g., American, white, Midwestern, female) as well as a microcontext (e.g., recently divorced, unemployed, estranged from family, generally unhappy, questing for resolutions). A theory of conversion that remains "generic," that is, describing the context as simply "human" or "ancient Jewish" or "modern" or "American," will not satisfy all the important dimensions of the experience of converts.

Cultural Context

For instance, our *culture* shapes a conversion by providing what sociologists call "symbols" and "myth-dreams" on which, into which, and around which Christianity builds its case for conversion. Maggie's advocate appears to be the Roman Catholic tradition as a personalized tradition while Angela had several advocates: her parents, especially her mother; her youth pastor; her friend sitting next to her and with whom she walked forward; and "Bob." Maria's advocate can only be inferred: the church catholic and local? her parents? siblings? a youth pastor at the Covenant church? a friend not mentioned? a group of friends?

The interaction of the Christian faith in a macrocontext is important to recognize. For instance, (at least white male) American culture shapes expectations by giving Americans the sense that there is an equal opportunity for all. Armed with this, some Americans convert to Christianity under the assumption that, if anywhere, surely the church will provide an equal opportunity for all. The key advocates for this church, say, the pastor or some friend, support this expectation. This then feeds into the "religious message" of Christianity that all are "one in Christ" (Gal. 3:28) and before long we have churches that emphasize "equality for all"— except for women ministers! except for interracial marriages and relationships! except for the poor! except for the uneducated! What the "white American male" hears in the Christian message then is shaped in part by his culture, and anyone who has spent any time with Christians in another part of the world confronts this fact immediately. A convert in other parts of the world, say, in Iran where Maria was raised, does not have this "equal for all" expectation for the church, and neither would she have the above-described motivation or experience in the conversion process. We can expect that first-century converts to Jesus had similar expectations shaped by their culture.

Scholars have studied the context as a part of the conversion process, and we give three facets of that context here to illustrate the role it plays. First, the *social milieu* in which someone is raised provides transportation and communication that make conversion even possible. Maria probably does not make the institutional transition from Orthodoxy to evangelicalism if she does not move to the United States; her social milieu in Iran was more restrictive. Angela may not have been led to the crisis of her personal decision had she not had the freedom to attend the youth rally that day. Had John Henry Newman not been part of an intellectual, tract-writing society, the ideas that led to his conversion to Roman Catholicism would never have crystallized.[13]

Second, modern scholarship makes much of the fragility of the *human self* in Western societies. It is argued that our unsure world leaves the human self open to the need for, or, in pathological terms, susceptible to, conversion. The human self is especially susceptible to coerced conversion, when a person becomes entangled in a group that consciously controls minds to produce "conversions."[14] Angela's experience, though surely at a minor level, illustrates what can happen, and her feelings afterward reveal her discomfort with what happened to her. Even a dim imagination can think what group pressure can become.

Third, we also know surges in conversion are related to *social cycles* of religious transformation in a specific country or place. Religious influence is more cyclical than linear in development. Thus, a faith will sustain itself through steady growth, experience a peak dominance, and then decline; but the pattern will also recycle itself.[15] (This is the overall thesis of a set of books in the Old Testament, most notably Joshua and Judges.) Furthermore, if a country or region is going through a crisis cycle, more conversions occur; if a society is highly stable and happy, fewer conversions occur. Such a pattern may be more difficult to observe in the pluralism of Western societies, but we find confirmation in history (when a given culture was more monochromatic) and in the development of a faith in a local, monochromatic village.

Recently, Robert L. Montgomery has shown that macrosocial conditions influence the susceptibility of a society to outside religions and, at the same time, that religions provide stability for resisting outside religions and social threats.[16] The role the context plays in conversion has been studied intensively, and Rambo summarizes this research with seven hypotheses: (1) conversions are not as frequent in indigenous, stable cultures, except among the marginal; (2) conversions occur in an indigenous culture in crisis; (3) conversions occur more frequently between compatible cultures; (4) conversions occur in different patterns in cultures that are pluralistic; (5) converts convert on the basis of perceived advantages to themselves;[17] (6) converts selectively adopt and adapt their new faith; (7) the convert and the advocate (broadly defined) are in a dynamic process of interaction. These seven hypotheses illustrate how intensely scholars have examined the part context plays in the conversion process. Each, of course, could be studied in its own right, but this need not be done here.

The Christian Context

Recent study of conversion by social scientists has failed to grapple with what I think is an important factor influencing conversion: whether or not a person was "raised Christian." There are vast implications for the entire process of conversion if a person was socialized in a church or Christian context or, to use the humorous words of a group of Christian writers, "grew up born again."[18] Such a Christian context sets the course of conversion. For many, the "crisis" is muted almost to the point of "noncrisis" and the quest dimension of conversion becomes a journey on a natural, well-worn path. Consequently, the encounter becomes an old (if also fundamental) fact of life while the commitment mutates into a developmental series of awakenings, decisions, and gentle nods of the soul. The dead giveaway of conversion, a changed life, is sometimes not even seen; instead, consequences begin to emerge as a part of the developmental scheme of that person. Such a Christian context, then, reshapes dimensions of the conversion process into ongoing features of the Christian's identity development. Let me add, however, that such an experience is far from routine. Many kids who "grew up born again" experience serious and heavy tension with the faith of their parents and church, and thus increase the intensity of several dimensions of the conversion process (crisis, quest, encounter, commitment, and consequences).

Implications of Context for Conversion

If we think about converts we know, we might see various contextual factors coming into play, here more and there less. I can but continue the scenario previously outlined with the example of a divorced, white woman from an estranged family. She would convert, whether consciously or not, for her own advantages (as all converts do)—to find family, or to find forgiveness, or to find a social world in which she can live with a sense of belonging, or for other reasons. If conversion is shaped by seeking an advantage, it is not necessarily "selfish"; instead, it is the proper desire of humans made in God's image to find satisfaction. Augustine's famous line expresses this perfectly: "You [God] made us for Yourself and our heart is restless until it finds repose in You" (*Confessions* 1.1.1). To return to our convert: she might join one church over another because the former is known for accepting and helping divorced women, and she might choose against the latter because it is known for treating divorced people harshly. In so doing, she might be apostasizing from a former group and either intensifying her religious experience or simply affiliating with another; she might also be involved in either an institutional transition or a large-scale transition. Let us say that this woman was raised Roman Catholic, or Southern Baptist, or United Methodist and is converting to another Christian denomination—each of these contextual factors will influence her conversion. To think all converts are the same is to deny the marvel of human singularity, the glorious identity that each of us has, God's very image imprinted in us.

An illustration of context influencing conversion can be found in a famous convert to Roman Catholicism. G. K. Chesterton, a man of letters and stories, raised as he was on myths, fables, and fairy tales, needed a faith that spoke to his deep need for "story." Here are his words, in his own story of conversion to faith:[19]

Well, I left the fairy tales lying on the floor of the nursery, and I have not found any books so sensible since. . . . I have explained that the fairy tales founded in me two convictions; first, that this world is a wild and startling place, which might have been quite different, but which is quite delightful; second, that before this wildness and delight one may well be modest and submit to the queerest limitations of so queer a kindness. . . . [Chesterton then details his shock with a materialist philosophy and his arrival at the conclusion that repetition in nature might not be "automatic necessity" but "theatrical *encore*" at the hand of the creator.] This was my first conviction; made by the shock of my childish emotions meeting the modern creed in mid-career. I had always vaguely felt facts to be miracles in the sense that they are wonderful: now I began to think miracles in the stricter sense that they were *wilful*. I mean that they were, or might be, repeated exercises of some will. In short, I had always believed that the world involved magic: now I thought that perhaps it involved a magician. And this pointed a profound emotion always present and sub-conscious; that this world of ours has some purpose; and if there is a purpose, there is a person. I had always felt life first as a story: and if there is a story there is a story-teller.

One is reminded here of a similar sentiment of C. S. Lewis, who, after his conversion,[20] said,

[In writing to Arthur Greeves of his conversion after discussions with Dyson and Tolkien] What I couldn't see was how the life and death of Someone Else (whoever he was) two thousand years ago could help us here and now—except in so far as his *example* helped us. . . . Now what Dyson and Tolkien showed me was this: that if I met the idea of sacrifice in a Pagan story I didn't mind it at all . . . and was mysteriously moved by it. . . . The reason was that in Pagan stories I was prepared to feel the myth as profound and suggestive of meanings beyond my grasp even tho' I could not say in cold prose "what it meant".

Now the story of Christ is simply a true myth: a myth working on us in the same way as the others, but with this tremendous difference that *it really happened* . . . remembering that it is God's myth where the others are men's myths. . . . Therefore it is *true*, not in the sense of being a "description" of God (that no finite mind could take in) but in the sense of being the way in which God chooses to (or can) appear to our faculties. The "doctrines" we get *out of* the true myth are of course *less* true: they are translations into our *concepts* and *ideas* of that wh. [*sic*] God has already expressed in a language more adequate, namely the actual incarnation, crucifixion, and resurrection. Does this amount to a belief in Christianity? At any rate I am now certain (a) That this Christian story is to be approached, in a sense, as I approach other myths. (b) That it is the most important and full of meaning. I am also *nearly* certain that it happened. . . .

Both of these (world-famous) converts found what had been placed into them by the contexts of their faiths: the need for the aesthetic beauty of a story. Not only did both find in the story of the Bible an answer for that need, but both also discovered story as a vehicle for expressing their Christian beliefs as their lives unfolded. But context shaped their conversion.[21]

Maggie was raised in the United States in an Italian-Catholic family; Angela was nurtured in the United States in an evangelical home; Maria, however, experienced a different context entirely: Iran, immigration, and an old faith adapted to her new American culture. The following story of B. J. reveals a different context—and out of that context a different set of factors emerges in a conversion process.

B. J.'s Story

As a youngster, times were hard coming from the projects (low-income housing). There were a lot of different things I saw in the projects, not only saw but participated in. My mother was never home and I was the only child for a long time before my little brother came into the picture. Coming home from school I always had to go to my grandmother's house; she only lived across the tracks. Before I could go out and shoot ball, my grandmother would make me read a chapter out of a book. She always spoke about the Lord when she felt it was appropriate. I could say she was a big part of my education. After a while I did not have to read the books anymore and going outside became my hobby. However, without a father or a big brother figure I had role models such as gang bangers, drug dealers, and street ballplayers. I never had that special person to tell me what was right and wrong. I had to experience it at my own risk and that risk was very risky. At one point I thought I was going to become a street millionaire. Watching the downfall of all my friends made me realize that it is not all that easy. Staying up all night, making money all day, getting high and drinking was the lifestyle. I was living "ghetto fabulous." The reason I put myself in that predicament was because I thought being a hustler was the only way out of the ghetto. I was making moves with my friends but they made much more money than me because I attended school and played ball everyday. That was something my mother did not appreciate. If I did not go to school, I would have been tossed out of the house, and my belongings would have been tossed with me. She always made sure that I would get back on the bus. Once I was on the school bus, there was no way I could go back home. School was too far away to catch the bus and it was racist on the south end of the city. That was the eighth grade. Yes, I was bad—no curfews, hanging out with older guys that were out of school or who did not even make it to high school.

It was the summer of my tenth grade year when I started to realize that easy money was not good money. In that month I got arrested for trespassing. It was not a felony charge, but being in custody made me wake up mentally. My aunt came and got me out of the Junior Correctional Youth Center (JCYC), and she gave me a speech on the way home. She did not know I was deep into the game. I remember her saying that as long as I stayed in school she would take care of me. I thought about it, and during the summer most of my friends were getting arrested with felony charges. On the night of August 14, 1994, the guys and I were out on the block like any other night. A car kept riding by; no one was paying attention to the car. The car drove by one last time, letting off a whole clip [of bullets]. We were all terrified; we did not know what to do, run or shoot back. After the car skirted off, my cousin Jabari was laying in a puddle of his own blood with two bullet holes in his head. The ambulance came but it was too late; he was dead on arrival. After watching my cousin's death, it took a lot out of me. The reason I was surprised: because Jabari was an innocent hard-working man with a daughter. I felt that the Lord was telling me something. The Lord was telling me to get myself together because a life is a terrible thing to waste. For several weeks going to school was hard for me. The only thing I could think about was my cousin. I was fifteen years old in the tenth grade. I did not hang around with my old-time friends because they either dropped out or were incarcerated. I started hanging out with the basketball team, and we became closer than I ever imagined.

The years passed by, and it was my senior year in high school; I still had the hustler mentality, but I did not hustle anymore. My aunt held her word, and I still had the material things a hustler has. Thanks to my aunt I was stress free, having fun, getting perfect attendance, and playing ball. . . . [B. J. then rehearses his successful basketball career, which included a college scholarship.] I came home in spring '99, and I started going to church with my grandmother and aunt. I would go with my grandmother one week and with my aunt the next. Now I love to go to church because every sermon relates to me.

I have been through some tough times. I feel that every path the Lord put me on was for me to experience and to show me how much life is really worth.

B. J.'s story, so unlike the stories of Maggie, Angela, and Maria, nonetheless speaks of similar features: the quest for meaning, the lessons of life, and the impact of conversion. But what B. J.'s story illustrates for us here is that context shapes conversion. Redemption for B. J. means deliverance from drugs, pursuit of an honest life, and refocusing his life on his God-given talent to dazzle the crowds with quick moves, electric passes, and deft shooting of a basketball. It means centering his life around his aunt and his grandmother, his primary advocates. It means faith in Christ and church participation. But we should ask ourselves one question: Would an encounter with the message of Jesus not look different for B. J. than it would for Angela, or Maggie, or Maria? Contexts shape conversions. And everyone has a context.

Dimension 2: Crisis

For a person to be open to, or susceptible to, a conversion experience, a *crisis* of some kind is almost always present—and that crisis can be fundamental to the person's existence or relatively mild. Social scientists have studied such crises in depth and have shown that there is a spectrum in the intensity of a crisis; further, the duration, scope, and source of a crisis will vary from person to person. Angela's crisis is different from Maria's; and Maria's is different from Maggie's; and B. J.'s crisis is unlike Angela's, Maria's, and Maggie's. A crisis was present for each; but the substance of that crisis varied from person to person. Angela's was all about God's love and a fear of death; Maria's was about bitterness and the transition to a new culture; Maggie's is unknown, though her story clearly moves through such a crisis; B. J.'s resulted from the thunderous jolt to his very being when he saw his loved one dying in a pool of blood. Once again, it is obvious that conversion takes on different levels for different people. Accordingly, we should avoid thinking all go through the same crisis, and we should also check the notion that we can create, through some arranged experience, the same crisis for every person.

One problem facing us here is that the crises of St. Augustine and Martin Luther are so well known and interesting, so resonant at times with other Christians' experiences, that their crises have been elevated to the paradigms of Christian conversion. The closer one's experience approximates their conversions the more significant or genuine the conversion. But, dangers lurk here: the conversion experience of these Christian giants is the result of their personal histories and contexts, and since not everyone has similar experiences, it is dangerous to expect Augustine's and Luther's experiences to be normative. Lutherans have, in fact, attempted to secure the "Lutheran experience" by the way the gospel is presented: first law to make people feel guilty, then grace to find the resolution from guilt. This experience of Martin Luther, however, might not be the same for every person.

In the history of Christianity, the Puritans are especially known for leading converts to a crisis. One thinks here of the impact of Jonathan Edwards's *Sinners in the Hands of an Angry God*, Richard Baxter's *A Call to the Unconverted to Turn and Live*, and Joseph Alleine's *Alarm to the Unconverted*. There is no reason here to dabble in criticism or evaluation of the Puritan framework of conversion, but it should be noted that few have explored the nether regions of the Christian crisis more than they. The Puritan conversion experience is, however, the product of a set of contextual factors, most of which do not exist in the modern Christian setting.[22] Consequently, while their explorations shed light on what crisis is all about, their demand for similar crises illustrates once again the tragedy of forcing conversions into a mold.

In short, we need to keep in mind that "crisis" does not always mean "major traumatic experience." A crisis might be nothing more than a gentle nod of the soul, while walking in the park or commuting on a bus, even if its implications are far-reaching.[23] Some social-scientific studies have argued that "sudden conversions" or major crisis-type conversions derive from a specific sort of personal history or psychological health, and that some persons are therefore more susceptible to a sudden conversion.[24] If we respect this scholarship, we should also not expect all to undergo the same crisis experience.

A crisis, which is the tension between expectation and reality, results from various factors. Rambo mentions ten catalysts for crisis that accompany conversion:[25] (1) some convert because of a mystical experience;[26] (2) some have near-death experiences; (3) others find their way to conversion because of illnesses and the need for healing; (4) conversions frequently occur to those who are in a crisis because of a general dissatisfaction with life; (5) conversions are sometimes connected to a desire for transcendence;[27] (6) some find release from a crisis through an experience of an altered state; (7) scholars today are aware that some persons have a "protean selfhood" that is quite capable, and in need, of conversion(s);[28] (8) some convert to the Christian faith because of the crisis resulting from a pathological condition and, by converting, resolve fundamental tensions or find fulfillment; (9) apostasy can create a crisis and lead to conversion as a form of compensation; (10) crisis can be generated by external factors (politics, international issues, encounter with a charismatic figure, tragedy in the family).[29]

In short, if one finds a convert, one is entitled to ask if one of the above-mentioned catalysts prepared that person for conversion. Here we touch again on something important for religious conversion: people convert for a variety of reasons. Not all conversions are rooted in an intentional quest for religious meaning even if the result of an experience leads to religious conversion. Other factors—like illness and a need for healing, or interpersonal needs for a social group into which one can fit and find acceptance, or personal decisions to join a particular social vision—these factors sometimes drive a person to a conversion. In the influential story about her journey to the Amish, Sue Bender speaks of her former life as a "Crazy Quilt" because there was "no overall structure to hold the pieces together. The Crazy Quilt was a perfect metaphor for [her] life."[30] What led to her "conversion" was a crisis resulting from a general dissatisfaction with life. Most converts to the Christian faith speak of life having a clearer meaning after the conversion.

In the following stories various crises emerge in these students' lives and, as a result, a spiritual conversion occurs or at least a corner is turned. The first example, from Jeremy, illustrates how a mystical experience can lead to a conversion. The second, from Rosanna, reveals how physical injuries and tragedy can lead to a reshaping of our lives. In the third, from Jennifer, we find how a person's rebellion against her primary socialization can lead to an eventual crisis. And finally, Jackie's story illllustrates how context interacts with a personal experience of death. In short, we see that conversion occurs for a variety of reasons.

Jeremy's Story

Jeremy was reared in a Christian home; his father was a pastor who shifted into three different parishes during Jeremy's life. Jeremy eventually drifted away from the faith of his father for a variety of reasons, most of which were serious to him. Through the good graces of his youth pastor, who never gave up on him, Jeremy was invited to a retreat. I now turn to his words:

> The key to my development in my faith was in confirmation that year. I had been told over, and over, and over, and over what and who God was, but never really knew him. In the middle of the year, all of us first-year confirmans [*sic*] took a retreat up to [camp name], the local camp. On that retreat we had a question and answer time with the pastor, known as "Stump the Pastor." I went to the retreat thinking I'd get absolutely nothing out of it except the one day of missed school. That night changed my life, when we were closing in prayer. When the prayer was over, I couldn't open my eyes because I felt something entering the room from the outside and flowing over all fifty of us. The entire room was silent, and nothing else was moving. It felt like a blanket was being wrapped over me. I was so scared, and so confused, that I began to cry. The blanket wrapped around me and gave me the feeling of comfort and peace. I realized during the event that it was the Holy Spirit and wanted to share my encounter with the guys I so hated who were there. As I shared that night with the other guys in my youth group, they knew exactly what I felt because they, too, had felt it. That was the first time I really encountered God, and from that point on I wanted to further get to know what I had felt.

Now I am not sure what happened to Jeremy. But I do know that Jeremy sensed something dramatic and it changed his life: that is what conversion is. His crisis that led to conversion was a mystical experience.

Rosanna's Story

For eighteen years I've been living my life without God. My mother comes from a strong Catholic background, which consisted of her whole family attending church three times a week in Mexico. As for myself, I did not want to attend church even once. As a child, I had to attend church every Sunday, even when I did not want to. . . . Having such a strong religious belief in my family, I could not understand why I despised going to church. As a result of life-changing situations, it would only be a matter of time when my perception of religious beliefs would change.

[Rosanna then details her basketball career and a season-ending ACL injury.] I slowly started to turn to God, praying and asking him to help me recuperate in time to come back and play basketball. Successfully, I came out of surgery and in no time I was walking around and later running, but I would not be able to return to basketball my junior year and that disappointed me greatly. I thought to myself, "Why is God not listening to my prayers?" After this I swore I would never attend church. I was very selfish at this period in my life, 'cause I just wanted what was best for me, and only me.

When my senior year came along, I tore my ACL [anterior cruciate ligament] again, this time my left knee. I was devastated because it would be my last year in high school and I would not get the chance to play. . . . When the time came for me to undergo my second knee surgery, on that same day I was notified that my boyfriend had been murdered while leaving his apartment. My boyfriend had a long family history with gangs; he had been part of a gang since I was thirteen, and I knew this was only trouble, but I seemed to be able to overlook it. I thought my association with him would never harm me in any way. But at that time I realized that if I had been with him it probably would have been both of us dying instead of just one. The first thing that came to my mind was that all these obstacles set in front of me could have been a warning that I need to change my habits. That moment in my life helped me to understand that everything that was happening to me had a purpose and there was a reason for this to be occurring. I realized that God does not let things happen to you if he knows you may not be able to handle it. He simply permits it in order to make you a stronger person and to help you grow.

I wondered if my prayers would even be answered, considering that the first time they were not. Soon enough God heard my prayers. Amazingly, I returned to basketball in less than five months; luckily, it was only the middle of the season and I had time to play. . . . I knew it had to be a miracle, because my doctor even said there was no way my knee would recuperate in time for me to play.

In many ways I felt as if I was converting and becoming a Catholic, even though I already was. I began reading the Bible and attending church more often. Yes, indeed, my spiritual journey was somewhat rough because it felt as if I were on a roller coaster. My life was going up and down, and at that time I realized that the reason why it felt like a roller coaster was because I would accept God into my life one moment and I would forget about him the next minute. I came to the conclusion that God had to be present in my life at all times, not only when I had crisis problems, but also when I continued with my regular life.

Rosanna's twin crises—a heavy burden to bear for a teenager—of physical injury and personal tragic death drove her to find answers in the faith she had virtually denounced. But instead of growing bitter as a result of crisis, she found resolution in faith, in the faith of her parents.

Jennifer's Story

In high school I came to a place where I completely rejected Christianity, on a personal level as well as because of the hypocritical institution that I thought I saw. I could not and would not live a half-hearted Christian life, so I flat out denounced my Christianity. All of a sudden a whole new world of freedom was opened up to me, where I could be one of the millions living a life free of restraint, floating through days of earthly pleasures and nights of living hells of fears and devastation. There is nothing worse than the feeling of being separated from a faith that was once yours. Yes, I wanted it back, yet I could not, and this inner civil war almost killed me. Of course, my spiritual separation from God showed itself in my physical life as I was in high school and rebelled in this secret life in which drinking and drugs and sex were a common part. I led a double life basically. I drifted from atheism to exploring other religions and finding that they had nothing to offer that was any better than Christianity.

I entered North Park with many wounds and much bitterness, and I can say that it has been a crazy three years. God has been calling me back to Himself in that slow, insistent voice of His, and it has changed me. How? And what has been the magical formula? The thing is, I just don't know. It doesn't make sense to me that now it all of a sudden does make sense. It just does. I have gone through intense illness, losing my best friend in a car accident, and a severe depression in order to realize that I am sick of the struggling. I am tired of wrestling with the questions that have no answers. That is what faith is, I guess: not coming up with the answers, but believing through the questions, looking at your life and knowing that there is more.

I think it has come down to common sense. I know God isn't about logic, but from where I am coming from, it is the most logical decision. Once I get over the hump of believing, which I have, because no doubt there is a spiritual realm to this world, after realizing that other religions are a load of crap, even the New Age stuff which offers personal empowerment and exploration into the depths of the soul, then it makes perfect sense to me to give my life over to God. If I have the choice to have meaning and love and a power greater than myself directing my life, then I would be crazy not to believe. . . .

So this is my story in a nutshell, leaving out much. I believe that some lucky people in this world can be told things and believe them for the rest of their lives. I, on the other hand, have had to make my faith my own, and in order to do this, I had to get away from it for a while, in order to come back. And it is a completely different faith this time around.

Jennifer's experience of wandering from the faith in which she was raised is hardly unique. My experience with college students and friends with whom I was reared reminds me of an old but ever-occurring story. Jennifer's experience led to a crisis of logic, a crisis of personal meaning, and a social distance from both faith and community that precipitated her conversion to the faith of her family. Her honesty, even her strong language about other religious beliefs she found unhelpful, and her passion, all reveal evidence of conversion—a revised autobiography.

Jackie's Story

When a mother learned that I was studying the process of conversion, she handed me the following story of her daughter, Jackie, who at her confirmation reflected on what her church had done for her in socializing her into the faith, and tied into that experience was the death of her grandfather. Her confirmation story is as follows:

I have been involved in First Presbyterian Church of [city name] ever since I was born. My parents are members here, and I was baptized in this church. I have made a lot of friends through this congregation that have been there to help me grow throughout my childhood. All of my Sunday school teachers have taught me about Jesus, God, and how to grow as a person. Probably my best experiences with this church have been meeting new people, making new friends, and learning about God.

I believe that God has been there for me ever since I was born. This church has taught me to believe and trust in Him, and He will always be there I need Him. When my grandpa passed away, I had to trust in God that He would take him to a better place. Jesus Christ has taught me how to teach others, and to be the best person that I can possibly be. I learn this in the Gospels. If I'm ever in trouble, I say to myself, "What would Jesus do in this situation?" And it helps me get through my pain.

I have faith in Jesus Christ, God, and the Holy Spirit. Whenever I'm in trouble, or need advice, I go to them and everything eventually turns out for the best. . . .

I want to be confirmed at this time because, like I said before, I have always been part of this church. I was baptized here; I have always gone to Sunday School here; and I think it will be a really neat experience to be able to be a member. Also, I want to become more involved in this church, and this is my first opportunity to do so.

There are going to be tears in my life at the end of this school year. [Jackie tells of her school being split and fears losing contact with her friends.] I think God is watching over me through all of my tears, fears, and rage. We can't live a perfect life—God has to put obstacles in there so we can grow as people and become better people in this world. . . .

I think this confirmation class was a great experience for me. It taught me to have better trust in Jesus, God, and the Holy Spirit. I have faith that God is always there for us when we need Him, and nobody can tell you different. My faith has definitely grown through this class, as I learned to think more about God and how He is always there in our everyday lives.

Two observations: first, Jackie has been socialized into the faith through the catechism and teaching of her parents and church; second, two crises in her life have led her to ponder some of life's more profound questions—the death of her grandpa and the forced separation from her friends when a school district had to divide—and these questions revolve around pain and why there is pain in this world. Jackie's Christian context gave her the opportunity to learn from such experiences and provided for her foundations on which to build her faith.

Converts always emerge from a unique personal context, and this context gives shape to the particular crisis that generates a conversion experience. However, emphasizing conversion from the angle of context and crisis can give the impression the convert is a passive recipient of external forces that leave the convert without a say in the matter. The next dimension of conversion settles this issue decisively: converts are frequently in a *quest* to resolve their frustrations, frustrations that can be spiritual, social, emotional, psychological, physical, and so forth. Instead of passive recipients of external forces, converts can be active questers for what becomes their conversion.

Dimension 3: Quest

But aren't converts "victims" of manipulative ploys? Admittedly, sometimes. Are they always manipulated? Are they always victims? Only according to a crusty and peevish determinist. Recent trends in sociology, in fact, suggest otherwise. A significant issue for modern sociological study of conversion is the *degree of activism* present in the potential convert. Studies show that a convert can be placed on a "quest spectrum" that moves from passive to apathetic to rejecting to receptive to active.[31] We need not think of a person, head down, braving the winds of spiritual opposition because the quest, too, can be of an aggressive or gentle determination. Whether consciously or not, the potential convert is seeking what will become the benefits of a conversion. This questing can be understood as a seeking for answers or for inner resolution, as a heartfelt yearning for peace and contentment, or even as an unconscious, but palpable, desire for meaning.

Because C. S. Lewis wrote his first book before his conversion, an epic ballad entitled *Dymer* that "sorts out his options" (and he alludes to all sorts, including especially his "Christina dreams")[32] with no lasting joy or sense of resolution to that quest, we have a special insight into the quest dimension of his conversion. I suggest one read *Dymer* before *Surprised by Joy*, for the latter's description of conversion is his final settlement with the former's quest.[33] The same may be said of John Henry Newman, who once said of his own conversion the following: "that my mind had not found its ultimate rest, and that in some sense or other I was on a journey."[34]

In the examples from students we have so far rehearsed, we might say that Angela's, Maria's, B. J.'s, Rosanna's, and Jennifer's conversions demonstrate an active quest as an attempt to resolve a crisis. Angela was unsatisfied with her rally experience and so sought out a resolution in prayer in her own room, but there is no expression of something out of shape prior to her attending the rally. Maria found another church to be more helpful, while B. J. knew where to turn after seeing his loved one die. Rosanna's inherited faith was activated when she found God at work in her recuperating knee, and Jennifer fought the faith but, after the wrestling sapped her energy, returned actively to regain her old faith. Jeremy, on the other hand, seems to be a classic example of the convert who was surprised by a spiritual occurrence, so surprised that it changed his life. There is little evidence of the quest in his life, though one suspects that deep within his heart was a search for what he found by accident that night in prayer.

Questing, then, is a dimension of conversion, but questing has its own conditioning factors. Once again, not all quests are alike, and not all persons are questing for the same thing. Several factors influence the quest dimension of conversion: Is the person structurally free to quest? Is the person emotionally, intellectually, or religiously available for a quest? These factors influence not only *the viability* of a quest for conversion but *the manner* of the conversion.

Mark's Story

Students who wished to participate in this study of conversion were asked to use the categories of modern sociologists as much as possible as they wrote their stories of conversion. Notice how Mark, a pastor's son, explains his availability to conversion.

For me, I did not become structurally available to conversion until I came to college. The reason for this was because I finally was able to escape from my past: the expectations, family life, and my former stereotype as a pastor's son in society. At college I was able to start over again without having my father's job affect my social standing or having people have unfair expectations of my life. The second condition involves being emotionally ready for conversion. My experiences at the play *The Final Destiny* [he alludes here to a mystical experience with "spiritual forces" while in high school that convinced him there was a God] and my experience with a spiritual presence prepared me for the emotional part of the conversion experience. The third condition is one of being intellectually ready. This occurred during my junior and senior year of high school when one of my friends challenged my faith and made me question what I believe. This started my quest for knowledge and faith in God. The fourth condition deals with being ready religiously. This has not been much of a problem for me because I have been involved with Christianity and churches all of my life. Being prepared in all of these different areas enabled me to move closer to conversion and gave me motivation to convert.

College is one of those times in life when conversions are more frequent than at other times. It is the time when many of us work out our self-identity. Mark illustrates why: it was here he experienced the freedom from his parents that gave him an opportunity to think about the meaning of his life. But questing at this time of life is also surrounded with potential problems. Three factors surround young adults: they are in a condition where change is frequent and easy; they are seeking answers to life because of their psychological individuation; and they encounter advocates (see below in dimension four) of all sorts. If the advocate forces the issues on a potential convert, the quest for faith may dissipate like a bad investment. If too many advocates charge the young adult, hope for resolutions to life's questions may transform itself into despair. Further, questing can be hot and cold: at times, the potential convert intensely yearns for answers and resolutions; at other times, the same person may be quiet and at ease when a gentle whisper satisfies a longing. Conversion can't be reduced to a formula any more than love can be set out as an equation.

Discussing the issue of a quest leads into the issue of *why* someone converts. Again, not all convert from the same motivation though it is certainly true many orientations within the faith of Christianity too easily settle the issue of motivation as having only one acceptable form: religious meaning or a desire for release from guilt and sin. The acceptable motivation is shaped by the group's definition of the Christian gospel. Because the potential convert's motive and the advocate's message and mission interact to shape the process, limiting conversion to religious motivation inhibits us from seeing the full picture of those who were converting to Jesus.

There are at least six major motivations for conversion, and these are expressed in sociological, rather than theological, categories: (1) to find pleasure or to avoid pain; (2) to embrace an intellectually satisfying conceptual system; (3) to discover self-esteem; (4) to settle lasting and satisfying relationships with others; (5) to experience, enhance, or establish power;[35] and (6) to encounter meaningful transcendence. These meet deep, fundamental needs of human existence: physical, sensual, spiritual, personal, social, relational, and structural. We can thus *expect* conversion to meet those needs.

It would be inaccurate to think of these motivations as purely nonreligious, but space forbids an extensive discussion here. Two comments are in order. Anyone acquainted with the history of theology knows that many of these motivations can also be expressed in more religious and theological terms. Take, for instance, "to find pleasure or to avoid pain." Not long ago, a noted conservative evangelical, John Piper, wrote a book called *Desiring God* in which he contended that the essence of the Christian's purpose was to glorify God *by enjoying him forever*. In fact, Piper (much to the dismay of other evangelicals) subtitled his book *Meditations of a Christian Hedonist*—which for him meant seeking God in order to enjoy God and to be as fully happy as God intended humans to be.[36] Piper evidently sees knowing God as a relationship that brings ultimate pleasure to a person.

And one should not hesitate to mention that many Christians have indeed converted in order to avoid pain, to avoid their perception of what hell would be like—and it appears that this motivation influenced Angela, though she carefully explains that she did not want avoidance of pain to be her primary motivation. The ancient Seneca impressed on his correspondent Lucilius a similar perspective on the brevity of life and ultimate human finality: "No man has ever been so far advanced by Fortune that she did not threaten him as greatly [with mortality] as she had previously indulged him [with blessings]" (*Epistle* 4.7). We all desire to go on and on, to enjoy our lives, as Brian Doyle once said, "until the end of Until."[37] So some convert to avoid the darkness beyond the Until.

Conversion to enhance or establish one's power informs our study of Jesus, for certainly "power" is involved in Jesus' vision of what can take place through conversion: he has a vision for the restoration of Israel. A sense of power often emerges from an *experience* of power, say, a conversion or healing or relationship or membership in what is perceived to be a power group, which gives a person the hope of enhancing or establishing power. A sense of control or power was behind some of John Henry Newman's quest, and it led him to the door of the Vatican. Only in converting to Roman Catholicism did Newman find resolution for the dismay he sensed over England's growing liberalism, pluralism, and church disintegration.[38]

Of the stories so far rehearsed, certainly Jennifer's story is the most concerned with a quest. But the following story of Ondrej illustrates the quest stage as effectively as I know.

Ondrej's Story

A Polish immigrant, Ondrej has this story to tell of his conversion to the Christian faith. His story illustrates nicely the interplay of the soul's quest for meaning as well as an individual's perception of God's work in one's life.

I was born into a family that confessed the Roman Catholic faith. From my early childhood my parents would take me to church. I also had to participate in religion classes throughout my elementary as well as high school years. However, instead of teaching me to appreciate God, the schooling had the opposite effect. As I was growing older, my participation in the "religious" would decrease and would, finally, cease altogether. . . .

In my late teenage years I would go to church once a year, or even more rarely. Other "things" would consume my life, among others, sport, parties, sex. Sex was becoming my obsession, and after some years I became addicted. The only goal in my life was to get pleasure. In addition, I wanted to be admired and even worshiped; therefore, I would spend hours in training, bringing my body to perfection. . . . What about God?

In those years, I would pray sporadically, but only if I was in trouble or in desperate need of another dose of pleasure that would feed my pride. I prayed that God would put on my path girls that I could take advantage of. This only shows how limited my thinking was, and the degree to which I was consumed by the desire for pleasure. Believe it or not, I thought God was answering my prayers. . . .

After a while, I noticed, the more I strove for that praise through my pleasures, the more empty I was. Then I began to ask myself a question, which I later directed to God, "Is there anything else in this life, or is this it?" and "God, if You are there, show me Yourself."

[Ondrej speaks then of a desire for justice and truth that he had had since he was young, though he was unable to live up to his ideals. His desire for pleasure seemed always to win.] This period of struggle lasted several years. At the end, I was certain of one thing: I was trapped without any way out, trapped in my inability to be the person that I was longing to be. I tried to do everything, start all over again, forget about my past, but every single time my attempt ended up in a failure. That was it. I lived without hope. Life was meaningless.

Of course, there were a lot of things that would bring joy to my life. However, at the core of my existence there was nothing that could disperse the darkness. All the joy that I could get from my life was too shallow, incapable of bringing even a spark of life to my soul. . . .

By that time, I was into reading the Bible, beginning with my new quest. I would compare the things that I read in the Bible with the surrounding world. The Bible was right about things it described, that is, in matters I was capable of comprehending. I began adjusting my life to the teachings of this Book. Obedience would bring benefit; on the other hand, disobeying would result in greater or lesser trouble. Thus, I treated, looked at, the Bible with honor.

Meanwhile, after many years of absence, my feet crossed again the threshold of a church. The first thing that struck me was the number of young people there; another was its liveliness. I was not used to rejoicing in church; nevertheless, it was no longer alien to me. Regardless of these things, there was something distinct about this experience: it was this refreshing wind that gently touched my soul. I wanted to come back because my heart tasted something that was definitely good, not just good, but deep, penetrating, rich.

On account of these experiences, the process of changing my practices in some areas of my life notably picked up its pace. I began to view God in an increasingly serious way. It caused me to think, meditate more on topics concerning the sense of life. I was compelled to reevaluate my system of values and beliefs, which led me to some unpleasant discoveries. This inward survey pointed to my standing before God in purity—now in a more vivid way than I expected.

Since I had the Bible, the cluster of confusing data gradually was becoming clearer. Piece by piece, everything began to form a picture. This made sense of not only my everyday life, but also, of the universe. After years of searching, I finally found something that gave me hope for solving this overwhelming mystery. I could meditate again upon the essence of life, with a spark of hope in my heart.

The focus of my considerations was gradually shifting: from the surrounding world (outward) to myself (inward) in the light of the person and teachings of Jesus Christ. I had heard about Him since my childhood, but never honestly faced Him, never truly confronted my behavior, my life with Him. There was always a distance that I would not allow anyone to cross, including Jesus, for one simple reason: it was my territory, where only I possessed the right to rule. [Ondrej reflects on this "right to rule" in his life.]

However, the closer I would get to God, the more vividly I could see my faults, my shortcomings. The reality began to hit my heart. Gradually, my real self started to emerge to the surface. It was ugly and stinky; I was not able to hide my selfish and manipulative motives any longer. Everything was exposed, and I could not find enough courage to face it. Nobody could. A thought of living another day with myself was terrifying and depressing.

During this span of time meditation upon the cruel end of somebody so innocent, so good, and righteous as Jesus occupied my mind with an increasing intensity. However, I remember one evening in my room when a picture depicting an event in the life of the crucified Jesus became very vivid, very real, very relevant to me. On that evening my reflection upon Jesus' death reached its highest point, its peak. I was convinced, as one can only be, of the fact that my selfish actions, my promiscuous style of living, my stubborn, unrepentant heart nailed Him there. Because of my foolish, shortsighted autonomy (read: rebellion), Jesus, God's anointed, had to suffer death. A deep sorrow enhanced my whole being. I was moved to the core of my existence. Every part of my being was weeping in a lavish remorse. The real "I," stripped of everything else, stood before God giving the account of my wretched life, asking Him for forgiveness, desperately wanting a second chance, a new beginning. Yet this time, my only desire was to please God, to live as God wanted me to live.

Of the students I have taught at North Park, few have had Ondrej's lacerating self-perception about sordid matters or his theological alertness. Credit for this alertness, however, is almost entirely the result of his questing, his searching for answers to life's most serious questions. His exploration of the life of the Epicureans left him empty, cold, and searching for something more satisfying. Others have seen Jesus on the cross and felt his pain;[39] not all have come to terms with it as soundly as has Ondrej. Not only does Ondrej's story illustrate the quest stage, but it also exhibits a profound encounter, a stage to which we now turn in chapter 3, which decribes the last three dimensions of conversion: encounter, commitment, and consequences.

Chapter Three

Conversion

From Encounter to Consequences

The potential convert, before he or she has encountered the new Christian faith, is already on the way to conversion before realizing it. Most converts emerge from their particular world (context) with tensions in life that need resolution. Such tensions create a crisis of some sort, whether it is an undetectable tremor or a cataclysmic volcano. This (all-at-once or ongoing) crisis leads the convert to find resolution through a quest for conversion. But conversion will not occur without an *encounter* between the potential convert and the new faith. The encounter dimension of conversion involves an advocate, the advocate's strategy, and the interaction of the advocate with the potential convert.

This "story" of conversion requires nuance. Not all Christians sense that a "crisis" was important to their conversion. For some, conversion is a gradual, easy process, like a series of gentle nods of the soul. While it remains useful to speak of a crisis for such people, we need to mention two caveats: first, for such people the crisis is as natural as mental development, emotional maturation, and physical growth. Second, the term "crisis" itself may be an exaggeration for such persons. These convert to Jesus smoothly and without hesitation or resistance. A close examination of such a person's life, however, reveals moments of realization as well as subtle, personal encounters, not to mention conscious acts of faith. It remains useful, however, to discuss in this chapter the following three distinct dimensions of conversion: encounter, commitment, and consequences. Once again, however, we must recall that these are dimensions, not chronologically distinct steps, even if the logical order correlates mostly with their experienced order.

Dimension 4: Encounter

Most converts encounter a potential Christian group through an *advocate* of some sort—whether it be a charismatic figure, a religious group, or a family member. The advocate then, in most cases, is a representative of a group. Because of the susceptibility some have for being manipulated, it is worth our while to examine the advocate in more detail. Advocates, as I have said, are not always "evangelists." Simone Weil was evidently converted through the aesthetics and message-evoking structures of the church with its Eucharist.[1] Even Ondrej (see Ondrej's story in chap. 2), whose conversion reveals a higher-than-average individualistic emphasis, experienced advocates through his parents taking him to church, through the church's leaders at that time, and through the Bible as a Word-advocate. When he converted, the church and its leaders were no doubt advocates. To return to the advocate more abstractly, sociologists say an advocate has a *strategy* that gives shape to the whole process of the convert encountering the religion. The role an advocate plays in conversion has been graphically described by Nancy Mairs, after she came to terms with her (once abandoned) faith:

> Now poverty had a face: Rosa's, the Byrds'. . . . Now peace activism had a face: Matthew's, Lucie's, Bob Drinan's. . . . Mine? Yes. This is how conversion begins, and carries itself along, not with bodiless principles to be embraced by the "mind" or "heart" or "soul" but with a face, a real one, the kind you can take between your two hands and look at long and with love.[2]

Advocates

Advocates have one necessary feature: for dynamic communication to take place, and for conversion to follow, the advocate *must correlate substantially* with the convert and his or her world. That is, the advocate must be able to enter into the potential convert's symbolic universe and show significance. The "magic" of chemistry is needed as can be seen in the following stories. Angela's continued story (see chap. 2) includes reflections on good advocates versus ineffective ones. Brett tells how Felicity advocated the Christian faith through her life, her love, and her words; and Jacob shows the significance an advocate can play when a potential convert is in a camp setting. Three advocates, each performing a normal role in the conversion process: a mother, a peer, and a camp counselor. These advocates were able to enter into the world of our converts because they were able to correlate with the world and needs of the potential convert.

Angela's Story (continued)

[R]ambo] states in his book that the advocate—in this case "Bob"— must "correlate substantially" with the potential convert. Because I did not know "Bob" prior to our two-minute prayer and discussion time, there was no chance that I could correlate substantially with him. In addition, my advocate attempted to use an appeal to power (the power over my own destiny) to convince me, when it would have been more appropriate for him to use a cognitive or pragmatic appeal. Consequently, I had no interaction with "Bob," and I went on to the sixth stage [Rambo's commitment stage] of my pseudo-conversion unprepared. I experienced a commitment that was forced. The consequence was my previously unexplained feeling of weirdness and awkwardness.

My real conversion began at the encounter with my mother, long before I ever attended any play. She, I believe, was my real advocate, and she did "correlate with me substantially." Her interaction with me was great, and this enabled me to make a commitment in my bedroom that night and reap the consequences of having a faith that was based upon a cognitive appeal and real observations of the consequences of faith.

A negative experience with an advocate. Now two brief stories of a more positive nature.

Brett's Story

It is quite surprising to me to ever think that I would be attending a Christian liberal arts college. In fact, the idea of my ever going to North Park was a joke when I went to high school. All my life I had lived as a non-Christian. I grew up in a family that believed in God but never gave Jesus a chance. The morals that I learned as I got older were primarily from my parents and my friends. My mother always taught me that God loved good people and sent bad people to hell. I had decided from that point that as long as I did good deeds, I could win favor in God's eyes. I also recognized that as long as I didn't murder or commit a terrible act on another human being, I had a free ticket to heaven. But this wasn't sure enough. I wanted more out of life. I always wondered about the question "Why are we here?" I wanted to know what the purpose of life was, which fits into Rambo's crisis theory stage 2, which states that a convert has a general dissatisfaction with life and is looking for more. It wasn't until I had met a new friend of my best friend that my view was about to change.

Her name was Felicity, and she was a new friend I had made through my best friend Billy. Felicity is a Christian and did whatever she possibly could to bring God into my life. She told me stories of Jesus and made Him very real to me over time. Maybe it was at this time that I began my official quest to find out if Jesus was right for me. After hearing stories of Jesus and the power he possessed, I had decided that I might be hungering for what he had to offer. This incident reminds one of Rambo's suggestions about the quest: to find pleasure or avoid pain, to embrace a satisfactory conceptual system, and to discover self-esteem. All of these things I longed for—which may be the reasons that I accepted Christ on [date given]. I guess you could say, "I made the decision." My life has never been the same since then. I began going to Felicity's youth group and attended her church regularly. It was God who worked through Felicity and the people at [church name] that made me realize that I was called to minister to people in any way possible. The people at [church name] showed me a kind of love that I had never known my entire life. However, it did not stop there. They truly wanted to know where I was in my walk with Christ, whether it is hot, cold, or in between.

Jacob's Story

I was born into a Catholic family. [Jacob then tells his story of having a bad experience in that communion.]

My mother, being the child of a Methodist minister, grew more and more intolerant of the Catholic Church and started going to the Covenant church in the city we lived in. At first it was a little weird having one parent going to one church and one to another church, but pretty soon our whole family was attending the Covenant church. . . . At this point in my spiritual walk, I had taken communion, been baptized, and by some standards, was already a Christian. But for me, I did not yet consider myself a Christian, at least [I now consider that I was] not [a Christian] at this point. So as I was attending the Covenant church, a Bible camp was suggested to my mom for me to go to during the summer. At first, I was totally against the idea. I didn't know very many of the kids at the church yet, and my mom was wanting me to go to a place totally unfamiliar. After some poking and prodding, I decided to go. . . . I had a counselor named Toby. This guy was and still is very interesting. He had a godly character, and he did a lot of things that week that I still incorporate into my life now. The first thing he did was light a candle at night for devotional time. This was really impactful to me. Something about the light in the darkness struck a chord in me. The second thing he did was listen to me, and when I mean listen, he really listened to me, he heard me. There was a time he knew I had a question on my heart that I wanted to ask, and he spent the time asking me about it and listening to me. I still remember his voice in my head as he asked me what was wrong. The next day, I had just gotten back from swim time (which was always super fun for me) and somehow Toby and I were sitting down on the steps of Cabin #15, and he asked me if I was a Christian. I don't remember how the whole conversation went about, but before I knew it, I was praying with him, and was asking Jesus into my heart. This is what I call my conversion to Christianity.

[At this point, Jacob explains the entire series of events as God's working in his life.] Jesus had been working on me for so long. He helped me realize that what had been going on in the Catholic Church was not personal for me, and it wasn't what I wanted. God was also present in providing a place like [camp name] for me to meet Him, come to Him, and want Him in my life. He worked out all circumstances to get me into Toby's cabin that week, and to provide a time before craft hall and after swim time at the beach [date] to ask Jesus Christ into my life, forever.

We should give a little more attention to the correlation that takes place between an advocate and a convert. The dimensions of that correlation include at least the following: contextual connections (ethnicity, class, economic background); religious sympathy; an acceptable theory of conversion; how the career patterns of the advocate fit into the convert's world; and the various inducements to conversion the advocate can present. Angela's advocate, her mother, correlated powerfully—mostly because of love, trust, and a desire for the mother to see her child embrace the faith. Felicity corresponded with Brett's world through love, by being a peer, by having a message Brett was ready to hear, and through the power of a life that induced interest on Brett's part. She had something Brett thought he needed. Finally, Toby was able to enter into the world of Jacob because he listened and gained his trust; by listening to Toby, Jacob was willing to ask questions that emerged from a heart of doubt, frustration, and longing. Toby was able to offer Jacob what Jacob most wanted— a personal relationship with God.

But the interaction of an advocate and a convert goes both ways: from the angle of the potential convert, the conversion process corresponds to what the advocate is like and what the advocate expects and what the advocate says. As athletes might relate to a sports figure who advocates a conversion to the Christian faith, so an intellectual finds more resonance with a scholarly discussion about faith, while a musically oriented teenager needs an advocate who can sing the language of contemporary pop artists and culture.[3] And the advocate adapts to the potential convert—this adaptation, for instance, is seen when Jacob related how Toby "listened" and, by sympathetic listening, was able to speak the language of Jacob.

The Advocate's Strategy

We can say more about the advocate's interaction with the potential convert. Their encounter is shaped by the advocate's mission and strategy. Four observations make this clearer. First, the advocate's mission begins its roots in the advocate's (and group's) Christian faith. Second, the faith of the advocate shapes the "style" of the advocate. That is, the advocate's style can either be focused on large numbers (diffuse style) or narrowed to a specific group or set of persons (concentrated style). Third, this style leads to a "mode of contact" that can be public or private, personal or impersonal. Fourth, the advocate's strategy is shaped by the "benefits" the advocate perceives coming from the message he or she has.

In accomplishing the mission of advocacy of the (specific) Christian faith, the advocate *makes an appeal* to the potential convert. But the appeal can be varied. Thus, it can be (1) a cognitive appeal (a system of meaning), (2) an affective appeal (emotional gratification), (3) a pragmatic[4] appeal (techniques for living), (4) a charismatic appeal (perceived or real satisfaction through a relationship to a leader),[5] or (5) an appeal to power (social, cultural, or political control). An appeal to power has different shapes: from the *real* (even if unrealistic) hope of controlling a society to a *perceived* hope of control by the marginalized in an eschatological future (the day of the Lord in ancient prophets of Israel). In short, even if the advocate's strategy is mostly unconscious and inherited from a cultural tradition of advocacy, a strategy is used to support the mission and to gain converts. This strategy influences the potential convert's quest as well as the encounter between the advocate and the potential convert.

Toby's strategy was to convert Jacob; this is why he asks in our narrative, seemingly out of the blue, if Jacob is a Christian yet. Felicity, too, desired the conversion of Brett, and "did whatever she possibly could to bring God into [his] life." Angela's mother's goal, though unexpressed in this narrative, was undoubtedly to lead her child into the faith. All of these advocates believed, we can infer, in the traditional gospel message of Christianity as articulated by their particular church and thus led their converts into those same beliefs. Further, each of the advocates here used the "concentrated" style where personal contact was made: Toby was alone with Jacob; Angela's mother was alone with her; and Felicity apparently was with Brett in a closed environment. It should also be observed that Angela's quest was ignited by a "diffuse" effort at the play where lots of kids were present to hear a public, evangelistic presentation.

We don't have the evidence to determine the kind of appeal the advocate used in each case. Angela tells us that her mother was more of a correlating advocate because she used a cognitive appeal, while "Bob" used a power appeal. If we think back to B. J. and Rosanna, whose stories appeared in chapter 2, we may find evidence for a pragmatic appeal. Was not part of B. J.'s motivation for conversion the result of his family's warning him that life in the drug lane would lead to death? Conversion enabled B. J. to get back in the house and live outside of danger. Rosanna had a similar experience when she learned of her boyfriend's death. Jeremy's conversion probably provides evidence of an affective appeal—he was led to a sense of emotional gratification. Brett's conversion, in part, results from a charismatic appeal—in converting he was able to establish a personal relationship with Felicity, a person he admired. Jacob, no doubt, found through Toby a cognitive appeal as he discovered answers to his questions. Judgment on the genuineness of each conversion by examining which appeal was used would be inappropriate. If Angela, in part, was motivated by "everyone else doing it" or fearing separation from her friend, mixed into such motives also was a more serious quest, and, as can be seen from the consequences of the narrative, a stable conversion took place.

The Encounter

When we come to the *encounter proper* no one model exists to cover what is obviously a very complex and highly adaptable process of someone advocating a religious conversion encountering the potential convert. If one discusses this issue too long, only specialists will stay interested, or, as Sophocles once said of presenting too many details, "This is how to make a short journey long" (*Antigone* 232). I shall make, to reverse his words, "my long journey short."

The encounter is dialectical: both advocate and potential convert are reshaped by it. This deserves emphasis lest we are prone to think in simplistic categories. The advocate must present the message, see the response of the convert, and interact with the response; the potential covert will listen, interact, adapt, adopt, and convert or take the exit door. This rational process by the convert is currently being given more consideration as part of the conversion process.[6] These deliberative factors come into play in the encounter over time and with different degrees of intensity. Some people follow up the encounter by initiating a deeper process of conversion while others only find the message curious and interesting, in the same way our little bichon frise examines a stray turtle on a walk and then finds other elements of nature more to his liking.

Dallas's Story

Dallas grew up in a home where the mother was zealously Christian and the father only generally supportive. He was made to attend church with his mother. Further, he states, his mother developed a kids' Bible study for the neighborhood. He then tells us:

I had always been in public school all my life. When I was in the fifth grade my mother put my brother and me in private school. I begged my mother not to make us go because we wouldn't have any friends, and

I wanted to stay in school with all my other friends that I grew up with, but my mother wasn't trying to hear it. When I first started, it was totally different from public school; we had to wear uniforms, carry a Bible, and we would pray. The schoolwork was hard because not only did we have to learn the regular stuff in school but we had to memorize Bible verses; we had to go to chapel every Monday. It was hard for me to adjust to the new way of schooling. It was hard for me to relate with the other kids because some of them had been in private school all their life, so they would talk about things I wouldn't know anything about. (Now that I think about it, I didn't want to go to private school when I was little but now I go to a private college!) I was having problems with keeping up with the school work and the Bible work; I would be in the house all day doing homework while all my other friends would be outside playing. I didn't like private school because they had the right to spank you if you were bad.

But, I think private school helped me with my spiritual journey because I did learn more about God than I knew when I got there. I went to private school for only one year; then I went back to public school. From sixth grade to eighth grade we would still go to church, but my mother really didn't have to make us; if she didn't wake us up to go to church, we would stay asleep. But she did wake us, and we wouldn't cry about how we didn't want to go. We just got up and went.

[In high school Dallas went most of the time, sometimes, he says, only] to play basketball after we got out of teen church. I know it was the wrong reason for going but I was young and didn't understand how important it was to go to church and read the Bible. [Dallas is a football player and relates that he chose North Park because "my coach attended here" and advised him to go there. But, as he says, he came only to play football though he admits] this was the type of environment I needed to be around.

In conclusion, I really don't know where I'm at spiritually, but I do know I'm not happy with where I'm at right now. I am trying to change that, though. I am reading my Bible more and going to Bible study with some other people who are on the football team. When I was little I started out on the right path, but as I got older I wandered off the path. The reason, I believe, is because I worry too much about what other people think about me. But I have learned if they're your friend, they would accept you no matter how you act or what religion you are.

Dallas had two primary advocates, his mother and the private school that structured Christianity around him. His mother continued to pray for him and work on him to integrate the faith; the school, so it was believed, would make that faith more plausible. However, Dallas's personal world is not yet open to a full integration of his faith. Further interaction is probably necessary before Dallas will come to terms with the Christian faith.

The Interaction of Advocate and Potential Convert

This dimension of the encounter describes one of the most interesting dimensions of conversion, one that has been illustrated abundantly in the stories already presented. As the advocate persuades, the potential convert evaluates, chooses, agrees, confesses, believes, and undergoes a process of what we might call "catechesis" or "indoctrination" or "instruction" or "deliberation." Perhaps it is easiest to begin with John Henry Newman's personal reflections on his own "story." Responding, as he was frequently in need of doing, to the charge that he was a concealed "Romanist" while an Anglican priest, Newman rehearses his own, intense interaction with Anglican and Catholic theology in the following words:[7]

> For the first four years of the ten (up to Michaelmas, 1839), I honestly wished to benefit the Church of England, at the expense of the Church of Rome:
> For the second four years I wished to benefit the Church of England without prejudice to the Church of Rome:
> At the beginning of the ninth year (Michaelmas, 1843) I began to despair of the Church of England, and gave up all clerical duty; and then, what I wrote and did was influenced by a mere wish not to injure it, and not by the wish to benefit it:
> At the beginning of the tenth year I distinctly contemplated leaving it, but I also distinctly told my friends that it was in my contemplation.

Using the theory of Arthur Greil and David Rudy,[8] we can understand the interaction dimension of conversion best by studying the *encapsulation process*: the initiation and exposure of the convert to a self-contained world of constructed religious meaning to facilitate conversion. Parents of all faiths shelter children from outside influences; pastors warn parishioners about inadequate theologies; and both Christians and potential converts attend retreats "to get away from it all" so they concentrate their spiritual energies. Each of these is a form of encapsulation.

We need a little more theory before us to understand this dimension of conversion, so we will look at three *shapes* of encapsulation and then four *features* of encapsulation. Encapsulation takes on at least three shapes: (1) *physical encapsulation* removes the potential convert from his or her previous society;[9] (2) *social encapsulation* restricts the potential convert's contacts with his or her previous society; and (3) *ideological encapsulation* regards other worldviews as inferior and thus inoculates the convert from other systems of thought.

Penetrating each of the above three shapes of encapsulation are four features of encapsulation: (1) encapsulation presents the potential convert with new *relationships*[10] to existing members of the Christian faith and these relationships compensate[11] for old, dying relationships, and they confirm the rightness of the conversion (Brett's relationship with Felicity); (2) it offers *rituals* that both deconstruct the previous world of the convert and reconstruct the new faith in Jesus; and (3) encapsulation reorders the new world through a new *rhetoric*.[12] Although the normal convert to Jesus is unaware of this feature of conversion, language is the sole means by which the convert makes sense of the newfound faith. More important, converts always reconstruct their personal autobiography in line with their new faith. They now have a "new story to tell," and we have learned that one element of this new story is the assigning of motives and causes to the world ("God did this so I would do that" or "This happened so I would be led to this person")—we call this "attribution theory."[13] Finally, (4) the encapsulation process sets out a set of expectations or *roles* for the convert to play in the church.

Let me summarize these four theoretical observations. The web they form is not as complex as it first appears: the process of interaction between the advocate and the potential convert, or one who is actually converting, involves what sociologists call "encapsulation." Thus, the advocate isolates the relationship of the convert with the religious group so a conversion can take place. The term "isolate" needs to be understood as having both positive value (all relationships isolate to some degree) and negative implications (some isolation is forced and manipulative). Encapsulation, when it is occurring, focuses on relationships, rituals, rhetoric, and role definition. These are the spheres influencing the convert who is encapsulated. The impact of encapsulation, ideally, is a transformation of self-identity, but this identity is formed in relationship to the group or advocate. Through this transforming relationship, the convert finds meaning, a faith, and a "grasp on the big picture."[14] Thus, identity, formation of meaning, and group have a special dialectical relationship and the group provides a "plausibility structure" for converting.[15] In the oft-quoted words of Peter Berger and Thomas Luckmann:

> Commenting on *extra ecclesiam nulla salus* ("outside the church there is no salvation"): To have a conversion experience is nothing much. The real thing is to be able to keep on taking it seriously; to retain a sense of plausibility. *This* is where the religious community comes in. It provides the indispensable plausibility structure for the new reality. In other words, Saul may have become Paul in the aloneness of religious ecstasy, but he could *remain* Paul only in the context of the Christian community that recognized him as such and confirmed the "new being" in which he now located this identity. . . . Religion requires a religious community, and to live in a religious world requires affiliation with that community.[16]

Angela's conversion was incited when she was momentarily encapsulated in an auditorium to watch a gospel-message play. The slight form of encapsulation the pastor tried to create was not acceptable to Angela though later she was able to integrate her newfound faith into the larger community of faith. She formed a self-imposed encapsulation in retreating to her room to pray. Jeremy's conversion occurred in a camp where he was separated from family and from his non-Christian friends. Ideally, this geographical separation permitted focus on the spiritual issues of his life. Jennifer's college experience, while not a clean-cut form of encapsulation, did provide her with an open environment with plenty of options for Christian friendships and discussions, and the same can be said of Mark's conversion, which also took place in a college environment. Jacob, too, found God in an encapsulated experience at a Christian camp. The attempt by Dallas's mother to encapsulate him did not achieve, at that time, the desired results.

For each of these forms of physical encapsulation, however, there were other forms going on: the camp experience, as well as a Christian college setting, provides for both social encapsulation as well as ideological encapsulation. At a camp and at a Christian college, isolation from former friends often occurs and certain behaviors are not accepted. Such an environment forces the question of faith to the surface and shapes behavior by providing taboos. In both of these environments, too, relationships are established from both angles: zealous Christians seek to initiate conversations about the faith and potential converts find like-minded questers. Others, however, can be turned off by such an environment. The rituals of the Christian faith can be present: the Eucharist or baptisms, structured Bible reading, set and spontaneous prayers, attendance of special events, participation in dorm Bible studies, and involvement in Christian service projects can all, each in its own way, reconstruct a new world of meaning while, at the same time, squelching an older, less Christian worldview.

The eccentric faith of Nancy Mairs, a woman who has struggled with faith her entire life, finds occasional surges through rituals. She says "that in 'going through the motions' one might not be performing empty gestures but preparing a space into which belief could flood if it were going to (thought it might not, ever)."[17] I confess that I was raised in a non-liturgical and antiritual environment (though we had our own nonritual rites!). In spite of that past, I have come to appreciate the widespread presence of rituals in the ancient world, including within Judaism, the Jesus movement, and the various branches of earliest Christianity.[18] In seeing rituals as faith-generating sacraments, we are not far from considering worship as a part of conversion: "Worship itself thus became the major instrument of my conversion," says Kathleen Norris, and it "was the boring repetition of worship language, and even the dense, seemingly imponderable, words of the creeds that had pushed me into belief."[19] All of these features are surrounded by a new rhetoric that seeks to assign everything to its place. Each faith community in the holy catholic church has its "code terms" that provide organization for the helter-skelter of life. Each convert learns the language of the community into which the convert is entering.

Annika's Story

After relating her childhood religious experiences, Annika speaks of some wandering in her faith. During college some issues came to the fore that made her think about her religious life. She says,

The summer after my freshman year I spent the summer working at [camp name] in [city]. It was in this place of beauty and God's mighty hand that I experienced a conversion of intensification, which Rambo defines as "the revitalization of a person's faith already within a religious group." I was an object of "encapsulation," being in the camp setting, both physically and ideologically. I was in a new place and a place in which God's presence was very tangible. It was the perfect place for a transformation to occur, I was surrounded by other Christians for fellowship and learning. I also had a lot of time to sit and think about my life and the decisions that I was making, most of which were not good.

Having so much time to think about things essentially brought me to see the crisis in my life. To apply Rambo's catalysts for crisis, I was experiencing a general dissatisfaction with life. I was also dissatisfied with my choices and the lifestyle I was making for myself and began to feel a lot of convictions. I was "emotionally and intellectually available" for the conversion and the quest I was about to begin of finding Christ and "discovering self-esteem" and/or self-identity in Him. I feel the things that brought me to this point were the context in which I was raised [she said earlier that she was raised in a Christian home "by two loving Christian parents who instilled Christian morals of love"], the small feelings of desire and conviction I had felt during the school year, and being at camp challenged me to really think.

Final Thoughts on Encounter and Encapsulation

Critics of the process of encapsulation, clearly a dimension in the conversion of Annika, are quick to point out that encapsulation can easily become manipulation and brainwashing.[20] Indeed, manipulation does occur, and it is a tragedy involving the wholesale disrespect of a person's will and integrity. When conscious manipulative devices are used to "force" conversion, we are justified to label it, with utter seriousness, "spiritual molestation" or "religious rape." And this form of manipulation cannot be attributed only to those sectarian movements and cultic bands who physically remove potential converts from their previous society to force conversion. A similar form of manipulation occurs whenever the potential convert's will is not permitted freedom (recall the sentiments of Angela and Dallas who felt, at times, that the appeal was beyond their control) and whenever the integrity of a potential convert is not respected. One of my criticisms of the orientations to conversion I discussed in the Introduction is that, at some level, each of those orientations expects each person to have a similar experience of grace. Expectations are one thing. However, when a person's experience varies, the issue of manipulation arises. If the orientation demands uniformity, manipulation occurs.

Manipulation is not to be isolated to the corners of the religious society. It can occur between parents and children, between religious advocates and students, between pastors/priests/rabbis/shamans and their audiences. Having said this, we should not give up on appeals to conversion as simply a rude exercise in manipulation.[21] Genuine encounters can take place and do when the advocate and the potential convert respect one another and themselves as they ought. We should also observe that frequently the encounter is stimulated by a quest on the part of a potential convert. If Jeremy and Jacob were not expecting what happened to them, neither were they forced into it. Both Jennifer and Mark seemed to be open to an environment that would lead to a conversion, even if they entered the door sideways at times! Annika, quite self-consciously, describes her encapsulation as divinely willed and just what she needed in order for her conversion to take place. Hers was apparently an aching heart in need of conversion.

Further, when we look at the encounter and encapsulation, we should not forget the fundamental importance society and friendship play in our lives. I believe, theologically, that God has made us to enjoy both his presence and the presence of other humans in fellowship. We are most fully human when we interact in love and trust with others. We each have what Jim and Brian Doyle call the "the great human itch . . . to belong to a family of any sort, all sorts—familial by blood, neighborhood, avocation, occupation, religion, politics, gender, whatever will bind us to others and hold us all in a strong net."[22] Brett's conversion was aided in part by a desire for friendship; Angela's was as well. Whatever else we might say about such a motive, it certainly ignited a significant process for these two. I am not surprised friendship plays a role in the stories of my students; and I suspect it plays a more significant role than many of them realize. Aristotle, in his classic study of friendship, said this well: ". . . for man is a social being, and designed by nature to live with others" (*Nicomachean Ethics* 9.9.3). Encapsulation leads to relationships based on spirituality, and this realizes the ancient goal not only of the Greek philosophers but also of the Romans, expressed most lucidly by Cicero, "that friendship cannot exist except among good men" (*On Friendship* 5.18). What Cicero means by "good," when transferred to our study, is that people of like mind and mission and spiritual longings are in need of truly loving one another as friends for, as he says later, "virtue knits friendship together" (14.48).

Encapsulation, in the process of conversion, is the formation of a select number of friends (also an issue discussed by Aristotle in *Nicomachean Ethics* 9.10.1–6), and these friends permit a new meaning of life to establish itself. If encapsulation can be abused, it is only because relationships and friendships are a necessary part of Christian conversion and these can be abused. As individualistic as Ondrej was in his conversion, the first thing he did after his conversion was to settle into the relationships that emerge from a local church. The same connections were established quickly by Annika.

Dimension 5: Commitment

If the encounter stage is "successful" from the advocate's and quester's perspectives, *commitment* takes place. Conversion ultimately involves a decision, even if progressive, a turning from one way of life to another, and a dramatization of that commitment in some ritualized form. The commitment stage needs to be seen as the climax of the process from context, crisis, and quest to the encounter and interaction. Again, we need not imagine that commitment has to be either sudden or formal; it may be the result of many tiny decisions in a deliberative process. It can be little more than a gentle nod of the soul on a bike ride in a wood, and the commitment, at times, can surprise the convert in its impact. As Roberta Bondi, who tells her story of conversion in a moving book, said of her own experience, "Without even being aware of it, I had committed myself to the God I was encountering in these texts."[23] Or it can be perceived as a call from God, as is the case with John Henry Newman, who faced God himself, and God—apparently still speaking in the King James English—said, "My son, give Me thy Heart."[24] Commitment involves decision, surrender, and testimony—none of which should be stereotyped even though each has been.

Decision

Commitment of Jesus climaxes a *decision-making process* of the individual before God (*solus cum solo*). Sometimes the act of decision is self-conscious and volcanic; sometimes it occurs after a process of intense anguish.[25] In Christianity, many converts express their commitment (1) in a creedal confession at confirmation, (2) in an adult baptism or a public Eucharist, (3) in joining a church, (4) in taking a public stand, or (5) in a private prayer alone in one's inner sanctuary (as we saw in the cases of Angela and

Ondrej). This decision can be a traumatic crisis, a rushing emotional experience, or a gentle nod of the soul. From a sociological as well as theological perspective, its settled effect on one's identity and behavioral habits is the determinative factor. In other words, the "moment" of decision is less important than its palpable results in life.

Surrender

The inner nature of commitment to Jesus can be seen as a *surrender*.[26] Lewis Rambo's model[27] describes surrender in a psychological grid: beginning with the "desire" to convert (the quest) and "conflict" over the implications of conversion as well as interaction with the advocate, the convert "gives up/in" or finds "liberation" or experiences a "breakthrough." Writing to a Mrs. Ashton, C. S. Lewis once claimed of his own conversion, "I became my own only when I gave myself to Another."[28] We see this in most of the previous examples, especially so in the examples of Maria, Jeremy, and Jennifer. For many, the days of conversion evoke memories of deep emotion and internal peace. C. S. Lewis once evocatively called such experiences "birthday cards from God."[29] His distinction between the emotional intensity (for some) of the early days of faith and the realistic routines of the normal life of a Christian remains important. Surrender to Jesus is not a one-time act; instead, it is a routine relationship finding expression in the give-and-take of normal life.

Witness

Following the surrender, a convert gives *witness* to the conversion and once again the importance of language (as self-reflective and socially shaped) comes to the fore in conversion. A convert's witness essentially is the expression of one's autobiography that divides life into pre- and post-conversion days. It functions to define that person's identity as a convert to the Christian faith. Witness occurs within a dialectical relationship: first, the convert's experience and perception—not to mention his or her desire to please and be admitted fully—and, second, the standards and expectations of the community.[30] For this reason, the intended audience of the witness to faith is the community of that faith that will listen, evaluate, and accept (or reject) the witness as evidence of true conversion. This community might be the advocate, a church, a parachurch organization, a set of friends, or a college community of faith. The testimony is designed primarily for that specific group.

A witness to faith can be either formal—as in confirmation, where it may be done in a group of those being confirmed, or in baptism, or some other form of public display—or it can be informal—as it might take place with friends, or in a private room, or in a generalized change of behavior. A sociological model of a witness to faith does not restrict it to one kind of public behavior. It may be nothing more than joining in the singing of some song. But each convert has a story to tell, and that story is a revised autobiography.

One thinks here of classic examples of the history of the church where the convert gives witness to faith by telling his or her story: St. Augustine's *Confessions*, St. Francis's *Imitatio Christi*, Blaise Pascal's *Pensees*, John Wesley's *Journal*, John Henry Newman's *Apologia Pro Vita Sua*, Charles Spurgeon's *Autobiography*, Leo Tolstoy's *A Confession*, C. S. Lewis's *Surprised by Joy*, or Malcolm Muggeridge's *Jesus Rediscovered*. Of more recent vintage, I think of the (sometimes deeply) personal revelations of Nancy Mairs (*Ordinary Time: Cycles in Marriage, Faith, and Renewal*); Anne Lamott (*Traveling Mercies: Some Thoughts on Faith*); Roberta Bondi (*Memories of God: Theological Reflections on a Life*); Kathleen Norris (*Dakota: A Spiritual Geography*, *The Cloister Walk*, and *Amazing Grace: A Vocabulary of Faith*); and Mortimer J. Adler (*A Second Look in the Rearview Mirror: Further Autobiographical Reflections of a 'Philosopher at Large'*). For many, the spiritual autobiography of Simone Weil evokes the story of the quest for God (*Waiting for God*). If we take a backward glance at the orientations, we should observe that these stories are so personal and individualized that most of them do not fit comfortably into any of the orientations.

In fact, William Zinsser, justly famous for his books and formerly master at Branford College at Yale, once conceded that he has wondered if he might not have been put on earth by God—"a God who wants to make sure that His best stories get told."[31] A contributor to Zinsser's *Going on Faith: Writing as a Spiritual Quest*, Jaroslav Pelikan said that famous converts who tell their story "begin to sift the story for those objective-subjective data that will make sense out of the higgledy-piggledy events of a life."[32] Roberta Bondi, in fact, says that when she was able to tell her story honestly and without inhibition to her Auntie Ree, the "winding cloths of Lazarus began to loosen around me."[33]

In the following two examples of commitment, which vary considerably in outward manifestation, we see illustrations of this fifth dimension of conversion: commitment.

Sophie's Story

Though raised in the church with Christian parents, Sophie asks,

D id those Sunday morning services impact me or cause me to make any life-altering decisions?" I would have to say, "No." . . . I may not have drank, smoked, or cussed like the rest of my friends, but I certainly wasn't a disciple for Jesus eager to spread His word. . . .

But then it happened . . . there I was boarding the bus to take me to [city] to camp, to the place where boys were met, parents were left behind, friends were made, and fun was had, but little did I know that God had different plans for me. . . . Normally, chapel is a place where you go to sing in motion to upbeat praise songs, survey the scene to find the guy who is the crush choice of the week, as well as doodle and write notes to your friends about crushes. But, before I had a chance to even break out the binoculars, he captured my attention (not meaning the cute boy across the way)! It was the speaker, and the most captivating man I had ever heard speak in my entire life, [name]. He began with a series of jokes to seize the audience's attention and proceeded to talk about how we should prioritize aspects of our life. The next thing I knew I found myself staying after both morning and evening chapel services just to speak to [him], getting one last bit of wisdom before I started or ended my day. . . .

Through the knowledge of God's importance and his gracious love for me, I was able to accept myself and allow others to accept and love me; something I had never allowed in the past. It was the passion and amazing speaking ability of [name] and his willingness to let God work through him that helped my rededication to God and Jesus Christ as my Lord and Savior the last night at camp. Through this experience, I feel that Rambo's theory of *affiliation* was exemplified in my own life for I transferred from little or no commitment or dependence on God to full commitment. One could also say that I experienced Rambo's intensification. . . . [Sophie's commitment reveals an element of decision and surrender. Her witness was, in fact, a public acknowledgment to her father of her faith. She goes on to describe what must have been a moving scene for her and her parents.]

Previously throughout my junior high and high school years I had chosen to shut my parents out of my life whether it be by not talking to them, refusing to go anywhere with them, yelling at them, or basically through my complete and total ignorance of their existence. So, my actual missing of them [which she began to notice on the bus ride home] called for red flags, streamers, balloons, and fireworks! Finally the time came, the bus stopped, and I proceeded to step off the stairs. There, in the distance, I saw my dad . . . it was like a distant light shining through him beckoning my presence. The next thing I knew, my feet began to move quicker and quicker to the point of a full-blown sprint ending with my arms wrapping around my father as tears streamed down my face. But, what's so amazing is that it was God who was carrying me, holding my hand. The whole time it was God who was leading me to the two human people who loved me and whom I needed the most. Previously, it was they whom I had tried so dearly to push away.

Mario's Story

My walk with God has been a journey full of ups and downs. It has been full of learning experiences that I would not trade for the world yet would not pay a wooden nickel to repeat. . . .

My parents were good parents who raised me right. . . . We were not the most religious family to ever inhabit the earth, and for most intents and purposes we were an average family when it came to faith in God and religious activity for a family in [city]. . . .

Making me go to church was probably the best thing my mom could have done for me. At first I did not want to go, but after a while it did not seem so painful and I actually wanted to go. [Mario then tells of a lifting spiritual experience on a church missions trip where he "let God into [his] life." He then tells of an injury that ruined his athletic career that led him to wonder about life.]

Well, in this period of soul-searching my mom figured it would be a perfect time for me to get more involved with the church youth group. When the youth group went on a spring retreat in April of '97 I went along. It was there that I fully committed my life to Jesus Christ. The speaker for the retreat was a passionate inner-city black female preacher who spoke about Shadrach, Meshach, and Abednego from Daniel, chapter 3, and how these three young men stood up for their beliefs in God even when faced with death. Seeing as I was searching for meaning in my life, what Shadrach, Meshach, and Abednego had done seemed most definitely like something of worth for me. That very weekend of April 19–21, 1997, my long search for meaning was finally over with me coming to realize that God and a relationship with Jesus Christ was the only thing that would ever be right for me.

Making that decision has and always will be the best choice I ever made. . . . I get to go to college and get a good education while getting to experience the many wonders that Chicago offers that I would never get back in [hometown]. I have had the opportunity to serve Lord in many different places, such as [cities named]. I have grown closer to many of my family members, specifically my mother, since becoming a Christian and have developed a new kind of relationship with my dad, brother, and sister. My life is different since I now live for God and not for myself or ice hockey, yet God has given me so much and filled me in ways unthinkable before that I would not change my choice to follow him for anything.

Mario's conversion, prepared for by his mom's attentiveness, shows elements of decision and surrender and, as his story continues, leads to significant changes in his life.

The process of conversion is but an ecstatic experience, if even that, if it does not result in changed behavior and self-identity formation. Conversion is about change, and it is that dimension of conversion that we now examine.

Dimension 6: Consequences

What happens to the one who converts? What are the results? Can they be studied as well? Two aspects of the changes to converts are especially important: (1) the behavioral and identity expectations of the religious group into which the converts are entering and (2) the behaviors and stories of the converts themselves. A suspicious psychologist might see religious conversion as regression or some other symptom of pathology;[34] an adherent to a particular religion might report a wonderful, life-changing encounter with God; and a Christian group may be thoroughly satisfied with hands held high. Sophie's father was undoubtedly thrilled, and Mario's own explanation of his experience bubbles with joy and confidence. Changes occurred. However, there are conversions, and there are conversions. We are wise to remind ourselves of the wisdom of Francis Bacon: "Nature is often hidden, sometimes overcome, seldom extinguished."[35] Not all apparent changes are real, and even then only some are permanent.

Since conversion involves a person, and since personalities are complex, Donald J. Gelpi thinks there are five levels of responsibility in personal conversion: (1) affective, (2) intellectual, (3) ethical, (4) religious, and (5) sociopolitical. Further, he claims, a thoroughly integrated conversion shows consequences at all these levels of responsibility.[36] Conversion thus can have broad consequences, sometimes at the sociocultural level, of both an immediate and long-term nature. Thus, the growth of Judaism prior to the emergence of Christianity caused social and political problems for Jews in the Roman world, and the rapid growth of the Jesus movement into Rome in the middle of the first century had implications for Judaism as well as for the traditional religions of the Roman empire.[37]

Furthermore, conversion has consequences for personal psychology (both pathological and developmental) and religious satisfaction (relationship to God, love, relief from guilt, personal mission in life). Several of the stories told earlier reveal a fundamental psychological satisfaction occurring as a result of conversion. These people felt better, felt happier, and were more satisfied with life. G. K. Chesterton speaks of the same impact: "I could hear bolt after bolt over all the machinery falling into its place with a kind of click of relief. . . . Or, to vary the metaphor, I was like one who had advanced into a hostile country to take one high fortress. And when that fort had fallen the whole country surrendered and turned solid behind me."[38] In the concluding chapter to his famous book *Orthodoxy*, Chesterton says, "It is only since I have known orthodoxy that I have known mental emancipation. But, in conclusion, it has one special application to the ultimate idea of joy. . . . Joy, which was the small publicity of the pagan, is the gigantic secret of the Christian."[39] Roberta Bondi's wonderful story of her encounter with Mother Jane at the Anglican Benedictine Abbey in Oxford, England, reveals this common impact of conversion: "In the days that followed [that encounter with Mother Jane who spoke to her words of grace], I slept and ate, thought and prayed in a state of peace that I had never known before."[40]

Perhaps the gentle words of Kathleen Norris express this most poignantly:[41]

> There is a powerful moment in any religious conversion, perhaps to any faith, in which a person realizes that all of the mentors, and all that they have said, all of the time spent in reading scripture, or engaged in what felt like stupid, boring, or plain hopeless prayer, has been of help after all. It is nothing you have done, but all of it is one event, God's being there, and being of help. The enemies you were facing, whatever obstacles seemed amassed against you, even your own confusion, have simply vanished. And you are certain that it is God who has brought you to this moment, which may even feel like victory.

Yes, internal peace and tranquillity are regular parts of the stories of converts. But an important issue remains for all those who think carefully about conversion: anyone who has seen a religious conversion knows from experience that the issue of permanence (will the conversion stick?) is also involved. Conversion needs to be ongoing if it is to be permanent. But ongoing implies that conversion is not an event so much as it is a settled impact on a person's identity and behavior with marked consequences. For the consequences dimension of conversion I shall continue with Ondrej's story before moving to another example or two. If Ondrej illustrates the moral and cognitive consequences of conversion, the example of Deidra shows the emotional and psychological consequences, while Walter provides an example of various consequences.

Ondrej's Story (continued)

The next day I noticed a change inside of me. It was not just a feeling of refreshment that I experienced before [he alludes here to a single incident after confession as a child]. It was far more; all of my burdens were taken away, and all of the stains were cleansed, and a new seed of life was planted. I knew that I was born into the eternal family of God. The Scriptures provided a further confirmation. I received this unquenchable desire to read the Bible. I would read the Bible in the morning, at lunch time, while doing the laundry, in the evening; I would constantly read the Bible.

Two months after my conversion, God sent a brother to disciple me. We spent a lot of time together studying, praying, exercising, etc. During a period of six months I could see, touch, and taste Christ in the life of this person. . . .

Day after day, week after week, month after month, the process of molding through surrender began to take place. Step by step, God would deal with issues that needed healing, correction, rebuilding. God has tested my faith, in order to make me stronger. I realize that there are a lot of trials before me, but I am convinced that I will pass all of them because God is faithful and will keep me on the straight path of truth.

Undoubtedly, one of the more famous results of conversion is a feeling of *peace.*[42]

Deidra's Story

Listen to the words of Deidra:

Throughout my spiritual journey I have had many ups and downs. I was "saved" in August of '99. Before that August I had always believed in God and Jesus, but I'm not really sure if I *really* believed. During my first week at this school, I was questioning whether God was really there or if it was just some myth made up to give hope to people. I picked up my Bible and started reading it. I think I read about Abraham being 123 years old, or something, and was like "Yea, right." I didn't believe it, and that worried me because I wanted to know if there was a God. So that night I said a prayer to God, and asked him to somehow show me that he was real. Within the next two nights I was given three signs, which I really can't go into detail about because they are personal. That Sunday at College Life [a Sunday-evening student-led worship service] I ended up accepting Jesus into my heart, and bawled my eyes out (Psalm 138:1). I had always had a conscience, but everything came out that night; things I didn't even know existed inside me. After that night, I experienced the most peaceful feeling all over inside of my body. It was very intense. The peace is still there, but not nearly as intense, and I'm not exactly sure why, because I do have a wonderful relationship with God (Psalm 139:23).

Walter's Story

If Deidra experienced relief from suppressed guilt, Walter expresses manifold changes, whose story I pick up a couple of paragraphs in.

In all my relationships, I have a tendency to never really expect people to love me for being me. I can love somebody, and I'm always quick to identify the best characters in all the people I meet, and I enjoy their personalities, but I have never had the confidence to expect the same of them. And indeed, the very few times I have attempted to do so I have ended up being hurt. Instead, the Lord showed me that His love is not like that of the world. . . .

Last spring semester I was not half the person I am now. I remember thinking to myself that *I* had ceased to exist, becoming instead only a shell of a man. I used to lie in bed all day long, sleeping through my classes only to emerge from my bat cave under the cover of night—a model case of classic depression. I had long withdrawn from my circle of friends, existing instead in my own world of dark thoughts. . . . I was not ready to go without knowing for sure that there was a way to make it. I made all the plans I deemed necessary in order for me to drop out of school. I felt bad enough as it was about how much my parents have sacrificed in order to afford for me to be here. I knew I was constantly disappointing them with my poor grades, which were far below what I am capable of, but I have always been one of a proud nature, and I was not ready to either budge or change my ways. It was at about this time that a friend of mine invited me to study the Bible with her, and I found that I knew all the stuff that she talked about as the strong Christian background I had enjoyed in my youth came back to me. . . . To cut a long story short, what was supposed to be my three months to find a way to stop being the hopeless, sorry, and pitiable liability I felt I was to my parents ended up being a time of really meeting and knowing the Lord. My first surprise was my parents—they forgave me! [He then speaks about his father's patience with him.] I had been so braced for a confrontation [with my father] and an ugly showdown, that when he gave me his blessing, it simply knocked the breath out of me and I collapsed like a deflated balloon.

[He then speaks of being invited to church. This leads him to reflect on his resentment of American missionaries—Walter is an African—and all the harm they have done to his country. This church surprised him.]

Getting my life back on track was not easy, but I was so low that I realized that I could not possibly get any lower even if I tried, and I was not trying, so that was something that gave me strength. [He compares the peace he found there with the peace of his home country: "My people of the coastal region say *Amani haiji ila kwa ncha ya upanga*, i.e., peace does not come other than by the edge of the sword."] . . . And I drank of this water [offered by Jesus] giving life to my parched soul and do bear solemn testimony that it's cool and refreshing, indeed a clear sparkling spring bubbling up to eternal life.

[Walter then returns to his friends and the conflict his conversion caused.] I knew that if my change were not so radical, or if it was toned down just a little bit then perhaps I would have been less isolated, but I was not going to back down. I was leaving behind depression and had found abundant life . . . and I was in no way heading back the way from which I had come, not if I could help it.

I threw myself all the more into the renewing of my mind. . . . [Then Walter tells of a winter retreat where he found a small group of Christians who loved him unreservedly.] Like the great Physician He is, He is not only healing me of my hurts and wounds, but He was also now getting rid of the scars that remained from those wounds so that I would not have to carry them on my person forever. . . .

Before we proceed to study Jesus' "model" of conversion, I want to include one more story. The following story of Kjerstin illustrates the socialization theory of conversion. In Kjerstin's story, everything is present in the model presented so far, but everything is natural, everything evolves, and it all comes together in a young woman who is a Christian but who has no "great story to tell." By the way, her experience is also a common experience of those who were raised in a Christian context. I make no apology for it; religious heritage plays a significant role in the conversion of many. One could easily shift the key elements of the story to a Roman Catholic, to a Serbian Orthodox, or to a Lutheran context and find the same basic plot. This young woman was raised in the Evangelical Covenant Church, the sponsoring denomination of North Park University.

Kjerstin's Story

Not only have I grown up in the Covenant Church, but I am Swedish, and have grown up in this culture, celebrating the Swedish tradition Lucia, and having traditional Swedish Christmas dinners. Most of my family's closest friends are church friends, as is true with my grandparents and other relatives. These church folks, it is safe to say, are a majority Swedish and tend to have last names that sound a lot alike (Johnson, Peterson, Erickson, etc.), not to mention they have more connections than you can imagine. Rambo's description of socialized conversion seems to fit me like a glove.

I was baptized as an infant on [date], when I was six months old. Although I do not remember this, I feel it was an important day on which my parents presented me to the church and said that they intended for me to grow up and be a faithful child of Christ. I was also confirmed at the age of thirteen and have continued to attend church ever since.

For as long as I can remember, I have grown up attending church. It was never a choice, just a given that every Sunday that is where we went, like school during the week. When I was younger I had no idea what church really was. I knew my family went there every Sunday, got all dressed up, and my parents were always seeing friends and talking for way too long. To me church was just a place where I did not understand what the pastor was saying, and I did not want to get left in Sunday School without my parents and be made to memorize Bible verses (except for when we got prizes for doing it). Of course, I knew the story of the Birth of Jesus, Noah and the Ark, and Jonah and the Whale, but my knowledge of what those stories meant was probably pretty limited. As a child, I recall saying grace before every meal with my family and saying prayers before bed. When I was confirmed in eighth grade, it was not because I really felt that strong urge to be confirmed in my faith in Christ; it was because that was what you did in eighth grade at [name] church, and in many if not most churches like it.

I think I had known for my whole life that I was a Christian, or at least I carried Christian attitudes. I was taught not to call people names, hit others, talk about people in a not-nice way, or lie; however, it was not until I was at [camp] in [city], at a retreat in third grade where I remember understanding what it meant to be a Christian. This is when I really remember for the first time understanding what it meant to be a Christian and have Christ in my heart. I do not remember everything about that day, but I know there must have been a great speaker who presented the gospel to me in a way that I understood it at such a young age. Although I did feel changed after this time in my life, it was not until much later that I really felt what it meant to be a Christian woman and live my life for Jesus. I grew up in an area that was not heavily populated by Christians, and for however many Christians there were, there was probably a pretty similar amount of [ethnic group] people around, too. This being said, it is probably understandable that I did not have any close Christian friends in high school to guide, support, and encourage me. Also, my church had been through a tough time, where I had four youth pastors in four years, so my church connection was not a place I could go and feel totally connected or on a spiritual high. It was not until I started working at [camp] during the summers that this "connection" happened. Being there taught me how awesome it was to be a Christian, how there really was a God and people to love you and care about you, encourage and challenge you. Working all summers at camp like I have has definitely had a huge impact on my spiritual life. . . . Once I started working there and feeling a connection, I realized that I could not go back to my old ways even if I was still in high school with the same people. But that was alright, because I started reading my Bible more, keeping my friendships strong with my Christian friends, going to [youth conference named], and really figuring out who I was.

Kjerstin's story is like that of many others who have been raised in the faith. One of the consequences of conversion is that a person enters "the church" and discovers many who have a similar story to tell. No one has told this better than G. K. Chesterton, who in his classic *Orthodoxy* says, "I am the man who with the utmost daring discovered what had been discovered before."[43] Chesterton's conversion to faith was intensely personal and yet the faith of many others; it landed him in the church. It remains for us now to reexamine this turning to Jesus with enough sociological theory to make better sense of the gospel records. But before we proceed to that task, I would like to look at one more recent study that gives nuance to the model just presented.

Contribution of Viswanathan

Gauri Viswanathan, in her book *Outside the Fold*, studied the social relationship of conversion and modernity. Ironically, this English professor at Columbia University adds an additional sociological dimension to the approach of sociologists. In deftly studying the literary, religious, social, legal, and political debates and interconnections of England and India, she contends that religious conversion is a significant *political* action, a form of both *dissent and assent*. Previous studies have given full sway to the assent side of the ledger, but to her credit we find an emphasis here on the dissent side. The Jesuit scholar Donald L. Gelpi pleads for religious persons to integrate their conversions fully so that they take on a sociopolitical nature; Viswanathan contends conversion itself *is* a sociopolitical act.[44] She focuses on several different figures who in some manner are involved in conversion—John Henry Newman, Pandita Ramabai, Annie Besant, and B. R. Ambedkar—but she relates that conversion to its sociopolitical context. She concludes her own argument as follows:

> I shall offer as the principal argument of this book *that conversion ranks among the most destabilizing activities in modern society*, altering not only demographic patterns but also the characterization of belief as communally sanctioned assent to religious ideology. Although it is true that, in the context of majority-minority relations, conversion is typically regarded as an assimilative act—a form of incorporation into a dominant culture of belief—*conversion's role in restoring belief from the margins of secular society to a more worldly function is less readily conceded.*[45]

In other words, conversion is an act of protest against some socially shaped community, whether it be the dominant society or a minority movement. From another angle, conversion is cultural criticism.[46] After all, it is not rare that converts express anger and even hostility to their former society. We can recall here how Jennifer spoke of some of the religious ideas she sampled during her wandering years. Since Viswanathan's study is so diffuse and exacting, I shall take but one example: the conversion of John Henry Newman from Anglicanism to Roman Catholicism.[47]

Born to evangelical parents in 1801 and educated at Oriel College (Oxford), Newman became the gifted, charismatic leader of the Tractarian movement with its attempt to revive the Catholic elements of Anglicanism. The revival, however, was inadequate to stem the flow of liberalism and pluralism, and it did not counter sufficiently the legal, tolerant acceptance of minority religions. Consequently, Newman took off his Anglican collar and converted to Roman Catholicism (1845), eventually being named a cardinal-deacon. His relationship to the Roman Catholic authorities was not without its own difficulties but need not be detailed here.

What seems from a religious and theological approach to be a "case of religious conversion" under the eyes of an observant social historian, such as Viswanathan, becomes also a case of social, cultural, and political protest. Thus, "what appears to emanate from a religious discourse is as concerned with negotiating secular parameters as it is with establishing the claims of religious subjectivity."[48] In short, Newman's conversion is understood here to be as much sociopolitical and religious protest as it is personal belief: the conversion to Roman Catholicism is Newman's embodiment of protest against legal toleration of religious minorities and the diminution of authority in the Anglican communion. His assent to Roman Catholicism rides on the back of deconstruction, that is, dissent from England, from Anglicanism,[49] and from growing liberalism.[50] If Newman's conversion finds a new transnational community in Roman Catholicism, it is because that assent is a "grammar of dissent from all forms of rational, codified systems of thought that exist to induce membership into a national interpretive community."[51] Viswanathan's fullest statement, which best expresses what I shall use to modify our model of conversion, is as follows:

> The most striking feature of the emergence of a culture of conversion-as-dissent is its contrast to a monolithic, exclusionary culture in which conversion functions as a sign of assimilation to the dominant group. Conversion in the latter sense is a gesture of acquiescence, a capitulation to the pragmatics of survival, where individuals either adopt the religion that will admit them to certain rights and privileges or accept the consequences of being rendered outcastes [*sic*] if they do not convert. *Indeed it would be fair to say that conversion in an era of religious tolerance functions as an expression of resistance to the centralizing tendencies of national formation.* The blurring of differences between religious groups that marks the secularization process, by

means of which discrete religious sects are transformed into comparable denominations of a trunk-like religious system, simultaneously produces a defiant reaction by certain groups to preserve difference even while they acknowledge the need for national identification. *As a mode of preserving heterogeneity against the unifying impact of the state, conversion acquires an oppositional character that conflicts with its customary description as assimilative or adaptive.*[52]

In short, for Newman conversion is national protest (against England), religious dissent (from Anglicanism), and social construction (a new society understood in terms of the Roman Catholic option) whereas maintaining the status quo is heresy, sociocultural capitulation, and un-Christian thinking and action. One hears this political dimension to conversion in what must be some of John Henry Newman's most pointed words: "On the morning of the 23rd [of February, 1846] I left the Observatory [where he had spent the last night with his good friend]. I have never seen Oxford since, excepting its spires, as they are seen from the railway."[53]

Though Viswanathan's study could augment our discussion in other dimensions, I shall concentrate on the following, which I see as confirmations of our model of conversion. First, dimension one, *context*, though surely broadly defined, now acquires another nuance at the social level of protest and dissent. *Apostasy*, which emerges in dimensions one and two, though defined by Newman as "heresy," also gains an importance and centrality when conversion is seen in social terms: as dissent, conversion is always in some sense an apostasy. Dimension three, *quest*, finds an even sturdier foundation in the "active" dimension of the pursuit of conversion, as do the features of the conceptual system and power dimensions in that quest. Likewise, dimension four, *encounter*, finds another ally in Viswanathan as the power benefits of conversion take on a more central role in conversion as dissent; several features in dimension four of the interaction find a new emphasis: encapsulation theory, so beneficial for understanding conversion, should be seen in more "ecclesial" terms. That is, conversion inevitably drives toward a new community, whether that community be the Jesus movement or the Roman Catholic Church as perceived by Newman. Furthermore, "relationships" are in the context of dissent against the norm; "ritual" (especially in its more deconstructive dimensions) finds support in a form of protest; the "rhetoric" of attribution is a newly discovered perception that contains elements of dissent as well as assent as defined by a social group of fellow dissenters; and "roles" are shaped by this new understanding of conversion as dissent.

Next, if conversion is dissent, then dimension five, *commitment*, needs to be seen in more social terms: decision making becomes a social crisis, not just for the individual but also for the group—and this may well explain the emphasis Jesus gave to the cost of following him, especially when those costs take on family, vocation, and social categories. Both witness and motivational reformulation will find more elements of dissent than are seen in the typical sociological study. Finally, dimension six, *consequences*, needs to spell out more forcefully the social consequences of conversion because it is fundamentally an act of protest against the status quo, whether that be defined primarily in terms of politics, culture, or religious affiliation. In short, our model will be seen to be accurate to real-life conversions, but that model finds a more socially dissenting confirmation in the work of Viswanathan.

What about the stories I have related? Let me say, first, that giving these stories a social-protest angle does not mean that I am demeaning the religious dimension of conversion. In fact, following the lines of Viswanathan confirms in my judgment the essential human need for society and for group formation. That is, conversion is both personally integrative as well as socially constructive. The stories of B. J., Jeremy, Jennifer, Mark, Brett, Jacob, Dallas, Sophie, Ondrej, and Walter have social dimensions of protest in them. Just a couple of examples will suffice. B. J. found in converting to his family's faith that he could resist the dangers of his society and, in so doing, he offered a protest to that world. One notices in Jeremy a social antipathy to his father's religious world, but his conversion was simultaneously a social affirmation of that world as well as a sudden negation of the world in which he had been living. Dallas, however, seems to be affirming the world his mother wants him to deny while Walter has found in the church a society to which he can belong as an African living temporarily in the United States.

Here's the point: conversion to the Christian faith is a social statement and a political action. In "social statement" I include "church." Those who so convert are denying their former world and affirming the social vision of the group to which they convert. This is what it means, in the simplest of terms, to "join the church." Though often not recognized, the church is a social vision itself—a vision of what the group thinks God wants for his people on earth. If this vision is then extended into the larger society, and it frequently is (even in the case of those withdrawn from society like the Amish), then the church is simply carrying out its mandate. Thus, it is my conviction that Viswanathan has struck a vibrant chord: conversion is social protest.

Chapter Four

Jesus and Conversion

Context to Quest

I n what follows, the concern is not with Jesus' normative model of conversion but with a descriptive analysis of what he expected, what he did, and what he taught with respect to conversion—and I shall use the model previously described to delineate the model of Jesus. Our purpose is to describe how converting to Jesus occurred when we examine the Gospel traditions in light of our model of the sociology of conversion. In so doing we return to the questions asked in the beginning of this book: questions about the three orientations and questions about what was really going on in the conversions of those like Peter and Zacchaeus.[1] If the first look at the evidence of the Gospel stories did not reveal enough about conversion to discern just how conversion took place at the time of Jesus, we are now prepared, having surveyed a modern model of conversion, to ask how this model leads us to other elements in the Gospels that may help us discover more about converting to Jesus. Only then can we adjudicate matters swirling around the three orientations of conversion in the church today.

The lead question for the use of a social-scientific model for examining evidence from the ancient world is "What general process is apparent when Israelites converted to Jesus?" In light of that question, we can search for evidence that provides answers. Again, I am not suggesting Jesus had a (or "my" or "Lewis R. Rambo's") "sociological model of conversion," but we will discover that the evidence fits nicely into the scheme outlined earlier. Neither am I suggesting that he was so "ancient" he couldn't have thought such things. More important, the evidence from the Jesus traditions will be permitted to shape the model itself. Studies using sociological methods in general, and conversion in particular, have confirmed the value of using social-scientific studies to illuminate ancient practice and belief.[2]

The recent study of Thomas Finn suggests that conversion in a wide variety of ancient contexts took place according to the lines sketched out by the process model modern sociologists use. Finn concludes the following about conversion to ancient Judaism:

> The evidence shows that both kinds of conversion [to Judaism, within Judaism] required a clear-cut choice between an old way of life and a new way, a choice that demanded commitment. Choice and commitment permeate the process from beginning to end, with repentance as the cutting edge. The evidence, however, yields one caveat: *conversion is a gradual and continuing process*. Although there is a decisive moment when one is a Jew or, as at Qumran and among the Johannites, a true Israelite, the road to it is long and hazardous. Conversion is not sudden. And the road beyond conversion is equally long and hazardous.[3]

A difference immediately confronts us: although sociology teaches us how converts move into a new group, with that specific group defining much of what is believed and undertaken, the Jesus traditions reveal it is not a group that defines faith and action but *Jesus himself*. Converting in this sense is a conversion to Jesus and not conversion to a religious group. Having said this, it needs also to be noted that converting to Jesus is also converting to the group around Jesus: his followers. But this group is not yet the church. Instead, at the time of Jesus it is a reconfiguration of Judaism that over time emerges to form a "third religion": Christianity. But that is far down the road. At the time of Jesus those Israelites who decided to "join" his movement were essentially lone rangers who found Israel's hopes and expectations best expressed by this solitary prophet from Galilee, Jesus of Nazareth.

Jesus and Kinds of Conversion

In order to have a clearer grasp of what "converting to Jesus" means, we need to look at the five kinds of conversion we sketched previously: Was converting to Jesus an experience or process of (1) apostasy from Judaism, (2) intensification, (3) affiliation, (4) institutional transition, or (5) tradition transition? Since conversion is a complex set of factors, many of which are unknown to us even when we analyze modern conversions, we need to settle terms also with the issue of "according to whom?" That is, evaluating conversion differs person by person, group by group, orientation by orientation. What was for one person nothing but a "strange idea," for someone else may have been "radical apostasy." The convert may be completely or only partially at odds with his family, with his community, with a "rabbi," and with his heritage.

Apostasy?

It seems probable that *most kinds of conversion are apostasies from something or someone else.* After all, that's what conversion is: leaving one group/ideology for another. We observe, however, that some forms of "intensification" do not involve changing groups, and therefore apostasy is muted as a viable category of explanation. Intensification is an awakening to an existing faith with full integration into the group; the previous state involved much less participation. Thus, it is likely that a person "joining Jesus" was leaving some other group, but we must be cautious here.

One solid piece of evidence from the Gospels is the regular need on Jesus' part to repeat his challenge to those around him not to give in, not to return to their former paths, and not to succumb to other values. This suggests a lure of the past and its associations. A good place to anchor this notion is the parable of the sower (Mark 4:1–9, 13–20; italics added to call attention to the significant expressions):

> Again he began to teach beside the sea. Such a very large crowd gathered around him that he got into a boat on the sea and sat there, while the whole crowd was beside the sea on the land. He began to teach them many things in parables, and in his teaching he said to them: "Listen! A sower went out to sow. And as he sowed, some seed fell on the path, *and the birds came and ate it up.* Other seed fell on rocky ground, *where it did not have much soil, and it sprang up quickly, since it had no depth of soil. And when the sun rose, it was scorched; and since it had no root, it withered away.* Other seed fell among thorns, *and the thorns grew up and choked it, and it yielded no grain.* Other seed fell into good soil and brought forth grain, growing up and increasing and yielding thirty and sixty and a hundredfold." And he said, "Let anyone with ears to hear listen!" . . .
>
> And he said to them, "Do you not understand this parable? Then how will you understand all the parables? The sower sows the word. These are the ones on the path where the word is sown: when they hear, *Satan immediately comes and takes away the word that is sown in them.* And these are the ones sown on rocky ground: when they hear the word, they immediately receive it with joy. *But they have no root, and endure only for a while; then, when trouble or persecution arises on*

account of the word, immediately they fall away. And others are those sown among the thorns: these are the ones who hear the word, *but the cares of the world, and the lure of wealth, and the desire for other things come in and choke the word, and it yields nothing.* And these are the ones sown on the good soil: they hear the word and accept it and bear fruit, thirty and sixty and a hundredfold."

Jesus evidently had concerns about his followers, concerns about their longevity and their perseverance in retaining loyalty to him. The obstacles of fidelity are Satan, personal persecution, and the lures of the material world. We can infer that these calls to perseverance reveal that converting to Jesus involved an apostasy from some other form of allegiance, even if that allegiance be as crass as materialism (or mammonism—cf. Matt. 6:19–34). More likely, however, is that what we hear in the concern about the effects of persecution is that those converts to Jesus had emerged from groups who exercised various forms of procedures to gain the converts back—even if as general as mainstream Jewish society. If this sort of evidence is permitted, and more could be cited, we have evidence that some of those converting to Jesus were apostasizing from some other group.

Because the notion shapes much of what can be said about Jesus, it needs to be emphasized that saying those converting to Jesus are apostasizing from one group to Jesus' group does not imply that Jesus' group is already "the church." Neither were the groups as rigidly defined then as Christian denominations are today. Converts to Jesus were more often than not leaving their local flavor of Judaism to follow Jesus. In general, most were simply leaving one form of authority within Judaism—general, nondescript, Galilean, artisan-shaped Judaism—to follow Jesus as their form of faith. In so leaving, his converts did not think they were "joining a new religion" or "leaving Judaism." Instead, they were probing the authority of Jesus for their own lives as an intensification of their Jewish faith. The category of "apostasy" for explaining conversion to Jesus remains of limited use.

Intensification

What about intensification? It cannot be doubted that Jesus awakened those who were converting to him *to an intensified experience of their own preexisting faith.* Again, his converts remained Jews, and those conversions are "insider conversions."[4] This is seen perhaps, if only in a parable, in the story of the return of the prodigal son to his father (Luke 15:11–32). Here we find a Jewish boy gone bad; a Jewish boy who comes to his senses; a Jewish boy who returns home to find forgiveness and social restoration. His return is a reawakening of his former faith, an intensification.[5] Furthermore, the themes of eschatological fulfillment, so programmatically expressed in Mark 1:15 ("The time is fulfilled, and the kingdom of God has come near; repent, and believe in the good news"), forms the foundation for seeing conversion to Jesus as an intensification of Jewish faith. What was already held as normative and anticipated has now arrived. Converting to Jesus then means grasping a moment of fulfillment for the old faith. As Jesus' brothers' names expressed a faith in Israel's patriarchal heritage by Jesus' parents,[6] so Jesus' choice of the Twelve (whom we call "apostles") signifies an intensification of Israel's faith.[7] Converting to Jesus was for these an intensification of their (already existing) faith in God's covenant with Israel. Even though intensification is probably the most common kind of conversion, the process of intensification differs little from that of any other kind of conversion.

Affiliation

Is there evidence for affiliation, for some *converting to Jesus from no or minimal faith?* This question is important, for the second half of the first century C.E. will witness a massive reshaping of Jesus' mission. The apostle Paul, for one, spilled his blood for a mission that itself shifted from Jews to Gentiles. Paul's own mission, especially as described in Acts, begins at the synagogue but moves quite easily into the community "for all who believe" (Gal. 2:15–21). Thus, if converting Jews to Jesus was for Paul an intensification conversion, the expansion of that mission to Gentiles around the synagogue and beyond reveals other kinds of conversion: affiliation as well as institutional and tradition transition. We ask here if that reshaping had its roots in Jesus' own practice.

Three lines of evidence, each varying in their boldness, suggest so. I begin with a convert like Levi, son of Alphaeus (Mark 2:13–17), whom the First Evangelist names "Matthew" (Matt. 9:9). If anything like the hackneyed definition of a toll (and tax) collector obtains for Levi, that is, a "dishonest filch" or "legal pickpocket," as readers often find in Zacchaeus (Luke 19:1–10), we may assume he was either a Jewish "traitor" to Rome or at least a nonobservant Jew. And that "toll collectors" like Levi are associated with "sinners" suggests they were at least nonobservant Jews. If so, Levi's conversion would probably be less intensification and more affiliation.

A second line of evidence, just as bold as the previous one, points to Jesus' somehow convincing prostitutes to convert to him and his group of followers.[8] Prostitutes attached themselves to temples, taverns, and brothels and were little different from other ancient institutions for male sexual provision—concubines and courtesans. There is some evidence for Jewish women turning to prostitution and some for Jewish female slaves being forced into prostitution, but the majority of the evidence suggests Jewish males turned to Gentile women.[9] Thus, when we read Matthew 21:31 we should probably think of brothel prostitutes or (more likely) courtesans of Galilean upper-class males: "Truly I tell you, the tax collectors and the prostitutes are going into the kingdom of God ahead of you." And it is likely the woman in Luke 7:36–50 who pours ointment on Jesus was a *fille des rues*. If prostitutes and courtesans (Capernaum's proximity to Roman military stations makes their presence likely) found their way to Jesus, their converting to Jesus would probably be either tradition transition or affiliation conversion. There is a consistent line from Mark 2:13–17 to Matthew 11:18–19 and 21:31–32: Jesus dined with the undesirables and their number included prostitutes and courtesans.[10]

Another line of evidence, not so bold, is that Jesus ate with "sinners" (Mark 2:13–17; Matt. 11:18–19). If, as traditionally understood, the "sinners" are the "wicked," those who violated the Torah, then we have another group whose conversion would be an affiliation. However, if that group is defined more "factionally,"[11] that is, as those who were excluded by one group or another, and their "sinfulness" was no more than lack of connection with the defining group (e.g., Pharisees accusing non-Pharisees of being "sinners" because they did not observe their interpretations), then "sinner" might not be so much a conversion by way of affiliation as by way of "institutional transition," to which we now turn.

Institutional Transition

It is surprising, in my view, how little evidence there is for what I would describe as the classical model of understanding conversion to Jesus. Most understand converting to Jesus as *leaving one group, most notably the Pharisees, for Jesus' group.* This type of conversion is called *institutional transition.* Modern examples abound: Americans transit from one institution to another quite readily, from Baptist to Presbyterian, from Methodist to Quaker, from Roman Catholic to Lutheran, from Presbyterian to Roman Catholic. Is there evidence that those converting to Jesus were transiting from one institution to another? We might assume this to be the case, and there is good reason to think so: most people had some kind of institutional identity—or did they? Evidence for such is hardly clear, and it would be better for us if we drop our modern religious categories in the bin before we look at the Jesus traditions in this regard.

There is no evidence in the Gospels, for instance, that any Sadducees or Essenes became followers of Jesus—no direct evidence. We could take Nicodemus as an example of a Pharisee (cf. John 3:1–21; 7:50; 19:38–42). There is evidence, probably, that one of the twelve followers of Jesus was formerly a "Zealot." Luke tells us, at 6:15, that a certain Simon was called a "zealot." If we grant the (hotly disputed) hypothesis that there was a group called "Zealots" at the time of Jesus and, in addition, if "called a 'zealot'" means Simon was formerly a "Zealot," we would have unmistakable evidence for an institutional transition among the closest followers of Jesus. But both parts of this assumption are open to serious doubt, and it is best not to include this evidence.[12] One thus can argue on general grounds that conversions always involve "institutional transition," but since this category expresses a more precise notion, namely, that of switching precise groups, it is best to leave this category at the margins for understanding conversion to Jesus.

Tradition Transition

Finally, do we find evidence for *tradition transition?* We can guess—and it is no more than that—that the Gentiles who were touched by Jesus may have then connected themselves to him. We have evidence he did minister to some Gentiles, who added a touch of tarragon to the evening meals. As an example, we note the so-called Syro-Phoenician woman (Mark 7:24–30) whose daughter had a demon exorcized by Jesus. A similar type of event occurs to the centurion's servant (Luke 7:1–10, par. Matt. 8:5–13). We can assume both were Gentiles, pagans as we might call them, but there is no evidence either of them became associated with Jesus or with the followers around Jesus. However, it is entirely possible the centurion himself was a "Godfearer," in which case his coming to Jesus could be an example of either tradition transition or institutional transition.[13] It is probable the Gerasene demonized man was a Gentile (Mark 5:1–20), and John records that some "Greeks" asked to see Jesus (John 12:20–22). But, again, there is no suggestion any of these converted to Jesus' movement. It is possible the woman from Samaria may well have "converted to Jesus" (John 4:1–42), but the evidence is sketchy at best. What is more striking is that on one occasion Jesus evidently prohibited "evangelizing" Gentiles (Matt. 10:5–6). We can affirm confidently that converts to Jesus were not drawn from "other religions": there is simply insufficient evidence to see tradition transition as a significant factor among the converts to Jesus.

Conclusions

To sum up: first, it seems likely some of those converting to Jesus can be legitimately classified as "apostates" from some other group/movement or social identity. Again, this should not be reified or overemphasized. That many of his followers experienced some form of opposition reflects group tension. That is all we should say about apostasy. Second, the two major types of conversion experienced by those converting to Jesus are intensification of an already-existing form of Judaism and affiliation on the part of those who had been marginalized in Jewish society. It is possible that a few of Jesus' converts experienced an institutional transition, but even less likely that converts incurred a tradition transition.

It is historically unjustifiable and theologically dangerous to pretend that all those "converting to Jesus" were experiencing one and the same kind of conversion. Put graphically, what James and John experienced is not what Zacchaeus experienced, and what he experienced is not what the prostitutes experienced. An important insight from sociological studies of conversion is that people convert for various reasons and for their own advantages.[14] If so, it would be nonsense to force all the "conversions to Jesus" in the Gospel traditions into one mold and then extrude from that mold a "convert type" or "conversion message." What Jesus said about the kingdom's incursion in strength, for instance, to the woman caught *en fla-grant délit* (John 7:53–8:11) would adjust itself dramatically when the audience becomes a Pharisee or an Essene or a Roman commander or an Alexandrian Jew visiting Jerusalem at Passover. The makeup of Jesus' followers, in other words, made the room hum when they gathered in the evening for dinner.

Jesus and Context

When speaking of converting to Jesus, context is everything, but it is too big to describe adequately here. In what follows I want to set out two features of the context for converting to Jesus: first, the socioreligious context in which Jesus operated and second, the various features of conversion that emerge from understanding such a context. This section, longer because it sets up what follows, will necessarily remain general and suggestive.

Jewish Socioreligious Context: General Observations

Judaism revolves around four core symbols: Torah, nation, Temple, and land. These four core symbols, however, are not static. Instead, Jews expressed their relationship to these four symbols in different contexts in a variety of ways. While a Jew in Babylonia may have valued the Temple, his or her expression of that value was not the same as that of the Galilean Jew who made the trip to Jerusalem a few times a year, and neither was the Galilean Jew's relationship the same as an Essene's (now living in Qumran) or a Sadducee's (now living in Jerusalem). Nonetheless, within this variety these four pillars of Judaism stood tall and proud. The Torah governed not only behavior but also space (in progressive concentric circles moving out from the inner sanctum) and calendar (Sabbath, annual and monthly cycles). In saying that Jews had a "way of life" I am purposefully setting such an orientation over against a great deal of bleary Christian thinking that assumes far too often that a creed unified and distinguished ancient Judaism.

The Galilee

These right behaviors, so carefully regulated and guided within the contours of the concept of purity, find expression in three larger social contexts for Jesus: the Galilee, Judea, and Rome. Of most importance for Jesus is the Galilee.[15] Located approximately seventy-five miles north of Jerusalem, the Galilee was a loose collection of mostly Jewish, "lower-class" villagers[16] in more than two hundred villages that was divided into southern (the lower Galilee) and northern (the upper Galilee) regions. The Galilee produced wheat, olives and olive oil, wine, and fish. Jewish life centered around households, with several families sharing a courtyard, an oven, a millstone, and a cistern. Apparently, "city hall" was responsible for the wine and olive presses, and it is likely that Jews gathered together weekly, perhaps even more often, in synagogues.

More importantly, the Galilee contains elements of *independence, religious piety* (later rabbinic Judaism has important roots in the Galilee), and *revolutionary spirit*. The land was fertile; the population not fallow. Such blessings fostered confidence and self-sufficiency. When Antipas assumed control of the Galilee, he rebuilt two cities for his regime. Thus, "Jesus and his initial followers, who formed a movement rooted in villages, were from a generation struggling to adjust to and/or resist the dramatic changes that had so suddenly come upon their communities."[17] If the economy was as stressed as many historians think today, then Jesus' call to cancel debts (cf. Luke 11:2–4) certainly electrified some Galilean hopes. If one respects the regional differences between the Galilee and Jerusalem, it would not be far off target to assume that Jesus' reaction to the priestly leadership of Jerusalem, even if it perhaps got its origins in John the Baptist, was at least fanned into a bigger flame by the Galilean resentment of that same leadership (cf. Mark 11:15–18; 12:13–17; 12:18–27; 13:2). Further, if the breezy winds of Roman and Greek culture entered into the Galilee through the presence of Roman leadership, it can also be said that inherited walls kept those winds at bay, though the fragrance (some would have said "stench") was everywhere present.

Thus, when Jesus was but a child, an event occurred less than four miles north of Nazareth, in Sepphoris, that expresses what can occasionally happen in the Galilee. A certain Judas, son of a certain Ezekiel who himself had been captured by Herod the Great for sedition, gathered a mob and assaulted Sepphoris, a Roman fortress, stole the weapons and possessions, and proceeded to terrorize the surrounding areas (Josephus, *Antiquities* 17.271–272). At about the same time, Galileans participated in Temple disturbances in protest of the actions of Sabinus, a procurator of Caesar (17.254–268). All of this illustrates disturbances caused by the death of Herod the Great—protests of the policies of the megalomaniac. And while it would be an overstatement to suggest that rebelliousness characterized the Galilee, these disturbances reveal that Galileans were capable of revolt. Evidently, Galileans had some proprietary rights and interests over what took place in Jerusalem with respect to the nation. It would be unfair to characterize the Galilee as a hot house of rebellion, but it would be fair to think Judea and Jerusalem saw the Galilee as backwoods. Geza Vermes was possibly on to something when he wrote,"Jesus became a political suspect in the eyes of the rulers of Jerusalem because he was a Galilean."[18] Perhaps it could be said for some in the Galilee that their greatest possible good would be to create as much mischief for Judea and Jerusalem as possible. In other words, the Galilee was in a sometimes precarious state of equilibrium.

Judea and Jerusalem

The second social context for the Jewish life was Judea and Jerusalem, the capital of the nation. Run largely by the priestly establishment but housing representatives of all the varieties of Judaism, Jerusalem functioned as the religious, legal, social, and economic center of the Jewish people. Annual pilgrimages to the city swelled its numbers to unmanageable levels, leading Roman authorities to garner special protective forces. These festivals gave Jews throughout the ancient world an opportunity to gain contacts, find new friends and renew old friendships, restore commitments to the Torah, and regain the prophetic vision for Israel. In short, Judaism's identity was shaped powerfully in the annual pilgrimages to the city to worship and pray. No feast was more vital than Pesach, or Passover.[19]

Politically, Jerusalem was administered by the high priest who was himself appointed by the Roman authorities. Unfortunately, tranquillity depended too much on the interpersonal skills of the specific high priest, say, Joseph Caiaphas, or the prefect in charge, say, Pontius Pilate. The latter, a (nonmetaphorical) cutthroat if ever there was one, upset the balance of peace more often than not through acts of silliness or stupidity. His memory was as short as his eyes were skittery. He learned the hard way that the four pillars of Judaism would not be toppled, as when he ordered soldiers to enter Jerusalem with standards on which were engraved the "image" (cf. Exod. 20:4) of Caesar, or when he used temple funds to build an aqueduct, or when he tried to soften his earlier act of images by placing votive shields in his residence—this time with only the emperor's name. Pilate had the knack of turning chaos into a habit. Each of these actions provoked a stubborn social protest.

High priests were by definition tangled into the Torah's stipulations about worship, sacrifice, and tithes; into the leadership issues throughout the land of Israel; and into complex, changing, and sometimes volatile relations with Rome and its emperors and underlings. About a century and a half before Jesus, a complex event occurred: Jerusalem regained control of the Temple as a result of the Maccabean revolt against Seleucid power, notably Antiochus Epiphanes. Shortly thereafter, the high-priest issue emerged as the number one item on the platform. When the establishment opted for a Pharisee-oriented priest, one group of Sadducean priests protested, wrote an informative letter about crucial ritual and philosophical differences (4QMMT), but lost the showdown. The group withdrew, formed a community at Khirbet Qumran, and bequeathed to the world a site and a library of information that is just now beginning to take on clarity and definition.[20] Problems within the leadership only made relations with Rome more difficult. As a result, the priests who eventually established themselves by the time of Jesus were those who had a proven track record in negotiating with Rome.

Rome

Rome, too, was a formative influence on Galilean Judaism, on Jesus, and on those who converted to him. Typical Christian scholarship sees Rome as "occupying" Judea and the Galilee to the degree that a Roman soldier seems to be suspiciously posted at every corner, with a few more hiding out at the market place. But this misunderstands Roman policy and exaggerates the evidence in order to foster rhetorically effective explanations of Jesus. As long as Rome got what it needed from its subjects—taxes,[21] peaceful negotiations, and general contentment—Rome left its vassal states alone. Furthermore, since Israel was generally supportive (its leaders maintained the party line), Rome's military presence was restricted to the coastal city of Caesarea, even if that presence was ratcheted up a notch for the major festivals when guards were stationed in Jerusalem to remind the crowds of Rome's vested interest in what happened. As long as Jerusalem offered its politically correct sacrifice for the emperor, Rome would maintain its policy of religious toleration. Thus, the Galilee of Jesus had no or little Roman military presence. However, the Roman fortified city just north of Nazareth, Sepphoris, functioned as the capital of the Galilee in some regards (cf. Josephus, *Antiquities* 17.271; *War* 2.56) and added more than a dollop to the mix. It would not have been hard, or taken long, for Jesus to peer into Roman culture. Recent archaeological work on this site has expanded our understanding of its significance.[22] It is also possible Jesus found work in this city and would have there encountered Romans, or as H. L. Mencken might have called them, the *"chic-oisie."*

However, even if there was little direct oppression of the Jews by Rome, it is highly likely that the average Jew, and especially the Jew with vivid hopes and expectations, hoped for the day when the Romans would be gone and the Jews would be left to run things their own way. That Sepphoris, a Roman fort, was just north of Nazareth would have reminded Jewish workers that the Galilee was not free. Holding such a view of Jews does not mean that Jews sat around grousing about Romans, or that they connived schemes by which they might assassinate the unlucky Roman who found himself alone in an alley! They didn't think Roman women grew beards. If they told jokes about them, they would have been three parts mirth and one part gall. Some Jews surely resented Rome, but Jews did not hate Rome. After all, Rome maintained peace for the whole known (to them) world and permitted their fellow Jews to make pilgrimages to Jerusalem, thus allowing an international communion.

These three directional winds—the Galilee, Judea, and Rome—gave birth to what sociologists call a "myth-dream," a grand scheme attributed to God of what he had planned for Israel, how he would bring it about, and when such things might happen. Included in such myth-dreams would be religious and spiritual dreams, fostered no doubt by prophets like Isaiah, Jeremiah, and (for the more priestly oriented) Ezekiel, as well as social, political, and economic dreams. The solitary figure of Simeon, embedded in the Lukan birth narrative (Luke 2:25–35), expresses what I would argue to be a typical myth-dream: hope for a national deliverer, concentration on Jerusalem as God's place to begin final salvation, restoration of Israel, and inclusion of Gentiles. Similar kinds of very Jewish hopes can be seen in the other figures of Luke's birth narrative: Zechariah, Elizabeth, Mary, and Anna (Luke 1–2). As for Jesus, then, Galilean Judaism had rolled out the "Welcome!" mat for anyone who wanted to announce the dawn of God's redemption. Jesus stepped on that mat and entered the Galilean dining hall and delivered his message about the kingdom of God arriving, even now! Galilean Jews, in no small number, had heard of the milk-and-honey days and were getting tired of the bread-and-water days. In Jesus they found someone who could restore the former.

Each of these contextual factors matters deeply for those converting to Jesus. Other factors could of course be placed on the table for consideration: culturally—that Jews had easy access to major trade centers and that roads were conducive for travel to and from Jerusalem; personally—that Jesus' personal family situation gave him a vision for Israel; and that his life of employment in and around Nazareth and Sepphoris gave him contact with the real world of both poverty and lucrative excess; that authorities, both locally and in Jerusalem, gave him a sharp eye for abuse and oppression.

Contextual Factors for Those Converting to Jesus

The Marginalized

Jesus' converts were predominantly drawn from the marginalized villager classes. He appealed to this class of people; they found in him the answer to their marginalization and to whatever needs they had. People convert to their own advantage, and it must be that the marginalized found in Jesus an advantage. We would be foolish to think the only reason people gathered around Jesus was spiritual. Galilean Judaism, with its disparate and scattered communities dotting the landscape, had raised a significant number of the poor. Crop failure, overproduction, building projects, and bad decisions all contributed. On top of that, Jesus also attracted those who were marginalized for other reasons: prostitutes, tax collectors, social oppressed, and the sinners. Galileans converted to Jesus out of a sense of crisis, and the crisis point seems to have been felt most deeply at the level of the marginal classes of the Galilee. Surely this best explains the attraction Jesus must have had to those who were physically needy: the demonized, the paralyzed, the deaf, the blind, the lame, and the lepers. An early tradition from Q says this:

> Jesus answered them, "Go and tell John what you hear and see: the blind receive their sight, the lame walk, the lepers are cleansed, the deaf hear, the dead are raised, and the poor have good news brought to them. And blessed is anyone who takes no offense at me." (Matt. 11:4–6)

In saying this, however, I am not suggesting that Jesus was concerned *only* with the marginalized. Jesus had a big heart and broad spirit—he was for all who would embrace his vision. Remember, it was he who gave the memorable line of inclusion: "He who is not against us is for us" (Mark 9:40). He attracted the marginalized but, in doing so, did not limit himself to them.

Another form of marginalization also makes sense: those who found themselves *religiously marginalized*. In previous writings, I have sought to redress the imbalance toward the overly spiritual in the teachings of Jesus; I have argued that there is a strong social dimension to his mission. However, I do not intend to minimize the religious in seeking for a balanced presentation. Whatever we might think of a marginalization theory for converting to Jesus—in which a sort of a religion of the dispossessed is what conversion is really all about—when those converting to Jesus found themselves gathered around him, it was a message about the kingdom of God, about God in his loving and compassionate nature, about an ethic of fiery resolution to obey God they heard from his lips. And this must mean the marginalization, at least in part, was religious, for the form of Jesus' message is heavily religious in orientation.

We know more: some of those converting were in fact ostracized at some level by those who had other religious ideas. If we take into consideration the "factional" theory of the term "sinners," as proposed by J. D. G. Dunn (mentioned earlier), then it becomes clear that whether or not the sinners were dubbed so because of flagrant violation of the Torah or not, they were also (at least) dubbed "sinner" because they differed in their observance from the accusing party, which in the Jesus traditions shakes down to the Pharisees. That is, in this view Jesus welcomed those who had been marginalized by the Pharisees. In saying this, I want to emphasize that I do not subscribe to the common view that the Pharisees were all bigots. We should not see them as actors in a farce who have wandered off the stage and accidentally bumped into someone who unfortunately took them seriously. The debates between Jesus and the Pharisees were understandable, from both sides, and Pharisees were fundamentally good Jews—Jesus just differed with them. Too, they differed with him. His vision for Israel had everything in its favor—except, in the opinion of the Pharisees and others, tradition and reality!

Conversion takes place among the marginalized, and we learn about the context itself when we learn from which quarters the marginalized are drawn. In this case, we learn that there were crises at the economic, physical, and religious level. "Marginal" can carry a heavy load when it is defined as a complex set of circumstances giving rise to a variety of needs to which Jesus addressed his vision of God's kingdom. And the term "crisis" must carry the same load.

The Crisis

The large numbers of those who converted to Jesus, even if sometimes the numbers might be exaggerated (as perhaps the case of the feeding incidents; e.g., Mark 6:30–44; 8:1–10), show a crisis was being felt at a broader level. The crisis was not large enough to cause a revolt, though it did come to the attention of Herod Antipas, to whom John did not truckle. There was a need large enough for Jesus to attract sizable crowds. The summary statements illustrate the point I am making. For instance, Matthew 15:29–31:

> After Jesus had left that place, he passed along the Sea of Galilee, and he went up the mountain, where he sat down. Great crowds came to him, bringing with them the lame, the maimed, the blind, the mute, and many others. They put them at his feet, and he cured them, so that the crowd was amazed when they saw the mute speaking, the maimed whole, the lame walking, and the blind seeing. And they praised the God of Israel.

Here we see a significant number of people gathering round Jesus to experience his form of salvation and give praise to the "God of Israel."

The Core Symbol: Kingdom of God

Jesus also appeals to the marginalized *by use of a core symbol: the kingdom of God.* Sociologists would call Jesus an "advocate" in this respect: as an advocate for the kingdom of God, Jesus appeals to those whose conversion finds their expectations met in the core value of kingdom. Scholars have long reproached Paul for not using kingdom language enough. A more sociologically nuanced understanding of religious expression and conversion suggests that Paul did not use it because other terms were better in his system of advocacy: terms like reconciliation, justification, redemption, propitiation, and gospel. For Jesus, however, "kingdom" was magic because his converts found in the category of "kingdom" an answer to their deepest longings. We then need to unpack what they were expecting.[23]

Since the appeal to the audience by Jesus the advocate is interactionist and not just a one-time sales offer, we can go back and forth between what is expected and what is given. First, what is expected is that God's promises to Israel, mostly made known to Abraham, David, and then the prophets, would be fulfilled. At a general level this includes such things as justice, peace, love, purity, obedience, and international centrality. Jews expected these sorts of things, and they would naturally associate the term "kingdom" with them. Second, while it cannot be said that the majority of Jews expected *the* messiah, or even a messianic figure, it is clear most would think naturally in terms of a deliverer who would usher in God's kingdom. Third, rather than expecting an individual, most Jews thought of Israel as a restored twelve-tribe nation when the final kingdom arrived. Jesus clearly evokes that symbolic expectation in giving prominence to twelve of his chosen followers (Mark 3:13–19). Fourth, all Jews would have expected the kingdom to arrive in glory, power, and majesty—a sort of flashing brilliance, a magnificent display of power, and a challenge so mighty the enemies would fall to their knees quaking and trembling about what might happen next. This expectation, however, is jettisoned by Jesus and replaced by another theme found in Israel's history: the inauspicious presence of God's work. To be sure, sometimes Jesus' kingdom displays itself in strength (e.g., Matt. 12:28), but more often it is like a mustard seed growing into a sizable bush (Mark 4:30–32), a small piece of leaven buried in some dough that influences the whole batch (Luke 13:20–21), a child who responds to the kingdom (Mark 10:14–15), or a quiet revolution recognized in Jesus' presence (Luke 17:20–21).

Fifth, satisfying Jewish expectation for a national holiness movement, a nation marked by obedience to the Torah, Jesus calls his followers to a radical relationship with God that outstrips some Jewish expectations for Torah observance. Instead of listening to parents and performing normal family responsibilities, Jesus calls his followers to obey him (Luke 9:57–62). But the emphasis he gives to common sense, to love of God and others (Mark 12:28–34), and to sorting things out hierarchically, beginning with God, gives to his followers some handles they might not otherwise have had. None of this is un-Jewish; it is all Jewish. What is more Jewish than the Shema—the call to love God and others as preeminent commandments? We need to observe that the call of Jesus to a radical discipleship appeals to the marginalized in part because it resonates with their expectations. And it apparently was a call that sounded a distinctly fresh note in the Galilee.

Sixth, we need to note that Jesus' expectations for the kingdom yet to come, the kingdom that still awaited fulfillment, also strike significant chords within Galilean Judaism: he expects the final kingdom to come soon (cf. Luke 19:11; Acts 1:6; Mark 13:30), and because his followers wanted it to come soon, they prayed for its arrival (Luke 11:1–4). That kingdom would be a judgment on unfaithfulness (e.g., Matt. 25:31–33) and an entrance into eternal table fellowship with the Father God of Israel (Luke 22:29–30). We can only reason that the Galileans of Jesus' day were hoping for such a kingdom.

To summarize, Jesus uses as the advocate for his vision for Israel a term that (necessarily) resonates with the core values of his audience, who are Galilean Jews marginalized in a variety of ways. That term is "kingdom." Unpacked, Jesus is an advocate for a restored Israel, an Israel that finds God's promises now being fulfilled and a new people being formed in the wake of that kingdom's arrival. If "kingdom" did not strike at the heart of his audience's core values, Jesus could not have garnered a following. The response shows that his term made pragmatic sense.[24]

The Poor

Jesus' offer in his context found a response because it was to that audience's advantage. I now turn around and look at the marginalized from their angle. The poor found some "wealth" in Jesus, even if that wealth was by way of communal sharing or by way of future promise. (More of this later.) The sick, the lame, the injured, the handicapped, the list goes on—all found healing in Jesus and converted to Jesus (if they finally did) to satisfy their needs. The prostitutes were attracted to Jesus, I suspect, because they found in him the message of the Father's unconditional love and a social community of acceptance. One also suspects the tax collectors gathered around Jesus for the noble motive of finding release from the guilt they absorbed from rapacious policies and from social ostracism. The Zacchaeus story focuses precisely there (Luke 19:1–10). While we cannot always be sure of the precise motives (even for our religious actions)—and speculation might tell us more about our own rather than some ancient beliefs—we can be sure that those who converted to Jesus found the conversion to their own advantage.

Different Motives for Different Converts

Finally, just as conversion has different "kinds" (e.g., intensification, affiliation, etc.), so also converts came to Jesus for different reasons, and as a result of their interactions with Jesus, they adopted and adapted his own vision for Israel. Thus, kingdom appeals to some on the basis of its connection with long-cherished spiritual and national myth-dreams (e.g., someone like a Simeon), but for others it might appeal to economic justice (e.g., a poor activist); a sense of vindication against Rome (e.g., if Simon was a pre-Jesus "zealot-type"); or the promise of physical healing. Each of these, of course, is the flip side of Jesus' offer of the kingdom.

But we dare not pretend all converts to Jesus came to him because they all had the same need and the same myth-dream. We must use our common sense: humans are wonderfully different, and a bundle of motives make up the drives of each of us. Only some kind of religious ideology would force all humans to convert for simply religious motivations. If the sinful woman came to Jesus for forgiveness (Luke 7:36–50), that does not mean that all women were guilty of sexual sins (e.g., Luke 8:1–3). The evidence simply does not permit us to say the poor came to Jesus to learn to pray or that lepers came to Jesus to learn the liturgies. The poor needed relief, and lepers needed cleansing. Further, it is certain that those who converted to Jesus, while they followed him at different levels (some absolutely, others not so absolutely), adapted what he was saying into their own personal framework of understanding. We might arrogate to moderns a lively self-identity and personal awareness, and we might also contend first-century Jews had more of a dyadic personality and social consciousness, but it remains a fact that first-century personalities were intact, and these converts to Jesus had to make sense of their own lives. After all, they were not all unthinking waifs and sycophants. This means that each of their own recrystallizations of Jesus' vision had a personally useful shape, a shape useful for the fullness of one's personal life.

Now, I need to back off these stronger statements because I believe all humans, both moderns and ancient Galilean Jews, have fundamental religious needs, and I do think Jesus met deep spiritual needs for a wide variety of Galilean Jews. He gave them a prayer; he promised rest for the soul; he offered them a loving, holy God whom they could engage at table; he structured an ethically responsible life of holiness and compassion; and he resocialized all sorts of Galileans as a form of forgiveness. If we want to interrelate all facets of life—social, political, cultural, economic, physical, familial—we dare not in this interrelating forget that first-century Galileans had just as much of a religious impulse and spiritual quest as moderns.

Jesus and Crisis

By definition, conversion resolves some kind of crisis in a person's life. Conversion crisis, however, needs to be charted along a continuum: from severe to mild intensity, from a prolonged anguish to a brief flash or a gentle nod, from an extensive to a limited scope in a person's life, from an external to an internal source, or from a radically discontinuous change to one marked more by continuity. The prototypical radical crisis may be seen in the examples of the apostle Paul, St. Augustine, and Martin Luther. Unfortunately, some forms of Christianity have equated a specific kind of crisis with genuine conversion, and that crisis is typically the "guilt-release-from-sin" and "dramatic conversion" form of conversion (as, so it is assumed, in the apostle Paul), leaving the majority orphaned and accused as unworthy. But this perspective is not only contrary to scientifically demonstrable studies, it flies in the face of the evidence of the Jesus traditions.

Minor Crisis Types

The ten "types" of crisis characteristic of conversion outlined in chapter 3 can now be compared to the evidence about Jesus.[25] I begin with types of crisis that may or may not be found, and then I shall look at three types of crisis that certainly characterized those converting to Jesus.

We do not know if converts to Jesus did so out of or in order to obtain *mystical experiences*. According to many scholars, Jesus himself was a kind of a charismatic, and the evidence suggests he was somewhat of a mystic. Luke 10:18 indicates a vision of some sort in which Jesus "saw" Satan's demise; the temptation was as much visionary as it was physical (Luke 4:1–13); the transfiguration, though "seen" by three disciples, was some kind of mystical experience (Mark 9:1–8); there is some kind of connection between healing and mysticism; it is remotely possible that Mark 7:34 and 8:12, in spite of Romans 8:26–27, describe Jesus' speaking in tongues; finally, Jesus' intense prayer life, perhaps most intense in the Garden (cf. Mark 14:32–42 and Luke 22:40–46), can at times be explained as some sort of mystical prayer. The individual bits of evidence are disputed, but it seems likely that Jesus had some mystical experiences. However, there is not much evidence Israelites converted to Jesus either as a result of previous mystical experiences or in order to gain such. The desire of the followers of Jesus to pray as Jesus prayed, now recorded in Luke 11:1, could be understood this way, but it is far more likely that they petitioned him for a formal prayer to mark off their community from other sectarian movements—and Jesus gave them what they needed (11:2–4).

The same can be said for the fifth and sixth kind of "crisis": *a desire for transcendence* and *altered states of consciousness*. Humans need God, and they are not at rest until they find God. Thus, God has made humans with a desire for transcendence. We find meaning in knowing how God views life. But when it comes to the Jesus traditions the evidence does not reveal Galileans or Judeans out on the prowl for God—this supports the conclusion above that the converts to Jesus were not from irreligious backgrounds, that their conversions were not "tradition" or "institutional" transitions, but instead more likely "intensifications" and "affiliations."

It is remotely possible that a few converting to Jesus had had a *near-death experience*. The evidence for this sort of experience does not meet our empirical qualifications, but one should at least think of Mark 5:21–43, wherein the leading story is the restoration to life of Jairus's daughter (vv. 21–24a, 35–43). In the face of grief and mourning, Jesus claims the little girl is only "sleeping," the mourners scorn his suggestion, Jesus takes in three of his followers, raises the girl back to life, and everyone stands amazed. Two issues defy explanation: Why does Jesus say she was only "sleeping"? Is it because he knew he could raise her from the dead, or did he know she was only having a near-death experience? Our distance makes an answer impossible. Further, we know nothing of what happened to Jairus's daughter after this dramatic experience. It is possible she began to follow Jesus—who wouldn't?! With appropriate changes, the same can be said for the son of the widow of Nain (Luke 7:11–17) and Lazarus (John 11:1–46).[26] Scholarship tends to look credibly on traditions about Jesus found in multiple Gospel sources/traditions. If so, scholarship ought to give the "raising from the dead" tradition a fair hearing for it appears in Mark, in L, in John, and in the Q tradition at Matthew 11:5. I hold it as a possibility that one or more persons converted to Jesus as a result of a near-death experience.

Religious conversions, sociologists tell us, occur frequently because of a *general dissatisfaction with life as it is*, and persons wanting more out of life are prone to find that "more" in religion. But can we find evidence for "wanting more" in the Jesus traditions as a motive for conversion? It is easy for moderns just to assume this viewpoint, assert it as so, and then explain stories about conversion, say Peter's or Levi's, in light of their assumptions. We cannot be so certain of such an explanation since the evidence for it in the Gospels is so sketchy. What we can do, however, is infer from "results" back to "desires" and then attribute such desires to those converting. Where there is the smoke of joy and satisfaction there is surely a preceding fire of sadness and dissatisfaction. For instance, we can infer from Matthew 11:28–30 that "rest," given to the followers by Jesus' comforting words and presence, meets the need of "restlessness" or "soul-heaviness." We can argue that some converting to Jesus found a release from their burdens, however those burdens might be defined—and we need not define them as legalistic. It may be tentatively assumed that some converted to Jesus because of general dissatisfaction.[27]

The eighth kind of crisis, *pathology*, can also be seen as a dimension of a person's general dissatisfaction with life. Pathologies can only be diagnosed after intense scrutiny by trained professionals, and my wife, a trained psychologist, tells me the symptoms of people in the pages of the Gospels are too general to admit of a specific explanation. It is thus wisest for modern scholarship to avoid this category when discussing converting to Jesus except to say this: some probably converted to Jesus for pathological motivations, but we can't detect who they were or their specific pathologies.[28]

Illness and Healing

The previous six crises are possibly present in the Jesus traditions for those who converted to Jesus; the following three I take to be certain. I begin with the crisis of *illness*. We rarely find a window into the heart and soul of the person who comes to Jesus for healing, but we can assume the crisis was physical. In ancient Judaism, illness or physical defects were a source of both physical suffering and an opportunity for social classification. Notice how the ill are all grouped together in Matthew 11:5. That is, healings by Jesus were acts of both alleviation and resocialization, as can be seen in Jesus' female disciples (Luke 8:1–3). The one made well experienced no more personal pain and no more social stigmatization. All of this can be seen helpfully through the lens of purity: Jesus was a contagion of purity, and he put people back in their natural order (which is what purity is) with respect to themselves and society.[29]

We can be sure that Galileans and others converted to Jesus because of a crisis in health. Notably, Mary Magdalene traveled with Jesus (Luke 8:2), witnessed his execution (23:49), and encountered Jesus after Easter (24:3–8); and it was she who was healed of seven demons (8:2). Peter's mother-in-law was healed, and she then served Jesus (Mark 1:29–31), just as a leper was purified and instructed to go through a purification ritual to be fully socialized (1:40–45). Exorcisms figure prominently in the Jesus traditions, among which surely the exorcism of the Gerasene demonized man stands above the others (Mark 5:1–20); this man is exhorted to tell others what the Lord had done for him. Jesus' healings not only witness then to the presence of the kingdom with Jesus as God's agent of that kingdom (Matt. 11:2–6; 12:28; Luke 17:20–21), but they enact that kingdom for those persons, socialize them into the Jesus movement, and encourage them to follow in the path of discipleship. Blind Bartimaeus, spoken about in Mark 10:46–52, was healed through faith and as a result followed Jesus "on the way," a metaphor for following Jesus as a disciple just as Jesus accepts the road of suffering.

External Factors

Another almost certain feature of converting to Jesus concerns an *external or political crisis*. Those who converted to Jesus had various motivations, but one motivation was surely *justice*. I would not put as much emphasis as some recent writers have on an anti-Zealot or antiviolence stance on the part of Jesus—a sort of modern '60s activist so wonderfully attractive to people of my generation—but I am quite convinced that Jesus' message of *peace* contained a solid core of social vision and national hope. This perhaps explains the conversion of Joanna, wife of Herod's steward (Luke 8:3). Alongside these two notions of justice and peace, we must place the accents Jesus gives to *economics*—a clear revival of the themes connected with the ancient Israelite vision for a Jubilee. Though more subdued than John the Baptist, Jesus may have had some antipriestly concepts. This could be expected of Galileans, and for anyone else who held atavistic concepts of the ideal priesthood: say, for instance, as is the case with the "rebels" at Qumran. Current connections with Rome and compromise simply riled the fever of those who found the levitical rules constraining or the taxes burdening. Jesus' decision to centralize his ideas around the term "kingdom" fueled the same fires: Who would talk about the coming kingdom but one who thought the present arrangement was falling apart? Finally, Jesus' particular emphases in ethical behaviors, say adultery, divorce, oath-taking, the *lex talionis*, and attitudes toward non-Jewish associates—take any or all of these—give one the impression that his own views were set into a context that had conflicting views. He was offering another constellation of what it meant to live as a nation before the God of Israel in a manner superior to other views.

This chastened perception of Judaism permits a Jesus who butted heads with the Pharisees. Regardless of how much Matthew 23 shows signs of editorial updating, the core tradition remains firm: Jesus saw purity in terms other than those seen by the Pharisees. His emphasis derived more from the Shema, used now deductively from the dual principles of love for God and love for neighbor, and less from the levitical stipulations. I doubt very much that Jesus thought the levitical rules were wrong; instead he thought they were getting in the way—and that is all we need for the point I am about to make.

Sociopolitical Vision for Israel

For Jesus' followers, converting to Jesus was to posture oneself into a sociopolitical stance. This interpretation can be overdone—recent scholarship shows it. But it still remains a solid fact that following Jesus was a choice not to follow the other options in one's ambit of life. I here am borrowing again from the important study of Gauri Viswanathan, who sees conversion as a form of "dissent" as well as assent. At its core, many of those who converted to Jesus embraced his notion of the kingdom of God and his vision for Israel's redemption. Most saw Jesus as a prophet of some kind who was announcing a dual message of redemption through his vision of the kingdom and a warning of judgment for those who refused to see God at work in his mission to Israel (this message is what the "unforgiveable sin" is all about: Matt. 12:31–32). By thus embracing Jesus' vision for Israel in that dynamic term "kingdom," these converts to Jesus were socially enacting a protest against the other options on the table—whether one wants to particularize them as Pharisaic, Zealotic, Essenic, and what not—or were a generalized group who were now intensifying their (previous, latent or active) commitment to the prophetic vision of redemption by associating themselves so clearly with Jesus.

Formulating conversion to Jesus in sociopolitical terms does not require that we make Jesus' followers a bunch of revolutionaries, nor does it rule out the concept that his followers had, from an early period, the makings of what came to be an "ecclesiology." However, such a view does state what sociologists of conversion would readily argue: conversion to Jesus implies a sociopolitical unit on the part of Jesus and his followers. If it is the case that a goodly number of Galilean Jews were converting to Jesus, then it goes without saying that they were more than amorphous amoebae wafting around on the Galilean hillsides with no apparent connection to one another but rather somehow in close enough proximity to Jesus to be together! The origins of the Christian doctrine of the church are to be found here: in the sociological necessity of like-minded persons attaching themselves to one another. It ought to be reiterated that this connection I find between followers of Jesus, on the basis of a sociological model of conversion, is not the formation of a new religion in lower Galilee. No, this movement around Jesus is a Jewish vision for a Jewish people: a new vision for Israel.

In short, the ninth and tenth kinds of crises can be profitably combined: apostasy and externally stimulated crises are fundamentally social shapings of conversion behaviors by a collection of similarly minded folk. Those who converted to Jesus left another central dimension to their experience and formed a new center. In the case of those who converted to Jesus as an act of affiliation, the dimension of apostasy forms little usefulness by way of explanation. But especially those who encountered Jesus as an act of institution transition, for which there is not that much evidence, the concept of apostasy becomes central to explain the conversion. For the majority of converts to Jesus intensification best explains their conversion: and in these cases the concept of apostasy is subdued but nonetheless present. For each, however, a sociopolitical action of joining a new movement remains important to the very act of converting.

Thus, converting to Jesus involved various crises, among which the most important are those of the alleviation of suffering, resocialization, sociopolitical reformation, and apostasy. At a lesser level of importance, the crisis involved mystical experience, a desire for transcendence, and a near-death experience. I take it as a distinct likelihood that those who converted to Jesus did so to satisfy their concepts of meaning and happiness, though I am unsure how useful the categories of protean selfhood and pathology are for explaining this crisis for the time of Jesus.

Jesus and the Quest for Conversion

Older studies of conversion shared the conviction that converts were to one degree or another passive instruments of forces outside their control, and these studies consequently saw conversion too often as manipulation. More recent scholarship has, however, flip-flopped: today, converts are seen as actively involved in their own conversion. Accordingly, conversion is understood as the climax to a *quest*. Does the evidence of the Gospels reveal potential converts on a quest?

A simple place to see evidence of a quest is in the Jewish historian Josephus, who claims he underwent conversion to various Jewish philosophies—his carefully chosen word for the sects or denominations within Judaism. While his words, especially when he has the opportunity to market his own virtues, are not always stated with propriety or modesty, nonetheless, here they are:

> I made great progress in my education, gaining a reputation for an excellent memory and understanding. While still a mere boy, about fourteen years old, I won universal applause for my love of letters; insomuch that the chief priests and the leading men of the city used constantly to come to me for precise information on some particular in our ordinances. At about the age of sixteen *I determined to gain personal experience of the several sects into which our nation was divided....* *I thought that, after a thorough investigation, I should be in a position to select the best. So I submitted myself to hard training and laborious exercises and passed through the three courses.* Not content, however, with the experience thus gained, on hearing of one named Bannus, who dwelt in the wilderness, wearing only such clothing as trees provided, feeding on such things as grew of themselves, and using frequent ablutions of cold water, by day and night, for purity's sake, I *became his devoted disciple.* With him I lived for three years and, having accomplished my purpose, returned to the city. Being now in my nineteenth year I began to govern my life [*politeuesthai*] by the rules of the Pharisees [*te Pharisaion hairesei katakolouthon*], a sect having points of resemblance to that which the Greeks call the Stoic school. (*Life* 8–12; italics added)

Traditional scholarship sees here Josephus's conversion to Pharisaism. The general tone of his several works and the specifics of this very passage suggest otherwise: Why would he find Bannus his master if he had found the Pharisees satisfying? It is more likely that Josephus is speaking here not of a conversion to Pharisaism but of his return to "public life" (*politeuesthai*) and, in his public life, of a willingness to be governed by the reigning Pharisaic political party's specific codes. In other words, it describes Josephus's willingness to "go with the flow."[30] More important for our purposes, however, is how active Josephus is in his own quest for spiritual formation. He personally examined, after a pretty fair education, the three major parties of Judaism: the Pharisees, Sadducees, and Essenes. After examining each of these, after passing the three courses, Josephus then becomes the disciple of a certain desert master, Bannus. What we see here is an active quest on the part of a first-century Jew for spiritual formation. While it was outside the limits of agrarian peasants to spend so much leisure time seeking the nuances of religious parties, we can be confident in seeing here the sort of activism available to a first-century Jew— given the opportunity and the interest. That is, if people are structurally, emotionally, intellectually, and religiously available, a quest for conversion may well take place.

Another factor highlighting the element of activism in religious exploration and conversion is the sociopolitical angle given to the discussion of conversion by Gauri Viswanathan. If conversion fundamentally is a form of dissent and assent, it is also an active quest on the part of the dissenting and assenting convert. Those who convert act out socially their vision for their own lives and are not simply passive recipients of a religious experience.

What was involved on the part of Jesus' converts when they were "questing" and found Jesus to be the end of that quest? We here overlap with the previous section on the kinds of "crises" one might undergo in the process of conversion, but the different angle on the evidence, this time from the angle of the potential convert, permits a greater depth of understanding of conversion in the world of Jesus. First, some convert because they are in a quest *for pleasure or to avoid pain*. One needs only to think of the many who converted to Jesus, and who physically pursued him, in order to find the end of suffering. Thus, the leper approached Jesus and bowed before him, beseeching his help and healing (Mark 1:40–45). The centurion, or his ambassadors, sought Jesus for help for the suffering servant/child (Luke 7:1–10, par. Matt. 8:5–13). And just as crowds gathered around Jesus' evening locations for healing (Mark 1:32–34), so also some friends dug their way through a roof to lower a paralytic into Jesus' presence for his healing touch (Mark 2:1–12). Enough said—some quested for Jesus to enable healing, to find physical pleasure, and to end suffering.

Second, it seems quite likely that some Galilean Jews converted to Jesus because they were questing (already), whether consciously or not, *for a conceptual system that gave coherence to their experience*. In particular, if we take into consideration the myth-dream of Galilean Jews, we can surmise Jesus' choice of the term *kingdom* captured the myth-dream for a significant number of Galileans. We can assume some Jews lived comfortably in a world of ideas, within the confines and hopes of their own myth-dreams, and Jesus grabbed hold of those hopes and gave them new life and urgency. They said, "Kingdom, now that's a good way of putting it. Yes, that's what I think, too." This theme of eschatology dominated both Jesus' vision and a fair number of early Christian writings. In this context, I can merely point to this dominant theme.[31]

Third, some converted to Jesus as a result of their quest *for self-esteem*. The term sounds as modern as "gigabyte." But people are people, even if they are ancient, and people need a sense of identity. If we go by modern analogies, the fact that Jesus spoke of God's utter love, welcomed all sorts to the table in the evening, and showed regard for the integrity of women in the nooks and crannies of Jewish society (e.g., Luke 8:1–3; John 4; John 7:53–8:11) supports the notion that persons converted to Jesus in order to find acceptance with God and thereby find a sense of self-esteem. Some modern anthropologists and social scientists contend for a fundamentally different conceptualization of the self in the ancient world (seeing ancients as dyadic), leading one to consider "self-esteem" too modern a concern. However, a brief reading of Seneca's *Epistles* or Plutarch's various essays reveals a more balanced perspective: ancient Romans and Greeks, and by inference Jews, could think quite individualistically, could have their feelings hurt, and could act to protect their egos.

That some converted to Jesus *to find relationships*, or a *surrogate family*, builds on the previous motivation in the quest for conversion. Environment shapes our world, as Peter Berger and Thomas Luckmann have so ably explained, and that includes what we think is normal, good, beautiful, honorable, and exciting, as well as what is abnormal, bad, ugly, and boring.[32] What appears to us to be oppressive, male-dominated chauvinism in the Galilee of Jesus might have appeared to be normal and capable of generating a happy life for them. I take that for granted. But even within this general framework, the emphasis Jesus gave to his little clutch of followers as a *family* leads me to think there was a crisis for many at the level of social relationships and communal satisfaction. With God as Father, Jesus becomes the creator of a new (metaphorical) family. Thus, he considers his mother and family as having less of a claim on his life than his followers: John 2:1–11 and Mark 3:31–35 (cf. Luke 9:57–62). In fact, it is clear Jesus called his followers to separate themselves from their families (Matt. 10:34–39) and to join the new surrogate family (Mark 10:29–30).[33] All of this, of course, is embodied in Jesus' regular table fellowship with his followers where he embodies his vision for family and instructs it in his new vision for Israel.

Once again, conversions take place to Jesus because some were in the *quest for power*. I don't think it is unfair to Jesus to suggest he wanted power—he wanted to be the king, and he wanted Israel to listen to him, to follow him, and to be enrolled in his vision for the nation. It follows to suggest some of his followers (but not all) jumped into his boat because they, too, thought current mixtures of power were flammable or rotten, and a cooling off or a remedy was needed (Luke 8:3—Joanna). Again, we are led to the term "kingdom," which must speak of power, and to the occasional question he was asked about taxes and Caesar (cf. Mark 12:13–17; Matt. 17:24–27). These are questions about who is in power and whether they should be in power; even if the answers are as ambiguous as their implications, the point remains that power was on the lips of those interested in Jesus. It was cleverness, perhaps more than cleverness, that led Jesus to get the tax collectors on his side (Mark 2:13–17; Luke 19:1–10), but it was also an issue of power. Jesus' choice of the Twelve is along the same line: it is a claim on the whole nation. The same applies, *mutatis mutandis*, to his entry into and occupation of the Temple. These are terms and actions and images of power, not violent power but nonetheless claims on the nation. Surely some caught the drift and rode Jesus to the cross for it.

Finally, some no doubt were on a quest *for religious transcendence, mystical experience, and spiritual happiness*. As I said previously, this motivation as a quest for those who converted to Jesus is not as notable in the Jesus traditions as some might think—but we can safely assume Jesus' very religiousness attracted a quest on the part of those around him. Perhaps no one has spoken more eloquently for this view of Jesus than Marcus Borg, who in his book of enormous influence, *Jesus: A New Vision*,[34] describes a Jesus who is a charismatic "spirit person." Jesus speaks of serving God (Matt. 6:24), and he relays a message of the heart (6:19–21). If these shape the center of Jesus' teachings, and if at some level their images strike what Jesus expected in discipleship, we are driven to infer that he ended the quest for some who were seeking God and religious meaning.

In conclusion, those who converted to Jesus were undoubtedly questing. It appears less and less that Jesus was one capable of finding passive recipients and taking them along with him. Instead, Jesus met the needs of those who were out and about seeking for various solutions to their underlying myth-dreams. In particular, the major foci of his offer to Israel correlated with the various forms of questing in his Galilean Jewish world, and the two met, set off sparks, and formed a dynamic movement. Those forms of questing appear to have been to end suffering; to find a meaningful conceptual system, sense of self-esteem, relationships, and family; as well as to find religious meaning. Further, we should not shove to a corner the imagery Jesus used and the attractiveness that his vision for Israel had for those whose desire it was to find power in society.

Chapter Five

Jesus and Conversion

Encounter to Consequences

Those Galilean questers who found in Jesus what they were looking for encountered Jesus and Jesus encountered them. The encounter phase of conversion involves the advocate (Jesus, who has a strategy), the encounter, and an interaction. The academic study of the sociology of conversion formerly gave far too little attention to the advocate's role in the encounter itself; this imbalance has recently been revised. Because they conclude that the relationship of the advocate and convert is dialectical and interactionist, sociological studies undermine the common assumption in Jesus studies that he differed from the protorabbinic and rabbinic model. Formerly, scholarship assumed that, with rabbis, the disciples approached the master whereas with Jesus there was a sovereign, authority-usurping call.[1] This contrast between Jesus and the rabbis, often drawn polemically, has been undermined by recent study. In fact, such a proposal operates in an ideal world that does not connect with the realities of either ancient Judaism or modern Christianity. The realities of conversion involve an advocate who interacts with potential converts and potential converts who interact with the advocate. The encounter goes both ways. We need to examine each element of this dimension of conversion.

Jesus the Advocate

Jesus was convinced he had been called by God to deliver a message to Israel about its possible restoration so it could fulfill God's design for his people. Such a calling was "in the genes" since his relative, John, had a similar calling (cf. Matt. 3:1–17; Luke 1:39–56). With this heritage, something peculiar happening to Jesus at the age of his bar mitzvah cannot be outside the realm of probability (Luke 2:41–52), but Jesus' own calling only comes to the surface with power at his baptism (Mark 1:9–11). From that time on, the calling manifests itself in his public preaching, healing, and prophetic actions[2] in the Galilee (Mark 1:14–15; cf. Matt. 5:1–9:34). This mission of Jesus is concerned with the kingdom of God, the expression Jesus chose to elaborate his vision for Israel and connect to like-minded Jews.

Unlike modern Christian faith, where we find a variety of advocates as agents of conversion, the Jesus traditions focus exclusively on Jesus the advocate. For earliest Christianity Jesus was clearly "more than" the normal advocate; for early Christians he was Messiah, Son of God, and Lord. Because of this elevation of status and role, those concerned with a social-scientific study of Jesus and conversion need flexible and adaptable categories. However, recognizing this exalted status does not prevent the category from being used profitably. We might say that the term "advocate" does not tell us all we know of Jesus, but it does fairly represent one role he played. Furthermore, recent study of Jesus concludes that he fulfilled the role of the eschatological prophet, and prophet fits snugly into the category of advocate.[3]

This "more-than-the-normal-advocate" dimension of Jesus forms a pillar on which we can build a more accurate perception of Jesus' role in the conversion of his followers. Sociology teaches us that there is a significant *correlation between the advocate and the convert* but that correlation need not be equivalent. Thus, if Jesus can say it is the norm for disciples to be treated as are their teachers and for students to be as their teachers, he can also expect his students to follow him (Matt. 10:24–25; Mark 8:34). The relationship of Jesus and his disciples was not simple equivalency. It was one of both correlation and noncorrelation. He was "more than an advocate" at times. First, this "more than" role for Jesus comes to the fore because he is Lord of his followers. Jesus, it will be recalled, chose twelve and made them leaders of his followers, but Jesus was not one of the twelve. He was above the twelve (Mark 3:13–19) even though they had a major role in Jesus' vision of the future (Matt. 19:28). Second, Jesus' relationship to his followers was *apodictic*, a term designating commandments of the Torah that have no conditions—"do this, don't do that" instead of "if this, then do this." Too much is sometimes made of the apodictic style of Jesus, but at least this can be said: Jesus' relationship to his followers was one of authority and lordship. In short, it was a master-disciple relationship and not a "fellow traveler" relationship. And this relationship continued: disciples of Jesus never imagined surpassing this rabbi.

This convergence of the Gospel presentations of Jesus as Messiah, Son of God, and Lord, along with the authoritative relationship Jesus had with his converts, gives shape to various "attributes" an advocate has in conversion. Jesus fits at the "secular" and "religious" level with his converts: he is male; he is Jewish; he is Galilean; he is an artisan; and he has a cousin whose father is a priest. Each of these attributes enables Jesus to be successful in carrying out his mission from God. For instance, it would have required something "more than more" for a Judean to carry out a mission in the Galilee, and it was probably strategic for Jesus to have been an artisan to be able to relate to the marginalized. It was probably to Jesus' advantage that he wasn't a priest or a professional; it helped that he was from Nazareth. His heritage gave him an entrée to the marginalized villagers in the Galilee. Perhaps even the scorn from his hometown villagers worked to his eventual favor (cf. Mark 6:1–6). His prophetic orientation had its own deep roots in the artisans of society. Take Abraham, Elisha, Elijah, and Amos for examples; Moses could also be appealed to. Commenting on the social location of Jesus as providing a basis for his mission, Walter Brueggemann says,

> He is a Nazarene, which is to say surely a marginal, faithful one. He is marginal geographically ([Matthew 1] v. 22) to avoid the final royal reality, and he is also religiously marginal (cf. Num. 6:1–21), for he stands as a reality always to contrast and finally to destroy the dominant reality.[4]

Another dimension that needs to show correlation between advocate and convert is "the theory of conversion." While this information requires argument in a circle, this much can be said: Jesus' conversion expectations were not only practicable but desirable for his Galilean audiences. It was possible in the Galilee for some men to drop their nets and become itinerants dependent on others for their sustenance, mendicants as it were. Jesus was flexible enough to permit some to stay home and carry on their normal lives. But fundamentally Jesus called his converts to surrender their lives to him and to his vision for Israel, and that meant living for the kingdom of God. Morally, it might mean giving up possessions and vocation, but it surely meant living before God righteously, peacefully, forgivingly, mercifully, that is, lovingly with others.[5] Accordingly, Jesus' primary forms of inducement are tied into the practicable goals of his converts: they could be with him; they could share table with other converts to Jesus; they could be part of this restoration of Israel; they could find God's approval—to wit, they could participate in the kingdom of God. Social, communal participation in the restored Israel is what is meant, at least in part, by the partial realization of the kingdom in Jesus' mission.

Jesus' Strategy

I have emphasized previously that the primary kind of conversion to Jesus is intensification, that is, the revitalization of a previously existing Jewish faith. In light of this general orientation to the mission of Jesus it needs to be said that Jesus' strategy was not so much evangelization (as defined by most today) as *the attempt to awaken Israel*, especially marginalized Galileans, to his prophetic vision for Israel. This vision was not just for the Galilee; he had a mission for the entire nation. As Jesus preached the restoration of Israel through the arrival of God's kingdom, so conversion to that vision for Israel would predominantly be intensification of their faith. Some converts probably underwent an affiliation conversion, those who moved out of the cracks of Jewish culture to firm association with Jesus' vision for Judaism. Some of his converts may have been previously classed as "resident aliens" (*ger toshavim*; see below). Within two decades this social classification would be reused by James to all Gentiles who converted to the Pauline gospel, even if living outside the land (Acts 15:19–21).[6] It is possible that James knew of the usefulness of this category from the period of Jesus. At any rate, the general strategy for Jesus, so narrowed as his mission was on his people (Matt. 10:5–6), was intensification of Jewish faith.

Within that general orientation, we can safely categorize Jesus' conversion strategy as "concentrated"—with modifications. If we go by results, we can infer that Jesus' method was not so much "diffuse" as concentrated. Clearly, the bulk of his converts were from among the marginalized of Galilee. However, there is clear evidence that Jesus was seeking to reach out "diffusely" to find converts throughout the entirety of Jewish society. First, his clear decision to call twelve, an undoubted symbolic number for the whole of Israel (Mark 3:13–19), shows a diffusion throughout Israel.[7] Jesus' choice is a call, if not also a radical claim, on his nation. Second, however, there are two separate traditions of Jesus sending out his followers, one time just twelve (Mark 6:6–13, 30; cf. Matt. 9:35–11:1) and the other time seventy (or seventy-two) (Luke 10:1–16). Both of these two traditions evince a vision on Jesus' part for extending his vision for Israel into the whole of the Galilee. And the Samaritan woman's proclamation witnesses to the same strategy (John 4:39). But if we define "diffuse" as systemic, in the sense that Jesus was moving politically from village to village, working from top down, seeking to get "leaders" and the whole village to his side—as David did in soliciting support for his kingship—then we would have to say that Jesus was not diffuse but concentrated in his strategy. The evidence supports this latter category: the focus of Jesus' strategy was an appeal to the marginalized, and through them he hoped to awaken interest in his vision for Israel.

Did Jesus stand in theaters and announce his message, in what was for Galileans the most glamorous form of media attention and communication? If we sort through the evidence for the *mode of Jesus' conduct* in carrying out his strategy, we would have to say Jesus opted for a public form of communication as well as personal conversation. Once again, Jesus' mode of conduct borrows from the prophetic tradition: prophets preached publicly (e.g., 1 Kings 22; Jeremiah; Obadiah), contacted key individuals (e.g., Isaiah contacts Ahaz in Isa. 7:11–14), and performed prophetic drama (Jeremiah breaks the jar in 19:11; Ezekiel spends 390 and then 40 days on his side in 4:4–6; Hosea marries, or remarries, a prostitute and gives symbolic names to his children in 1:2–5; 3:1–5). Jesus also preached publicly (Matt. 5:1–7:29; cf. Luke 6:12–49), even in the Temple courts to get even more attention (cf. Mark 11:27–40, pars.), and went so far as to predict the Temple's destruction (13:1–37, pars.). Alongside these "media events," we need also to note that Jesus regularly drew crowds and taught them (e.g., Mark 4:1; 8:1–10; 10:1). There is no record of Jesus intentionally taking action to speak to the leaders, though Luke records one instance with Antipas of indirect communication (Luke 13:31–33)— and his indirect form of communication may have gotten back to Antipas. After all, "that fox" was well aware of what John the Baptist was doing. But there is plenty of evidence for Jesus' own prophetic actions, including his participation with John in the Jordan river baptism (Mark 1:1–13), healing those who were ill (Luke 7:18–23), choosing twelve to represent his vision for the nation (Mark 3:13–19), open table fellowship with the marginalized (Mark 2:13–17), and instructing the disciples to shake off dust as a form of judgment (Mark 6:11). In his final week, we think of the complex of entering Jerusalem, tipping tables topsy-turvy in the Temple, cursing an adolescent fig tree, and turning the last supper with his followers into a memorial meal (Mark 11:1–25; 14:22–25). Jesus was, as someone has said, "the preacher with no off button."[8]

In addition to these very typical prophetic forms of communication, Jesus also engaged individuals in conversation and personal challenge. Luke's description of Peter's conversion (5:1–11) describes a realistic situation in which a challenge, response, and call are all reported. Jesus engages the Gerasene demonized man abruptly, powerfully, and personally (Mark 5:1–20), and he does the same with the Samaritan woman (John 4:1–42) and the sinful woman (Luke 7:36–50). The same can be said for

Zacchaeus (Luke 19:1–10) and Mary and Martha (Luke 10:38–42). With Mary and Martha we are carried once again into first-century Galilean homes with Jesus. Every evening someone hosted a dinner; around the table Jesus dispensed not just food but also his vision for the kingdom. We can assume it was an evening of informal conversation, personal riposte, and in-depth clarifications of what "kingdom" means. To each of these persons, but in a myriad of forms, Jesus offers a challenge and summons to embrace his vision for the kingdom. We know of these evening meals mostly because those who responded positively to the challenge told their story. We know less of the "would-be" converts of the tradition at Luke 9:57–62 because they probably did not—a tradition that sounds like it is reporting legendary stories of rejection of Jesus. We do learn more than we'd like to know about the rich young ruler who refused the pilgrimage from riches to rags (Mark 10:17–31). Jesus carried on habitually with both male and female converts, urging them to pluck up their courage and persevere in following him (cf. Mark 8:34–9:1; Luke 8:1–3). In light of this evidence, we can confidently affirm that Jesus' mode of conduct moved along a spectrum from public declaration to private conversation, with the latter the more typical mode.

A good strategist knows the benefits of converting, and Jesus evidently used the language of "rewards" as a way of expressing the benefits of embracing his view of the kingdom. Christians today, so schooled as they are in Reformation categories, find the use of "rewards" for discipleship either inconsistent with the doctrine of grace (a kind of merit theology) or with their (all too middle-class, European Protestant liberal) altruism: good is its own reward. Jesus embraced neither of these ideologies and thus, within his own world where the deuteronomic ideal stood tall and proud, spoke quite effectively to his audience about the rewards that were theirs for following his vision for Israel. Each of these advantages (rewards) meets a need and can be reversed to find that need. Before saying anything we must say this: Jesus' vision was, as I have said elsewhere,

> the grand and glorious revitalization of Zion, the flocking of Gentiles to Jerusalem to acknowledge Israel's God, the defeat of Israel's national enemies, the total restoration of Jewish society, and the complete moral transformation of the people of Israel, so that every Israelite would do the will of God from the inside out.[9]

Having the end in view shapes the present at hand—Jesus was not interested in "heaven," or in lots of material benefits, or in wild beasts becoming living room pets. His preoccupation was Israel and its redemption. For those who wished to join him, to convert to Jesus, he promised several things. We can mention the following:

For the present, Jesus envisioned his followers *being provided for,* no doubt through the good graces of fellow-minded Israelites. If he taught them to pray for bread, short of a new manna miracle every day, he must have thought in terms of others providing that bread (Luke 11:4 and Matt. 10:11–16). And he also taught them that those who pursued the kingdom first would have their needs met (Luke 12:22–31). This leads to a second present reward for his followers: *a new community.* Jesus' own community is no longer drawn only along blood lines but instead along faith lines (Mark 3:31–35). Jesus promises the same to Peter and those like him who wondered what was in it for them (10:28–30). *For the future,* Jesus seems to focus the promise on one central image: *eternal table fellowship with the Lord God of Israel.* Those who come to Zion from afar will get to sit with the patriarchs in the kingdom (Matt. 8:11), and Jesus promises his small clutch of followers in that last supper that he will share a table with them in the kingdom (Mark 14:25). If these are the benefits and Jesus any kind of skilled communicator and advocate, then we can infer that fellowship, family, and physical provisions were the central needs of his group— because these are what he promises. To backtrack, such a strategy appeals profoundly to the marginalized of Galilean society.

As stated in chapter 4, the benefits of conversion can be assigned to one of the following five categories: cognitive, affective, pragmatic, charismatic, and power. The previously mentioned rewards promised by Jesus fit quite neatly within these categories. Cognitively, Jesus provided a systemic explanation, so they embraced the vision: he used the category "kingdom." Affectively, Jesus offered family, fellowship, and personal relationships as a foundational dimension for his followers. Pragmatically, while they probably did not learn new "techniques" for living, Jesus did provide physical provisions through a network of supporting followers. Nothing could be more pragmatic for the marginalized. Charismatically, Jesus' own presence, with stories dashing to and fro about him like light images in digital electronics, would have satisfied the need of so many to find a leader and hero. And, finally, when it comes to an appeal of power, Jesus challenged the current view of power (through his image of suffering and cross as positives; cf. Mark 8:34–9:1), but he also supported the desire on the part of many "to take over" and control the mess in which Israel found itself. His vision was not of conventicles but of the kingdom of God.

Encountering Jesus

Conversion is complex, the tangled process of a myriad of motives with the uncanny ability to untangle itself within a newer and happier person. It is too complex to permit a simplistic taxonomy of what happens when potential converts encounter the myth-dream or the advocate. In the history of the church, the process of conversion has evolved, shifted, altered, and even reinvented itself. This bumpy history has produced at least three orientations in Christendom today, as I described in the Introduction: a liturgical, a socialization, and a personal-decision orientation. Since Jesus' mission to Israel was something new, socialization was only a part of the story, and liturgical rites seemed to have played a minimal part in the conversion stories that have survived. These two orientations, however, undoubtedly became two of the road bumps within a generation or two and remain important dimensions of the conversion process.

I shall examine, briefly, the records of two encounters with Jesus, one involving a convert and one evidently not: Zacchaeus and the rich young ruler. These illustrate the varieties of factors involved in an encounter with Jesus the advocate. Zacchaeus's story (Luke 19:1–10) has been told, nay sung, for generations but always for the same thing: to affirm life's limitations in being short! In fact, the expression used for Zacchaeus being "short," *hoti te helikia mikros en*, may refer to his being short "in years" and his inability to get to Jesus because of his (despised) status in Jericho. Nonetheless, even if the traditional view probably stands tall, the size (or age) of Zacchaeus has nothing to do with the central aspects of this story.

> He [Jesus] entered Jericho and was passing through it. A man was there named Zacchaeus; he was a chief tax collector and was rich. He was trying to see who Jesus was, but on account of the crowd he could not, because he was short in stature. So he ran ahead and climbed a sycamore tree to see him, because he was going to pass that way. When Jesus came to the place, he looked up and said to him, "Zacchaeus, hurry and come down; for I must stay at your house today." So he hurried down and was happy to welcome him. All who saw it began to grumble and said, "He has gone to be the guest of one who is a sinner." Zacchaeus stood there and said to the Lord, "Look, half of my possessions, Lord, I will give to the poor; and if I have defrauded anyone of anything, I will pay back four times as much." Then Jesus said to him, "Today salvation has come to this house, because he too is a son of Abraham. For the Son of Man came to seek out and to save the lost."

However powerful Zacchaeus may have been in the eyes of some, he remained nonetheless marginalized for Israelites who judged along purity and covenant lines: he was not only a cooperator with Rome but was also suspected of greed, theft, and all things big and bad (cf. vv. 2, 7). In spite of Zacchaeus's power economically, he was a quester in some sense for Jesus (v. 3). In a general way Jesus sought him as well (v. 10—*zeteo* in both instances). Zacchaeus may have been seeking better visibility, like paparazzi darting here and there to get a better angle on a celebrity, or just posturing himself to be in a spot to meet Jesus. In verse 5, a gap occurs, for suddenly Jesus speaks his name and says personal things. How did Jesus know who Zacchaeus was? Why did he say he wanted to, indeed that he "must" (v. 10), eat at his house? We can assume Jesus came to know these things by asking, by being informed by an interested person, or by knowing Zacchaeus from previous instances.

One of the problems for interpreters is that they too often assume that what is in the text is all that needs to be known in order to construct what happened. As first impressions needed to be revised for Peter's conversion (e.g., cf. Mark 1:16–20 to Luke 5:1–11), so a sociologically informed approach to this event with Zacchaeus might inform our first impressions of the tax collector's conversion. In this instance, we are to infer from general considerations that Jesus knew Zacchaeus from a previous meeting or that someone informed Jesus that Zacchaeus was interested in meeting him. That Zacchaeus knew (at least knew about) Jesus is confirmed by verse 6: Zacchaeus welcomes Jesus to his home happily, as if Jesus is someone he has wanted to know. That Jesus and Zacchaeus square off around the table illustrates physical, social, and ideological encapsulation. We don't know how long the conversation lasted; we don't know how long Jesus stayed with Zacchaeus (a few hours? an evening? a day? a week?). The encounter and interaction were sufficient enough to encapsulate Zacchaeus and lead him to conversion.

Once again, another gap occurs: Why is it that in verse 8 Zacchaeus blurts out his sins? Can we imagine that he did this because he felt Jesus' presence to be one of a "holy man," or is it more likely that the whole event, from verse 3 onwards, emerges out of a man who had been questing for Jesus on his own? I think the latter makes better sense. It is also likely, I think, that the encounter was an encapsulating experience to give the tax collector both insight and time to turn to Jesus. Zacchaeus then pledges to follow the economic reforms of both John (Luke 3:10–14) and Jesus. Zacchaeus's word would not have been trusted by defrauded Jews until they saw the money. To give half of his possessions to the poor (emphasizing the marginalized makeup of Jesus' audience and followers) and to pay back four times as much as he has defrauded to people was a courageous and just act. Several other lines converge into one question: when Jesus says that salvation has come to his house (19:9a), that Zacchaeus "too is a son of Abraham" (v. 9b), and that this all occurs because Jesus himself (here under the figure of the representative Israelite "Son of Man") is out and about to save the "lost" (one like Zacchaeus). These lines lead to a significant question: Has Jesus "restored" an Israelite (intensification or affiliation conversion) or has he redefined who is a son of Abraham (as did his mentor, John; cf. Luke 3:7–9; tradition or institutional transition)—that is, is it possible that Jesus has just turned a Gentile tax collector into a son of Abraham? This would be bold, not to say quite innovative! But the slim evidence we do have, drawn from the name itself (cf. Neh. 7:14; 2 Macc. 10:19), suggests otherwise: Zacchaeus is a Jew. His conversion, then, once again illustrates the orientation of Jesus—intensification of already existing faith, and in this case probably severely lapsed faith. Perhaps we should classify this conversion as *affiliation*. In either case, "salvation" is restoration of an Israelite so that he becomes a person of acceptable status.[11]

The advocate and the potential convert, in a highly stylized manner, encounter one another in this tradition. Jesus finds, cooperates, teaches, and pronounces a blessing on Zacchaeus; Zacchaeus seeks, finds, welcomes, and commits himself to Jesus' vision for the marginalized and the gypped, and he invests himself and his possessions into that mission of justice. We don't know what became of Zacchaeus though we would all like to guess that he did carry through with his extravagant promises—and that we know about him at all probably means that he did. Zacchaeus was probably looking for an opportunity to find forgiveness and to be resocialized, for those are his only benefits. I suspect his quest was motivated more by self-esteem and relationships, perhaps for a conceptual system like the "kingdom," for he seems not to be motivated by a need to mitigate suffering, to find transcendence, or to gain power (for he was surrendering that). Whatever his precise motivations, the text suggests Zacchaeus fully internalized the kingdom's call and embraced that vision. Consequently, he began to live the way Jesus calls his followers to live.

A second example of an encounter is the rich young ruler (Luke 18:18–30). Striking similarities and dissimilarities emerge in comparing the Zacchaeus and rich young ruler accounts.

> A certain ruler asked him, "Good Teacher, what must I do to inherit eternal life?" Jesus said to him, "Why do you call me good? No one

is good but God alone. You know the commandments: 'You shall not commit adultery; You shall not murder; You shall not steal; You shall not bear false witness; Honor your father and mother.'" He replied, "I have kept all these since my youth." When Jesus heard this, he said to him, "There is still one thing lacking. Sell all that you own and distribute the money to the poor, and you will have treasure in heaven; then come, follow me." But when he heard this, he became sad; for he was very rich. Jesus looked at him and said, "How hard it is for those who have wealth to enter the kingdom of God! Indeed, it is easier for a camel to go through the eye of a needle than for someone who is rich to enter the kingdom of God."

Those who heard it said, "Then who can be saved?" He replied, "What is impossible for mortals is possible for God." Then Peter said, "Look, we have left our homes and followed you." And he said to them, "Truly I tell you, there is no one who has left house or wife or brothers or parents or children, for the sake of the kingdom of God, who will not get back very much more in this age, and in the age to come eternal life."

As with Zacchaeus, the ruler—a synagogue ruler (8:41) or a magistrate (12:58) or a Pharisee (14:1)—acts on his own initiative (a quester) to encounter Jesus. His question, evidently emerging from things Jesus has been saying, sets the encounter into a decidedly religious category. "Eternal life" (*hayye olam*) may just as readily refer to an eternal existence in the land as to some form of heavenly spiritual existence (cf. Dan. 12:2). Jesus is a bit prickly after his question, but not so much because the ruler is asking about doing "good deeds" to find God's approval (for Jesus seems to support that in the dialogue; cf. vv. 20, 22), but because he has given Jesus himself the epithet "good." This means the ruler has given to Jesus a status or an attribute that belongs alone to YHWH (cf. Deut. 6:4–9). Jesus knows that his goodness is a gift from God. Abruptly, Jesus changes topics: from God alone being good to obedience of the second table of the Ten Commandments (Exod. 20:12–17).

Now the ruler is asked to measure his life against God's will—and the ruler replies, with a measured candor, that Jesus won't find poor scores on his grade card. There is no reason to distrust the young ruler's self-analysis; in Judaism, obedience to the Torah never meant sinless perfection. And neither was it pretentious to claim to be obedient to the Torah. (The list of virtues of Paul in Philippians 3:4–6 was a factual record of his case.) Like many Jews of his day, the ruler knew he had sinned against even these laws, but in accordance with the Torah's own stipulations, he had confessed his sins on Yom Kippur and was therefore not a transgressor. This is so hard for post-Reformation Christians to grasp that I want to say it again: this young man was considered, according to the Torah, a "righteous man," a *tsaddiq*, just as Jesus' father was a *tsaddiq* (cf. Matt. 1:19). There is no reason to delve into his motives or his hidden consciousness or to appeal to some other developments in theology to label him a religious, selfish prig. That is not the point here or in Jesus' response to him—the man was obedient. Such a view of the man does not make him sinless or stuffy. It makes him a good Jew. But for Jesus Torah conformity is not enough.

Jesus, since his mission is so concerned with economic justice and the poor, goes even further to find out if the ruler has the wherewithal to follow him—he asks him to give his possessions to the poor (v. 22). At this point in the encounter, as some interpret it, we learn that, in fact, the young ruler has obeyed the second table of the commandments (Exod. 20:12–17) but not the first. That is, Jesus points his finger on the man's basic idolatry—money is more important than God, so Jesus asks him to give up his possessions. This is a fair interpretation but not a very likely one. That kind of tricky dialogue might appeal to modern scholarship or be required to make one's theology snug, but it would be unusual for Jesus to express honoring God first by appealing to giving away one's possessions. Such a view is not impossible, but another explanation is more likely—namely, that Jesus' own regulation for his community, which the young man evidently wanted to join, in addition to acting lovingly toward others (Luke 18:20) was to surrender one's possessions to provide for the all-too-many poor (cf. 4:18–19; 6:20; 12:32–34; 14:33). He is being asked to convert to the marginalized. Such a demand might touch on the man's idolatry, but, more important, it shows the ruler that conversion to Jesus involves a radical economic commitment to the marginalized. The man "became sad," it says, because he was "very rich" (v. 23)—and he walks off the stage never to be heard from again, like a two-bit actor. Jesus then generalizes from this event to the difficulty the wealthy have in following him into the kingdom of God (vv. 24–25). Then, upon being questioned, he speaks about the promise of God's provision of family and eternal life to those who convert (unlike the young ruler) so radically that they surrender their very possessions.

Whether the interpretation I have offered is as commendable as that of traditional scholarship can be swept under the rug now: what we do have here is an encounter between Jesus and a potential convert. The young ruler quests for Jesus and then, when hearing Jesus' expectations, chooses to remain where he is and not to follow Jesus. The encounter dramatizes the options in converting to Jesus as well as the process of conversion itself. In both encounters with wealthy men Jesus forces the issue: wealth must be surrendered. In the first, Zacchaeus gushes forth with confession and promises; the young ruler, however, must be probed and challenged. Only in the second encounter do we see the oscillation, scrutinization, and deliberation that one suspects characterize nearly all encounters in which a challenge to convert orients the dialogue. While we might think the young ruler learned from Jesus and reduced his materialistic emphasis through a process sociologists call "syncretization," it was Zacchaeus who "indigenized" the challenge of Jesus and carried out his radical economic ethic.

Interaction

Once the initial "encounter" phase has taken place, an interaction occurs. Here, the advocate and potential convert clarify their relationship through a process of give and take. One might suspect that this dimension is not represented in the Jesus traditions since the disciples of Jesus are, after all, already converts. At one level this is true, but at another it misreads the evidence. The danger here is imposing a theological category (e.g., conversion as a sudden event) on the experience of conversion. In fact, in general, we find a tendency for Christians to equate a theological category—say, repentance, conversion, faith—with a particular experience of that category—say, baptism, the sinner's prayer, confirmation, First Communion, "going forward," membership in a church, ecstatic communion with God, or a healing. In most cases, identifying the two truncates the theological category while it exalts the experience.

We should not assume that those who are following Jesus as converts are done with the process of conversion. Once again, the theory that conversion is a single-event crisis in one's history, done once and for all, muddies the waters and prohibits a clear view to the bedrock teaching. In what follows I shall attempt to show that conversion to Jesus, even after a "successful" encounter like that of Zacchaeus, involved an interaction with Jesus that could have gone on for some time afterwards. It is not that conversion is never a "crisis" of a single moment, but crisis conversion is not the experience of everyone—in fact, crisis conversions are more dependent on whether the person was reared within a given religious tradition and how smooth the nurture within that tradition was. For the person with the "happy childhood syndrome," a traumatic crisis conversion may be nearly impossible.

The interaction phase can be seen through the lens of the theory of encapsulation, the more complete exposure of the convert to a self-contained world of constructed meaning. For us, this means asking if there is evidence for Jesus' exposing the potential convert to his vision of the kingdom of God for Israel in order for conversion to occur. Encapsulation has three shapes: physical, social, and ideological. There is evidence for each in the Gospel accounts, and this means that the interaction phase for Jesus was significant. In fact, older form-critical scholarship frequently referred to this aspect of the Jesus traditions as catechesis, or the teaching of the churches for converts, and saw the Gospels themselves as the record in many cases of that catechesis.

Physical encapsulation took place both when Jesus gathered around the table for fellowship in evening meals with a wide variety of followers (e.g., Luke 15:1–2 as the context for 15:3–32), as well as in his not irregular walks with his closest followers. A simple event of public teaching is a form of encapsulation so that Jesus can teach (e.g., Luke 6:17–49). Other narrative descriptions suggest some geographical encapsulation on the part of Jesus. In Mark 3:7–8 we read "Jesus departed with his disciples to the sea, and a great multitude from Galilee followed him" and in Matthew 15:21 Jesus attempts to withdraw from the rush of the crowd, but with his disciples in tow (v. 23). At times Jesus had to get alone with his disciples to explain himself, his actions, his plans, or his teachings (e.g., Mark 1:29; 2:13–17, 23–28; 3:13; 6:1, 32; 8:27; 9:2, 33; 10:32). Thus, Mark 4:33–34:

> With many such parables he spoke the word to them, as they were able to hear it; he did not speak to them except in parables, but he explained everything in private to his disciples.

Surely Mary's private questions were answered in her "encapsulation" with Jesus (Luke 10:38–42). During the last week Jesus would carry on in the Temple, disputing here and arguing there, but in the evening he gathered alone with his closest followers in part to explain and in part to get away (cf. Mark 11:19; 14:3, 17). The evidence is clear: Jesus regularly got away with his closest followers. We can't know for sure all they were doing, but it is unlikely all they did was grouse about the priests, synagogue services, and Rome. We do know he used these times to reveal his vision for Israel and to teach his followers. Encapsulation theory as an aspect of the encounter dimension of conversion puts such times alone with his disciples in a new perspective.

Encapsulation has a *social* dimension as well. If conversion and apostasy are defined by a group, then it follows that conversion will involve social encapsulation at various stages in the process of conversion. Advocates frequently instruct by socially constricting contacts with a former society so that the instruction will be more complete and powerful. Once again, I draw on a motif from our description of the work of Gauri Viswanathan: the conversion process leading to complete commitment and integration contains a social dimension of "leaving" the old group. A person generally leaves one group to join another group. Thus, conversion necessitates a kind of "social apostasy." In other words, a grammar of assent implies a grammar of dissent.[13] Jesus played a conscious role in this social process of apostasy and conversion. For instance, Jesus sat freely with respect to perceived regulations for those with whom an observant Jew was to eat. The byword about Jesus was that he was "a friend of tax collectors and sinners" (Matt. 11:19). By consorting with such persons, Jesus began to restrict his own contacts with those who saw his friends as "sinners," and he would have thereby also restricted the contacts of his own converts. We can be sure that Pharisees would have disapproved of at least some of Jesus' meals, and social constriction would at some level have taken place. It is normal in any society not to "fellowship" with someone with whom one disagrees; meals embody social regulations and parameters in most societies.[14] It can be said that this regular practice on the part of Jesus also reflected a "program of purity" for his new community of followers, as Bruce Chilton has demonstrated from different angles.[15]

Further, Jesus clearly explained to his followers that the authority structure was shifting from family to his own social vision for the new community around himself. For instance, in Luke 14:26 we read,

> Whoever comes to me and does not hate father and mother, wife and children, brothers and sisters, yes, and even life itself, cannot be my disciple.

And the tradition at Mark 3:31–35, whereby Jesus defined his family as those who did the will of his Father (read: who are following me and joining my kingdom vision), cuts the umbilical cord of conventional family authority. At times Jesus even asked his followers to abandon their means of sustenance, as is the case with the four brothers (Mark 1:16–20) and at least Levi (2:13–17)—we can be sure that more had the same requirement. In each of these instances—normal table fellowship, family, and vocation—Jesus encapsulates his converts to form a tighter unit, and this sets a precedent both *for* his vision and *against* another social construction of

meaning. Such a form of encapsulation, however, is not uniformly negative in the sense of denying to his converts a former society. In each it is
also a positive action: his followers discover a new fellowship, a new family, and a new means of sustenance. It is not simple deprivation, but trans-
ference from one society to another.

A third form of encapsulation is *ideological*, exposure to a worldview that
inoculates the potential convert from a contrasting worldview. Without
belaboring the point, we refer again to Jesus' vision of the kingdom with
support from Berger and Luckmann's important study on the social construction of reality.[16] "Primary socialization," the previous outlook on life
for the followers of Jesus or their "social construction of reality," took
place for Jesus' followers in a variety of contexts, some perhaps Judean but
mostly Galilean. In each of these his future followers would have "learned
a world of meaning" at the hands of parents, family, friends, and institutions by means of a language equipped to embody that meaning and give
that meaning to its users. In the process of converting to Jesus, however,
each of these converts would have needed a "secondary socialization"
process in which a new "world of meaning" would be mediated and an old
one in part discarded (to one degree or another), through Jesus' systemic
explanation of a new construction of reality. This new reality was
expressed by Jesus as "the kingdom of God" and, with it, a "plausibility
structure" provided to give it "legitimation."[17]

For complete success to be achieved, a total alienation from the former
construction of reality needs to take place—that is, if the conversion is of
a radical nature. Such types of conversion would include affiliation but
surely also institution and tradition transition. For Jesus' followers, most
of whom underwent an intensification kind of conversion, that new "construction of reality" would have involved only partial alienation along
with reorientation and reexpression of an older reality. When ideological
encapsulation achieves its end, the convert experiences "symmetry"
between experience and the newly reconstructed world "out there." All of
this, of course, is fancy language for the social processes of conversion, but
important insights are nonetheless gleaned. In short, ideological encapsulation requires a full explanatory system in order for a person to convert to Jesus from another "construction of reality." For Jesus, a "theology
of the kingdom" is a "social construction of reality," a "symbolic universe," that replaces and reorders the world of meaning his followers formerly knew.[18] His followers needed such an ordered world to make their
conversion complete and meaningful.

This threefold encapsulation process (physical, social, and ideological) expresses itself in four *features of encapsulation*: relationships, rituals, rhetoric, and roles. Encapsulation theory is abstract; these four features are the spheres in which encapsulation takes place. First, *relationships*. That Jesus defined his followers in some sense as a family, as can be inferred from Mark 3:31–35 or 10:28–30, suggests that for some of his converts, joining the Jesus movement was "compensation" for what they lacked or provided the pleasure they thought they needed. Here they found a father, a family, and friends. The regular companionship and table fellowship provided by Jesus strengthened the relational basis of those surrounding him and provided a catalyst for growth and development, and even courage to spread the word (cf. Mark 1:28, 45; 3:13–19; 6:6–13, 30). Furthermore, as a musical concert collects a gaggle of fans and induces even more adoration for the music, so a large web of relational networks all leading to Jesus would give to the convert and potential convert a sense of confirmation and consolidation of faith. To further the analogy to music concerts, so also would many have gathered around Jesus out of a sense of hero worship or the need to come into contact with a charismatic, holy man. Nonetheless, relationships are a decisive dimension of the encapsulation process of converting to Jesus.

Second, sociologists suggest that encapsulation will take place through *rituals* of both a deconstructive and (re)constructive orientation. If conversion is dissent and encapsulation is in part social and ideological reconstruction of reality, then it follows that rituals theoretically can forge both a deconstructive and reconstructive purpose. Three come to mind immediately: baptism, table fellowship, and the Last Supper, with the last playing only a limited role in the conversion process of Jesus' earliest followers. Since the Last Supper reconfigures the table fellowship practiced throughout the Galilee, we can focus on the first two.

Jesus was baptized by John in the Jordan as an act of reentering the land in order to bring into shape the kingdom of God (Mark 1:1–11, pars.).[19] For some time Jesus and John probably baptized alongside one another, but for some reason the evidence for Jesus continuing the practice in Galilee is nonexistent. We know this: his mentor did it, and his followers did as well. And we also know Jesus baptized for some time. We can guess Jesus continued the practice. If he did, and that is a big "if," the act itself was both purificatory and an expression of John's and Jesus' symbolic universe. As an act of purification, it would be connected to the use of water to cleanse and purify in order to make a person fit to enter into God's presence. It is not surprising that Josephus speaks of John's baptism as an act of purification, describing it as a "purification of the body" (*eph' hagneia tou somatos*; *Antiquities* 18.117). But since the act derives from the Jordan River and rehearses the entrance of the children of Israel into the land, baptism also must be seen as a ritual of entering the land, of ushering in the new age of the kingdom, and of restoring Israel.

As for table fellowship, there is clear evidence: Jesus regularly, provocatively, and symbolically engaged in a form of table fellowship that embodied his vision of the kingdom of God. This fellowship crystallizes his inclusion of all sorts, including the marginalized, as well as his distinct role as host and leader. The meal ritually permits all to function socially and covenantally at an equal level, and it becomes the source of a social vision. Further, table fellowship, like baptism, was a rite of undoing the past social convention with its inscribed symbolic universe and remaking the present. Around the table we will find those who were marginalized-but-now-centralized sitting with those who were formerly rich and who have surrendered their goods in order to enact Jesus' vision of the kingdom. Table fellowship thus embodies the "costs" of discipleship so prominent in the Jesus traditions about the call to discipleship because it "acts out" an egalitarian-type society (Luke 10:38–42). We can imagine Zacchaeus, as well as those who had abandoned vocation (Mark 1:16–20; 2:13–17) and social conventions (cf. Luke 9:57–62; 12:32–34; 14:33), all sitting together, eating and drinking and talking and praying, as an act both of (subtle) protest against their previous social conventions, as well as an act of attesting to the fullness of redemption in Jesus' vision of God's kingdom.

A third feature of encapsulation is that it took place at the rhetorical level as well. One dimension of rhetoric is the language Jesus used for his vision: kingdom, discipleship, hypocrisy, righteousness and justice, love, mercy, and poor versus rich. L. R. Rambo has said this well:

> Conversion then takes place, in part, through the process of learning a new language and learning to apply that language in situations that make it relevant to the convert and to the community to which the convert is speaking.[20]

Another dimension of rhetoric is that each convert has a "story" to tell—a "reconstructed autobiography" of the transformed self. Language is our attempt to interpret and make peace with the worlds we encounter, hiding some (like poverty, war, and disease) in the recesses of our mind and showing off others (like our family, our vocation, our faith). Each of us has a "grand story" of our own life, and when events occur in our lives, we shuffle our deck of cards and put the event into our grand scheme. When conversion occurs, we reorder the cards in such a way as to make sense of our lives. The stories in the earlier chapters of this book are rhetorical reconstructions. Everyone on Planet Earth tells a story, and so did the first-century Galilean Jews who converted or were in the process of converting to Jesus. Famously, Paul told his own story over and over, and its imprint is felt on several pages of the New Testament: Galatians 2:15–21; Romans 7:7–25; Philippians 3:4–11; Acts 9:1–31; 22:3–21; 26:9–20. We suspect the same of the Ethiopian eunuch, Lydia, and the Philippian jailor (Acts 8:26–40; 16:11–16; 16:16–40). Without digressing into a life of Paul and all the scholarship connected with it, we can say this: what was formerly an autobiography for Paul (being a good Jew and becoming noteworthy as a Jewish leader) became a new autobiography because of an encounter with Jesus on the road to Damascus.

We have precious little reliable evidence about this idea of reconstructed biographies in the Gospels, but we suspect that the little vignettes at the end of the first chapter of John belong in this category: Andrew evidently learned about Jesus from John, of whom he was a disciple (1:35, 40). He then told Simon (1:41), later to become Peter. Here Peter meets Jesus. Jesus then runs into Philip (1:43), from the same city as Andrew and Peter, and Philip finds Nathanael (1:45), who has the brackishness to accuse Nazareth of being backwater and therefore to question the viability of Jesus' leadership. All of this is, according to a sociological model of conversion, quite believable and probable: conversions take place through relationships and friendships with social status wrapped tightly around the mix. We probably only have these stories because these are the sorts of stories that these people talked about when they reconstructed their biographies. In fact, we have the stories about Peter, Andrew, James, John, Levi, Mary, Martha, Mary Magdalene, Zacchaeus, and others because they retold them. Looking at these same "autobiographers" from another angle, we can also say that in their retelling of their "stories" they also remade that story and reshaped perceptions of their lives. It works both ways: converts tell their new stories, and the stories, in the retelling, shape their conversion and their lives. The stories differ from person to person, but some general trends are noticeable.

If the encapsulation dimension of conversion shapes a new understanding of the self, we can posit that Jesus' emphasis on self-denial (Mark 8:34–9:1) had, as its direct aim, a new way of understanding the self. Jesus calls his followers to surrender their former selves and assume new selves that have Jesus and his vision for Israel as their central orientation. He promises those who so surrender themselves for him (and the gospel) that they will find great reward in acceptance from God and final vindication.

The same needs to be said about the "symbolic universe" Jesus taught: he didn't write out his ideas on parchment. Consequently, the Gospel records themselves are a part of the conversion process of the followers of Jesus, for it is in the Gospels that we find early Christians telling others about Jesus' symbolic universe—the kingdom—*as a way* of telling their stories of how Jesus entered into their lives. Kingdom, itself, is a mediated-by-followers category—we know it through their memories about Jesus. As such, it tells us about the conversion process of those so writing and believing.

Finally, encapsulation manifests these relationships, rituals, and rhetorical reshapings of life and meaning in the *roles* assigned to the converts. Jesus is the primary shaper of the expectations for converts, expectations involving behaviors and beliefs. Notably, the convert is expected to obey Jesus (cf. Matt. 7:24–27), to live under the grace of the present kingdom (6:33), to live lovingly with all (5:43–48; Mark 12:28–34), to forgive others (11:25), and to provide for the needs of others (e.g., Matt. 6:1–4). A more particular role found in the Jesus traditions, apart from perfunctory acts like acquiring a donkey (Mark 11:1–10) or getting Passover ready for the little community (Mark 14:12–16), is the missionary role of the twelve disciples (Mark 6:6–13, 30; expanded considerably in Matt. 9:35–11:10) as well as that of the Samaritan woman (John 4:39).[21] Their task was to extend and expand the mission of Jesus: they are given the same fundamental mission of announcing the kingdom and demonstrating that power through healings. We can be confident that the benevolent care of the women of Luke 8:1–3 is also a role assigned by Jesus of providing for his needs so he can carry out his mission. The women could give to the poor (unlike the rich young ruler but like Zacchaeus) and therefore function as noteworthy examples of what discipleship to Jesus is all about. That Jesus permitted women to accompany him would have raised eyebrows, and he thus becomes responsible for another break of social convention.

Encapsulation then is a worthwhile tool for examining how converting to Jesus took place. Those who were in process with Jesus found themselves physically segregated to find time and space for instruction; they were given social patterns that decreased opportunities to dwell in their former worlds and increased time with Jesus and his followers; and they were given a substantial ideological symbolic universe that could express for them their relationship to Jesus. Those encapsulation strategies manifested themselves in the various relationships, rituals, rhetoric, and roles in which the convert found himself or herself.

Jesus and Commitment

Decision is in fact a necessary dimension of all religious conversions and can be a useful exploratory device in understanding the Jesus traditions about conversion. If modern biblical scholars prefer to avoid the concept of "decision" because it invokes an unsophisticated populist form of the Christian faith, they shall also miss an opportunity to define more precisely how decisions take place. Sociologists can shed light here, for decision making transcends a sudden crisis and involves all the dimensions of a personality. Decisions need not be, and rarely are, traumatic moments. Decisions can be traumatic, and they can be a series of gentle nods of the soul. The evidence of the Jesus traditions fits into this spectrum.

Decision

In another book I outlined conversion in both positive (faith) and negative (repentance) categories because the Gospel evidence suggests that converting to Jesus was a "dialectic of denial and affirmation."[22] If we think through conversion, we will notice that the process of conversion is experienced dialectically rather than in separate steps. If we isolate the commitment to Jesus, *the decision*, we find that a convert to Jesus begins, however inchoately and subtly, with personal trust in Jesus as sent by God to restore Israel—and I would include in "to restore Israel" those who came to Jesus for little more than alleviation from suffering. We should avoid overly specifying how clearly defined those converting to Jesus were in what they thought about Jesus. In most cases, to be honest, it was far less than what orthodox believers today think of Jesus. Jesus' converts found in him either personal or social liberation, or both. Thus we have the following examples from scripture:

> And to the centurion Jesus said, "Go; let it be done for you according to your faith." And the servant was healed in that hour. (Matt. 8:13)

> "The time is fulfilled, and the kingdom of God has come near; repent, and believe in the good news." (Mark 1:15)

> "If any of you put a stumbling block before one of these little ones who believe in me, it would be better for you if a great millstone were hung around your neck and you were thrown into the sea." (Mark 9:42)

Here we find faith in its various nuances, each acceptable to Jesus: trusting Jesus to heal a loved one, entrusting oneself to the vision of Jesus for Israel, and children trusting Jesus for what is nearly impossible to know. This is the foundation for a commitment to Jesus, namely, trusting him.

A further aspect of this commitment-decision in the Jesus traditions is that it involves *deliberation*. Here the lines between "encounter" and "interaction" and "commitment" are confused, as they are in reality, but an isolation of the category of commitment reveals that those who so trust Jesus also deliberate over what they are getting themselves into (cf. John 4). Jesus told a parable that addresses the importance of deliberation in the commitment to his mission.

> "For which of you, intending to build a tower, does not first sit down and estimate the cost, to see whether he has enough to complete it? Otherwise, when he has laid a foundation and is not able to finish, all who see it will begin to ridicule him, saying, 'This fellow began to build and was not able to finish.' Or what king, going out to wage war against another king, will not sit down first and consider whether he is able with ten thousand to oppose the one who comes against him with twenty thousand? If he cannot, then, while the other is still far away, he sends a delegation and asks for the terms of peace." (Luke 14:28–32)

Appealing to a sense of social shame, Jesus urges those who are his followers to consider carefully what they are getting into. And this parable is focused to sharpen the commitment to the economic justice dimensions of his mission: "So therefore, none of you can become my disciple if you do not give up all your possessions" (14:33)—"a" if not "the" primary symptom of full surrender to Jesus and his gospel of the kingdom.

Ritual Confirmation and Consolidation

A second aspect of commitment to Jesus is *ritual confirmation and consolidation*. The wide-ranging need of humans to ritualize their behavior, especially their religious behavior, as well as the presence of entry rituals into paganism, ancient Judaism, and later Christianity, make it very likely that Jesus' followers enacted their faith through rituals.[23]

It is not clear whether converts to Jesus were all baptized as a ritual entry into kingdom life. If they were, the rite would have sealed their commitment to Jesus, for it would have been a public act of the sort that filters quite quickly throughout small Galilean villages. Unlike baptism performed on children today, this baptism would have been performed on, and enacted by, adults. Consequently, it would take considerable pluck to step forward, confess one's sins, express one's commitment to Jesus' vision for Israel in front of other villagers, and enter the waters that purified the Israelite. I deem it more likely that baptisms of this sort took place in the Sea of Galilee than that baptisms took place in a *mikveh* in a person's home or in a village center. Capernaum's closer location to water may be one reason Jesus chose that location for the center of his mission to the Galilee, though proximity to travel (and therefore more people) were more important considerations.

If baptism is less than certain as a rite, decision to eat with Jesus and his associates functions as a rite of passage for converts to Jesus. As with baptism's modern practice, so with meals: we should not appeal to "First Communion" to suggest at the time of Jesus a "first meal." The process of joining in the meals mirrors the process of conversion: it could be sudden; it could be progressive. But this is clear: the decision to eat with Jesus and join in his fellowship was part of joining the burgeoning movement. Inasmuch as table fellowship in Jesus' community embodies conversion to Jesus it is also a ritual. In fact, eating with Jesus was a highly visible and public statement because houses were not as private, distance between homes no thicker in many cases than the wall itself, and the courtyard in front of most semidetached dwellings a public forum. The harsh words Jesus makes about families, and leaving family members to follow him, find their best social context in table fellowship rather in a bohemian or cynic ideal (cf. Matt. 10:34–39; Mark 3:31–35).

Surrender

A third aspect of commitment is *surrender*. Readers of the Gospels today, if they are not blunted by overfamiliarity, ought to be struck by the sharp comments Jesus makes about the ego—which, for him, needs to be denied to the point of crucifixion![24] Surrendering to Jesus by giving up the ego is not pain: it is the joy of finding God to be the center of life as expressed in Jesus' vision for the kingdom. There can be a kind of conflict and tension over this decision, as can be seen in St. Augustine's highly introspective self-confessions, in St. Francis of Assisi's film-producing radical conversion, and in Martin Luther's struggle of the soul. It can also be a gentle nod of the soul, as can be seen in the diaries of C. S. Lewis. We can never know all about conversions of other people, but these examples alone should lead us to a chaste appreciation of different experiences. In approaching the evidence found in the Jesus traditions, then, we need to guard against making all conversions the same and turning the ego denial of Jesus into the struggle of the soul found in some notable converts.

The key text is Mark 8:34:

> He called the crowd with his disciples, and said to them, "If any want to become my followers, let them deny themselves and take up their cross and follow me."

The surrender to which Jesus calls the disciples, who had been with him for some time and now were being called again to surrender because conversion is a process, has two elements: first, Jesus asks his followers to *affirm him* and second, Jesus asks his followers to *deny themselves*. The image of assuming the "cross" trenchantly clarifies what self-denial means: those who deny themselves in effect put themselves to death. But Jesus is no self-absorbed, inward-looking, self-flagellating kook, and neither is he an annoying blister. For Jesus, to deny self is the sure way of experiencing the goodness of God in his kingdom; it is to find in Jesus soul-rest and to discover the joys of a loving, peaceful, and just society around Jesus' table. It is to give to Jesus one's heart. As Hans Conzelmann said it, "I understand that he not only wants *something* from me, he wants *me.*"[25]

This surrender then is an act of "double-speak": affirmation of all that God is doing in Jesus and denial of one's self-centeredness and self-absorption in securing one's life. Both are needed. In an act of auto-plagiarism, I quote: "To deny oneself without affirming Jesus and the kingdom is nothing but self-disciplined asceticism, a sort of picking oneself up by the bootstraps in an act of personal courage. To affirm the kingdom-through-Jesus without self-denial, on the other hand, trivializes the God of Israel by taking hold of his offer of restoring Israel without the necessary act of surrender that permits one to enter the covenant relationship."[26] This fundamental act of surrender, however, was not easy because it involved opposition and potential death. For that reason Jesus calls his followers to consider the cost, take on his kingdom, and give themselves to God's new work in Israel. I have given this notion of surrender a decidedly individualistic cast because the issue at hand is the convert's experience of surrender. In the world of Jesus, though, self-denial involves a denial of the context of that self, namely, the social collectivity out of which this convert emerges. Self-denial is in other words a social act of denying one's former social group; it is dissent.[27] Self-denial is part of what sociologists call identity transformation and figures prominently in what conversion is all about.

Public Identification

The fourth aspect of commitment to Jesus is *public identification*, or as sociologists might label it, "testimony" or "witness." Once again, we need to anchor our minds in the first century: the primary form of public identification in Jesus' mission was table fellowship with him and physical accompaniment. As I said, it is possible that Jesus' converts were baptized, but it is far from certain (cf. the tradition at John 3:26; 4:1–2). What is clear is that they staked their claim with Jesus by being with him (Mark 3:13–14, 15:40–41; Luke 8:1–3), and this meant dining at table with him (Mark 2:13–17)—a form of identification with Jesus that gives concrete reality to the words of Jesus in Luke 12:8–9:

> And I tell you, everyone who acknowledges me before others, the Son of Man also will acknowledge before the angels of God; but whoever denies me before others will be denied before the angels of God.

To our knowledge Jesus' followers did not have "testimony" sessions. Instead, one enacted one's stance with respect to Jesus by either sitting at table with him or simply by following him around. For those who truly converted to Jesus, this public identification with Jesus worked itself up into a "new story," a rhetorical reworking of one's personal autobiography. This biography need not be rehearsed aloud since essentially it is a self-perception. However done, this rhetorical refashioning will have taken place for any and all converts to Jesus.[28]

In addition, this process of commitment eventually manifests itself, as Gauri Viswanathan has contended,[29] in *groupishness* because conversion is a social act.[30] For this reason I lay even greater weight on the table of Jesus: here one expresses one's attitude toward Jesus' vision for Israel; here one expresses one's relationship to other converts to Jesus; here one expresses one's social vision; and here one expresses commitment to Jesus. At table with Jesus the group expresses itself as a social and spiritual vision for Israel. Commitment to Jesus is social commitment to Jesus' group and to Jesus' vision for the nation. Jesus' stern demands on separating from family are expressions of this groupishness, not some tension he had with his mother or father. And this group of converts, each person in varying degrees aligned with Jesus, also helped shape both the expectations for new converts and the process of conversion itself. Commitment then is a process of internalizing Jesus' vision as it is expressed by him and those around him as a new symbolic universe.

The Peter Paradigm, for Pete's Sake!

The process from quest to commitment, involving as it does the dimension of the encounter with the advocate, can perhaps best be seen in the example of Simon Peter in the Jesus traditions. If we take a maximum accounting of the evidence and include the earlier and later Johannine traditions, we can find a complete account of Peter's process of conversion. Here we see an advocate over and again encountering and interacting with Peter, and we see Peter interacting and deliberating with Jesus. We can begin with John 1:35–42. We learn here only about the encounter stage: Simon, through the encouragement and faith of his brother, Andrew, meets Jesus. In hindsight, it is at this time that Simon was being called to a special role in Jesus' movement (cf. 1:42).

The encounter and interaction of Luke 5:1–11 bring to the fore several dimensions of the conversion process. In the midst of fishing, a normal event in his life, Simon is asked by Jesus if he might use his boat in order to address the crowds more effectively (5:1–3). In a twist of fate, when done, Jesus asks Simon to toss his nets out for a catch (5:4), but Simon counters that he and his partners had been fishing all night—with an empty boat to prove failure. Though Jesus is no fisherman, Jesus' suggestion carries the day and Simon lets out the nets (5:5). The results are famous and over the top: Simon needs help, the nets are breaking, and two whole boats are filled to the point of sinking (5:6–7). Simon Peter (note Luke's change of language) confesses at this point that he is sinful (5:8)— why fishing with such great results leads Simon to a confession of personal sinfulness is impossible to say. Perhaps he knew more about Jesus than we suspect; perhaps the time fishing was used by Jesus to explain his vision of the kingdom and Simon's need to repent; perhaps the sheer awe of seeing so many fish entangle themselves in his nets led Simon to an overjoyed ebullience of spiritual joy (5:9); maybe all of these are involved. The others are also impressed (5:10), so they all (Luke changes to the plural here) drop their nets to follow Jesus (5:11). We have here an encounter: advocate, a strategy of leading Simon to follow, an interaction between Jesus and Simon, Simon making a fundamental commitment to follow Jesus— the fundamental commitment Jesus expects. But, in the event that Simon thinks he has crossed the line, the story goes on. We have more here than we can glean from the Pauline accounts of his own conversion; we have as much as, if not more than, we have from Luke's accounts of Paul's conversion. And we have even more to consider about Peter.

Once, when encapsulated by Jesus (Mark 8:27–9:1), the disciples experience one of Jesus' strategies to induce commitment: he asks them for a poll on how people identify him (8:27). The answers vary, but each thinks Jesus is someone special: John the Baptist *redivivus*, Elijah, or one of the other prophets. Clearly, Jesus is a prophet in popular opinion. Jesus wants a precise identification, and Simon blurts out: "You are the Messiah" (Mark 8:29). Surely here we must come to the threshold of conversion: Simon has now identified Jesus as Israel's long-awaited messiah. The strategy works because such an identification expresses commitment. But now an important interaction takes place: Jesus announces his impending death at the hands of Israel's leaders; Peter denounces Jesus' plans; and Jesus goes nose to nose with Peter over his inability to know what God has planned (8:31–33). Peter thus jumps at the chance to confess to Jesus—but he slips and falls on his face! Peter's confession is close yet still a continent away. At this point the address moves to a wider audience, but the general drift is applicable: to follow Jesus means accepting the way of suffering (8:34–9:1).

Peter has now confessed his sin, has confessed Jesus as Messiah, and has been given a special call to follow Jesus—but the process of encounter and interaction and commitment goes on. We move forward to the Garden: Mark 14:66–72. Tradition claims Jesus predicted the event of Peter's denials (cf. 14:27–31), and later Peter does deny Jesus—three times, as the story goes! Peter's denial of any connection whatsoever with the criminal on the cross saves his skin but humiliates his memory (14:72). I contend this event is part of the complex of encounter, interaction, and commitment. On the cross, Jesus is no longer a normal advocate with a strategy that calls for a commitment—he is now a living embodiment of his vision for Israel, and Peter sees him in all his rugged reality. This rugged reality, like the first mention of death back in Mark 8, is unacceptable to Peter. But so it is—he either goes on with Jesus or turns back. Peter goes on, limping through a difficult encounter with Jesus' vision, interacting negatively but still going forward.

At some point in the Easter faith of Peter, recorded both as a resurrection encounter in John's so-called second ending (John 21:15–20) and as a great spiritual encounter at Pentecost (Acts 2; cf. John 20:22), he is restored to his former faith. John's narrative describes an encounter and interaction with respect to Peter's denials and affirmations; the account in Acts simply includes Peter in those who are endowed with the Holy Spirit, but he is singled out for a mighty address to the nation. In my judgment this restoration of Peter is part of his conversion process: he encounters a new phase of Jesus' vision and responds, first negatively but ultimately positively, and presses on now to embody that vision in his own life. The next tradition about Peter is found in Acts 10 where, as a result of a mystical experience, Peter's life is changed and his orientation toward Gentiles converted: he abandons food laws. These experiences best explain how Peter can incorporate the cross of Jesus, that rugged reality Peter denounced, as the paradigm of following Jesus in 1 Peter 2:18–25. What was once a disgusting thought has become, as a result of an ongoing interaction, adapted to Peter's own scheme and adopted as his very own paradigm.

When was Simon Peter converted? To sum up, the question has three possible answers: (1) He converted at one specific moment, and readers will have to decide which moment fits their theory of conversion. (2) He was converted several times, a theory many readers would find incompatible with their theology. (3) Conversion was a process for Simon Peter, and at each new phase of encountering Jesus as his mission unrolled on the pages of the Galilean and Judean story, Simon Peter weighed his options, deliberated, discussed, debated, oscillated, and scrutinized, but in each phase he gave a new nod of the soul to Jesus' mission. In my judgment, there can be no question which answer is the most likely. Peter represents the prototypical disciple of Jesus as he also represents a normal conversion: a process of encounter, interaction, and commitment. New learning, new commitment.

Jesus and the Consequences of Conversion

Converting to Jesus brought benefits to all of those converting—those benefits, in fact, were primary motivations in their interest in Jesus. We can be sure that those motivations changed, like job descriptions, as the potential convert learned more and more about the kingdom. The primary benefits incurred to converts include affective, intellectual, ethical, religious, and sociopolitical dimensions. The deeper the conversion, the more representative each of these benefits becomes. Rabbis were aware of various motivations on the part of ancient converts to Judaism and gave some of them names: the true proselyte (*ger tsedeq*), the resident alien (*ger toshav*), the lion or fear proselyte (*ger arayot*), and the dream proselyte (*ger chalomot*). A discovery not long ago in Aphrodisias (Asia Minor) of a monument from the early part of the third century C.E. had inscribed on it a list that broke a community into Jews, proselytes, and Godfearers.[31] Godfearers, who are also known from the book of Acts (cf. 10:1–11:18; 13:16, 26, 43), were evidently "partial converts" to Judaism who, for various reasons, chose not to go all the way and be circumcised.[32] The Jewish acceptance of this mode of contact with Judaism gives us reason to think that some of those who were associated with Jesus could have been classed as "Jesus-fearers," if already Jewish, or "Godfearers," if Gentile, though the evidence for Gentiles in Jesus' group is thin and brittle. More important, we need to see that Jewish society would have willingly accepted various levels of commitment to Jesus, though Jesus himself may have looked askance on those whose commitment to him was less than sincere or complete. But that Galilean Jews were thusly connected to Jesus seems to me very likely. And, since conversion is a process through various dimensions, it is likely that nearly all of those who converted to Jesus went through a stage of being a "Jesus-fearer."

Some questers found in Jesus the mirage they were chasing. For them, those were the halcyon days. What are the components of this satisfaction? Those who converted to Jesus, as I have said before, found an *affective* satisfaction in the loving, compassionate vision of Jesus, with God as Father and all other converts as brothers and sisters. They also found an *intellectually satisfying system* in Jesus' vision of God's kingdom that can be seen as an innovative and fresh summing up of Jewish history and God's plans for his people. That Jesus was able to bandy about with the Jewish experts on matters of Torah, interpretation, and fulfillment (Mark 2:1–3:6; 7:1–23; Luke 4:16–30) also stimulated some of his followers. The developing tradition within the early churches on how to interpret the Torah and the Prophets and how to configure its prophecies as fulfilled in Jesus and the church owes a large debt to Jesus' own reflections on the same.[33]

Converting to Jesus satisfied the *ethical* vision of many Jews who found, on the one hand, some form of dissatisfaction with current Jewish practice (a common complaint) and, on the other, a challenge to their own conscience. The ethical strand of Jesus' teaching was repeated over and over and now is summarized in the reworked Sermon on the Mount (Matthew 5–7), which shows an interesting relationship to the letter of James and an early Christian document called *The Didache*. That Jesus gave his converts a sense of *religious* satisfaction, however anachronistic that term might be, is unquestionable. That he gave his followers a prayer to remember (Luke 11:1–4) and a distinctive name for God, "Abba," and that he spoke of ultimate things simply reflect concrete dimensions of this Galilean religious genius.[34] Finally, Jesus' converts found in his vision for Israel a *new Israel*, a new society, a group to which they could belong. That is, Jesus also satisfied both social and national, not to say cultural, needs in his message, mission, and group of followers. Whether we emphasize or simply conclude that this society was by its very nature a protest against the status quo only illustrates the sociopolitical nature of the Jesus movement.

Conclusion

G. K. Chesterton, a convert himself, once said, "The church is a house with a hundred gates; and no two men enter at exactly the same angle."[1] The purpose of this book has been to appreciate Chesterton's sentiment, once it includes women, by contending that conversion at the time of Jesus was a process. That process, in fact, was experienced differently by various of his followers. We examined conversion to Jesus in light of a model tied together from the threads of the sociological study of conversion. While it is a fact that some zip through various dimensions of conversion in one evening, another person may dwell in a single dimension (crisis, quest, interaction) for hours, days, weeks, even years before a threshold is crossed. The experience of conversion, as we have seen both in the Gospels and in the model explained in chapters 2 and 3, varies from person to person.

Talking and writing about conversion is sacred because it touches on the center of so many persons of faith and it reveals the soul, the inner person, of converts. If I have tried to anchor our ideas in social and cultural factors, it is not because I think religion and conversion are simply social factors. Without denying the importance of faith and spiritual formation, however, these dimensions of our experience are nonetheless also social dimensions of life. Conversion is profoundly a social act while at the same time it is a personal process. In fact, conversion is complex, and we rarely can unravel all its dimensions. When we do try to unravel all the dimensions at once we experience vertigo. If it is the case that conversions frequently take place at certain ages, then conversion must be understood within the stages of human development. Conversion then becomes both a religious act as well as a psychological-social-physical phase of development. If the empiricist wants to explain conversion as nothing but a set of social confluences, the Christian enthusiast, by overlooking the empirical, might fail to see conversion as an aspect of individuation from parents.

Jesus and a Model of Conversion

One sure result of this study is that the evidence of the Jesus traditions confirms the consensus model of modern sociologists of religion. Hence, we are led to believe that Jesus saw conversion as a process capable of variation. It is condescending on our part to think Jesus couldn't have thought of conversion in such terms—as if only modern, post-Enlightenment theologians can think in such abstractions. The evidence fits the model, with proper historical adjustments and permissions granted to the ancient evidence for gaps in presentation.

Cursory examination of the Gospel stories reveals a certain incompleteness of presentation about the process of conversion. However, once armed with a more comprehensive theory drawn from a wide variety of modern studies of conversion, we were able to draw out of the Gospel evidence sufficient observations to confirm the fundamental theories of sociologists. If the reader thinks the evidence is insufficient to prove the theory fully, I fall back on the humorous claim of one of Ireland's best writers, Frank O'Connor: "A trifle of incomprehension has never worried me when I felt really enthusiastic."[2] The evidence lacking is, in fact, but a trifle. If we attempt to put together a comprehensive pattern of conversion to Jesus, noting an observation here and adding a fact there, we are led to a pattern quite like that of modern sociologists. More seriously, the claim of L. R. Rambo is that the consensus model he presents fits the evidence to conversion for all religious conversions.[3] Granted his modern evidence, we are led to think that all conversions, both modern and ancient, fit the same pattern.[4] Our study confirms the model for conversion to Jesus.

But who best represents that model? This book argues, at least in a minor chord, that those who understand conversion through the lens of Paul's experience move the conversion experience away from the norm to the dramatic. Paul's experience of conversion was profound; it finds Christian counterparts in some of the greats in Christian history—notable leaders like Augustine, Martin Luther, John Wesley, and Karl Barth. But Paul's experience is hardly typical. Instead, what we find is that a sociological approach to the Gospel evidence reveals that Peter's conversion illustrates most completely the normal pattern. Consequently, I am calling Christian thinking to consider Peter as the prototypical convert to Jesus.

Conversions: Individuals without Individualism

A second conclusion is that Jesus' expectations for his followers and converts were not delineated in a single-line formula. Nor was the demand expressed similarly on every occasion. What Jesus said to Peter about dropping nets, what he said to the Samaritan woman about sin, what he said to the rich young ruler and Zacchaeus, what he said to Levi, and what he said to the various persons who chose not to follow him seemed to vary from person to person. So much is this clear that we are led to conclude that *for Jesus conversion was a highly personalized and individualized challenge to awaken to the new possibilities inherent in the kingdom which he was announcing.* Undergirding each of these calls, of course, is a fundamental challenge: follow me in the concreteness of your life and according to the challenge I make upon you. This was said eloquently long ago by the German Jesus scholar Joachim Jeremias:

> When we consider the individual demands made by Jesus, it is striking how *incomplete* they are. Jesus does not give instructions for all spheres of life; he does not offer a moral theology or a code of behaviour. Rather, his demands give symptoms, signs, examples of what happens when the reign of God breaks into a world that is still in the power of sin, death, and the devil. The *basileia* [reign of God] lays claim to the whole of life. Jesus uses illustrations to demonstrate the appearance of the new life. His disciples are to apply them to every other aspect of their life. They themselves are to be signs of the reign of God, signs that that something has happened.[5]

It is a mistake to think Jesus had a simple formula ("believe these three ideas" or "do these five behaviors") for conversion. It is far more accurate to say that Jesus revealed the implications of the kingdom for a variety of individuals, and each of those individuals was to take up that challenge as an individual. But this is not individualism.[6]

No, the challenge of Jesus must be understood within a larger social vision: Jesus was just as much concerned, indeed more, with Israel as he was with the "personal salvation" of those around him. Thus, the pages of the Gospels reveal a message designed for an intensification conversion experience rather than just a general religious message for scattered individuals to pick up willy-nilly. The vast majority of those who converted to Jesus were already Jews, and they were not converting to a new religion. Instead, they were intensifying, stepping up, renewing, and revitalizing their previous commitment to Judaism and the nation. "Conversion" then does not mean here an individual "changing religions" or "swapping denominations" but "rededicating one's life to God's covenant with Israel as made known by Jesus." In light of this observation we can say this: for

Jesus, the individual was challenged to join in his vision for Israel with the result that Jesus was not gathering "individualized" converts but individuals who converged with others around his vision for Israel. There is then an irreplaceable social component in conversion to Jesus. An ecclesiology, as it were. From a modern perspective, Kathleen Norris has in her grasp something quite important: "Christian conversion is, in fact, incarnational; it is worked out by each individual within the community of faith."[7] This expresses both nodes of converting to Jesus: social and individual.

Hand in hand with this bigger vision on Jesus' part is that the "conversion" stories of the Jesus traditions are not complete stories. Once we compare the stories of the Gospels to a modern sociological model we realize how much has been left out. We shouldn't blame the Evangelists; it was not their intent to describe how conversion took place in their world. But what we should also not do is pretend that they are complete conversion stories, and neither should we think they always give the most important elements. A nuanced understanding of the Gospel stories shows that, in fact, the elements are all there for the model we have used, but in no particular story are all the elements present. We need to read the stories for what they are trying to convey, to be sure. But if we are attempting to describe how conversion took place at the time of Jesus, then we will have to appeal to a broader range of facts than can be found in any one story. If we are forced to take one story as the most complete, we should take the Zacchaeus episode (Luke 19:1–10) or, if we can piece all the bits together, the various sorts of information about Peter.

At the Center of Conversion: Israel and Jesus

Another feature of the stories of conversion in the Gospels is that Jesus is always at the center. Jesus enlists people in the kingdom of God, with God and kingdom as his nodal points. But a striking feature of these traditions is that Jesus is God's special agent and those who enlist themselves in God's new work in the land of Israel must associate themselves with Jesus. This takes some real chutzpah. I have in another location called this the "egocentrism" of Jesus, but I do not mean by that any disrespect—in fact, I mean it in respect. Jesus' kingdom is undoubtedly *theocentric*, but drawing up close behind in the race of who is most important is Jesus. And, he is the one who speaks authoritatively for God's kingdom. Conversion, then, is conversion to Jesus. Religions have always had the ability to lose their way and to get off the tracks of their first principles; Christendom is not alone in jumping its tracks. At the heart of a true "Christian" faith is

Jesus and his vision for the kingdom. Unless Christian theology (and Christian practice) gets this right, it can't get its act in line with its master.[8] If one of the earliest Christian confessions is "Jesus is Lord," it only means that it follows this Jesus who announces the good news of God's gracious kingdom.

Jesus was not a rugged individualist. He called his followers into a social group. If this study has shown that conversion is a process, it has also attempted to show that conversion is defined by a group and expresses itself as a social act. The convert leaves one group to join another. The convert to Jesus is not a self-discoverer of personal religion in order to live in a congratulatory mode of personal existence for the next five generations. While modern scholarship has hesitated for a generation to say that Jesus started the church, and the terms used may well raise a caution flag for those who want to have a historical understanding, we can throw such a caution to the winds with this observation: conversion to Jesus by its nature was a social movement. That is, Jesus had an ecclesial dimension to his vision for Israel.[9] Once again, however, I am not saying that Jesus started a new religion: what Jesus was doing was creating a group of Israelites who saw things his way. That, *per definitionem*, is the beginning of what many now experience as the church. I am not claiming that "my" denomination is the result of Jesus' intention, but what I am saying is that there is an organic relationship between Jesus' call to repent, his vision for a restored Israel, and the church today—with all the loads and toads included as evidence that things don't always run according to plan. What I am claiming is that it is foolish to think Jesus was out and about in Israel, energetically preaching the kingdom of God as the climax of God's plan with Israel, but didn't expect any social manifestation. He did have a group in mind, and those who followed him composed that group. A group of followers, a church as it were.

Danger of the Conversion Experience

The danger of religious experience is that it seems to bring a desire for conformity with it but how one experiences the process need not be the same as how the next person will experience it. Our history, how we were raised, where we were nurtured, what was expected of us, what we expect of ourselves, what color we are, what sex we are, how smart we are, . . . need I go on? Each of these varies from person to person, so the experience of the process varies from person to person. What motivates one might not motivate the other. Each person has a motivation that drives, woos, or interests him or her in things religious, but, once again, it is the same process. What Paul experienced on the road to Damascus and what Augustine experienced in the garden and what Wesley experienced in the open air and what the earthy Anne Lamott experienced on the West Coast are all various ways of experiencing the same process. Each person's own history affects what dimensions of that process seem to rise to the surface. In my judgment, it is as wrong-headed to force each person to have the same experience as it is to think that every person has a different process. Humans experience conversion to God in various ways, but it is the same God whom they experience through a well-ordered but wide-open process.

And, if a danger is to want all to have "our" (read: the same) experience, it is just as wrong to identify a theological category with a specific experience. Paul experiences "repentance" with flashing lights; Leo Tolstoy senses shame over his past; John Henry Newman discovers a system that can adjudicate with order a society that is crumbling; C. S. Lewis finds meaningfulness in the "story" of Christianity; Dorothy Day hears a call to social action; while Kjerstin realizes the claim of God on her life in a series of gentle nods of the soul. Repentance takes root in more than one way. In fact, repentance is absolutely a private matter because only a person knows his or her heart. Repentance speaks of turning from the self and sin to God and his loving holiness. The point is not *how*, but *that*, one turns.

Consequences, Consequences, Consequences

How do we measure a conversion? Each of the three orientations, by definition and by the realities inherent to the process of experiencing conversion, holds up an implicit standard to measure conversion. If a bit simplistic, the following three expressions best describe what conversion means to each approach. For the socialized convert, conversion means *group membership*; for the liturgical convert, conversion means *faithful completion of the process of liturgy*; for the decision convert, conversion means *personal commitment*. And this tells us exactly what each thinks conversion is: it is becoming a church member; it is undergoing liturgy; or it is making a decision. But, we need to ask, *how did Jesus measure conversion?*

The answer to that question faces off with the fundamental focus of each of the orientations. Jesus saw conversion as consequences in behavior. Jesus did not ask any of his followers if they had been reared into his movement or Judaism; nor did he ask any if they had offered sacrifices, eaten kosher, and lived within the bounds of purity; nor did he ask any of his followers if they had made a heartfelt decision. Jesus, at a fundamental level, watched the life of those associated with him and by observation could tell if conversion was taking place. "You will know them by their fruits"—those are the words of Jesus (Matt. 7:16). It is about behavior; it is about consequences. He simply asked the rich young man to give up his money; he asked the woman caught in adultery to sin no more; he asked Peter, time and again, to follow him. And that is the point: conversion is about following Jesus. It doesn't matter *how* or *when* someone is converted; it matters only *that* they are converted or are being converted. Jesus measured conversion by behavioral standards—by love, by holiness, by righteousness, and by mercy. It is not about repeating a formula, or belonging to a church, or praying a prayer; it is about following Jesus as the shaping core of one's identity.

Back to the Orientations to Conversion

If the argument of this book is near the mark, it offers a challenge to how the orientations to conversion (see the Introduction) are to be understood. Groups shape the conversion experiences of those within their domain. When a group permits itself to fall into one orientation, and the evidence suggests this to be the lethargic norm, it shuts itself off from the fullness of human experience and from the mysterious ways of the Spirit. We know being "born from above" is the point, but we also know that such an experience is as noticeable and capturable as wind currents (John 3:8). If a group virtually demands that all its practicing members go through the same experience, whether that be a socialization process, a liturgical process, or a personal-decision process, that group shuts out of its expression of God's people those who don't have that experience. And there are many Christians who feel shut out of the worship of a particular church because of the structured uniformity of experience within that church. This robs Christians of the manifoldness of God's grace.

It is in fact sad that various churches, even whole denominations, have allied themselves with one orientation so much that other Christians do not even feel welcome. If we take a normal sampling of people, we should also get a normal spread of how individuals convert. But church structures prohibit the normal spread. Some of those who grow up in a church oriented to a socialized type of conversion may need a more traumatic decision, while some who grow up in the Christian faith within a decision orientation group might feel no need to go through some traumatic decision. Simply put: no group ought to force each of its members to convert through the same experiential process. Why? Because each orientation correlates with certain personal histories. When a church aligns itself with a single orientation, it raises the level of personal frustration, it leads to defections, and it blunts the sufficiency of God's grace.

Even more: when "force" toward one experience of conversion exhibits itself, bad things happen for all concerned. First, let me spell out some negative implications of the use of this kind of forced uniformity, and then I shall detail what I think can be the results when conversion runs its natural course for each person. When forced uniformity of conversion becomes a norm, a person's integrity, individuality, and identity are either questioned or violated. When this occurs, some persons develop what we might safely call "permanent religious adolescence." Instead of growing into maturity and spiritual identity, that person's own spiritual maturation comes to a screeching halt, full stop. To be sure, each church wants to see each person come to what it perceives to be adulthood, but in pushing uniformity onto the individual, that unconventional person may find the pushing so intolerably offensive that spiritual brakes are applied. People with this experience populate the Christian world and are sometimes unfortunately criticized severely. I could wish that each person could transcend the group force that is (almost) inevitably exercised by any and every church and find a more comfortable level of spirituality.

This spiritual adolescence about which I speak, especially when force leads to abandonment of faith, can linger into later years. Kathleen Norris is especially sensitive to this context: "In religious development, as in psychological development, we must become our own person. But denial of our inheritance doesn't work, nor does simply castigating it as 'nothing'. . . . There is a vast difference between blindly running away from old 'nothings,' and running with mature awareness toward something new."[10] Or, as Joan Didion has written, "I think we are well advised to keep on nodding terms with the people we used to be."[11] Stories abound of anger about one's religious upbringing, sometimes quite justifiable anger. Maturation can lead us beyond the anger to embrace our past, encompass it in the circle of a newfound faith, and lead us into more tranquil lives.

If some stay in the church without full maturation, others react to the expectation of uniform conversion experience with anger or rage, and others with an abortion of their own faith. Instead of churches grieving over what is occurring because of forced uniformity, far too frequently churches turn their heads and hearts away from such people. If it is the case that children who are abused and violated—emotionally, psychologically, physically, or sexually—frequently become enraged, angry, and violent, it should not surprise us that those persons who have been subjected to "religious violence" will also become enraged. More often than not these same people abort the development of faith that is occurring in their lives when the force becomes intolerable. However well-intentioned the practitioners of an orientation might be, the violated religious conscience still suffers. Surely we should recognize that, since adolescence carries with it the turbulence of metamorphosis, it requires special handling.

One of America's best-known (self-proclaimed) "apostates" is Mary McCarthy, whose life has recently been blown up into a Boswellian biography by Frances Kiernan.[12] This confident, stubborn, unpredictable, but charming, socially engaging satirist and very talented person endured— for want of a better word—a tragic childhood and adulthood, and found her only tranquillity in pointing her pen sharply at the printed page and scorching the landscape of her memories. One of her permanent achievements has to be the challenging of social roles for women. Her celebrated *Memories of a Catholic Girlhood*[13] records her anger and grapplings with her past and is wrapped up tightly in an earnest moral relentlessness. She perceived her past as a hypocritical and constricting religious authoritarianism. If ever a context shaped a (non-)faith, it is that of Mary McCarthy. She writes,

> When I left the competitive atmosphere of the parochial school [following the death of her parents], my religion withered on the stalk. [She concludes as follows:] Hence, as a lapsed Catholic, I do not trouble myself about the possibility that God may exist after all. If He exists (which seems to me more than doubtful), I am in for a bad time in the next world, but I am not going to bargain to believe in God in order to save my soul. Pascal's wager—the bet he took with himself that God existed, even though this could not be proved by reasoning—strikes me as too prudential. What had Pascal to lose by behaving as if God existed? Absolutely nothing, for there was no counter-Principle to damn him in case God didn't. For myself, I prefer not to play it so safe, and I shall never send for a priest or recite an Act of Contrition in my last moments. I do not mind if I lose my soul for all eternity. If the kind of God exists Who would damn me for not working out a deal with Him, then that is unfortunate. I should not care to spend eternity in the company of such a person.[14]

In my years of speaking in churches, discussing religious matters with people all over the United States, and corresponding with students, pastors, and readers, I have heard this same story more than I care to admit.

This is what the church must face until it learns to treat persons with the sensitivity they deserve.

Somewhere in this spectrum of what happens when a group expects religious conformity are those who "cave in" to the pressure. Some persons, more often than not between the teen and early adult years, simply can't bear the pressure, but instead of aborting their faith, they give in. What happens here? I would call this "premature religious development." If one knows this pocket of Christian experience, one knows that analogies are inevitably unable to describe the pathos experienced, but let me try. If you give a teenager a million dollars and turn him loose, he will more often than not never integrate himself maturely into an adulthood sense of economic responsibility. He may never know the human experience of studying for a profession, of yearning for an interview, of finding a job, of buying a first home, of struggling in relationships, of raising a family with its own financial ups and downs, and of experiencing the gratitude that comes later when financial burdens settle in middle age. Psychologists would claim the same for premature sexual activity, but I need not detail that here.

Similarly, in the process of spiritual transformation and development, when a young person suddenly caves in, the natural process of growth, development, and maturation aborts itself and that person suddenly becomes an adult—without the necessary growth to make that adult experience healthy. But what if kids are permitted to be kids? What if teenagers are given the freedom to experience those glorious years? And what if college students are allowed to experience the independence that comes with those years? If this is what fosters maturity at the psychosocial and intellectual levels, shouldn't those same freedoms be permitted in the spiritual development of people? In other words, humans can be expected to develop religiously through stages. Since we don't usually give kids adult responsibilities, so we should not expect spiritual teenagers to be adults in religious development. To everything there is a season. Faith develops within the psychosocial development of the person.

Conversion and Psychosocial
Development: An Amateur's Thoughts

I begin by quoting one of my favorite writers, Flannery O'Connor, mostly because her language says it better than I can: "I offer all my critical opinions on long sticks that can be jerked back at once because I really seldom know what I'm talking about but I'm willing to defend this one like a fox terrier."[15] Well, maybe not "seldom," but I do offer the following as tentative thoughts.

We can now leave this depressing story of the church's inability to see how humans develop religiously. We need to observe that the failure to integrate such an insight into the church's message of the process of conversion damages the conversion process. On the positive side of the ledger, we should note that those who are given the freedom to go through the cycle of the conversion process naturally experience a happiness and joy and health because their own religious psyche has not been violated. As we find normal adults who have been reared properly, with everything in its season, so we find healthy spiritual persons who have been permitted to experience what comes their way in its time. If their socialization into the faith was effective, these Christians find themselves spiritually and maturely participating in the family of faith; if their liturgical process was effective, they find themselves maturely worshiping with God's people; if the decision process was effective, they find themselves maturely following God's will in life. If they need socialization, they get it; if they need liturgy, they find it; if they need a decision, they are given an opportunity. Furthermore, those who grow up with freedom find a faith that is more permanent and meaningful than those whose faith is aborted or prematurely forced into adulthood. And we find that those who grow up with freedom in religious development develop an ability to integrate faith in the wholeness of a full life—it is not embarrassingly shoved into the corner of church attendance when peers challenge it, and neither is it buried into some privatized life when an opportunity for public declaration presents itself.

Social scientists have uncovered through a myriad of studies that conversion takes place in dimensions and faith can develop in stages. Psychologists like James Fowler, whose study has remained on the periphery of what I am discussing here, and others, like Stephen Happel, James J. Walter,[16] Walter Conn, and LeRoy Aden, who in differing ways correlate Erikson and Kohlberg into a meaningful synthesis,[17] have also unearthed "stages of faith." In general, Erik Erikson's stages of human development have wide approval.[18] We need not sign above the dotted line for any of the specific theories of those who integrate faith and personal development, but we may simply agree that faith develops in correlation with personal development. How would that appear? I offer a tentative sketch.

As we progress from infancy to mature adulthood, we go through crises and stages in which we actualize or don't actualize certain dimensions of life that affect our sense of identity, our maturation, and our happiness.

These dimensions of life are physical, emotional, social, psychological, and spiritual. According to Erik Erikson, the following crises occur for all of us: basic trust vs. basic mistrust (through 2 years of age), autonomy vs. shame and doubt (2–3), initiative vs. guilt (3–6), industry vs. inferiority (6–12), identity vs. role confusion (13–20), intimacy vs. isolation (21 and older), generativity vs. stagnation (35 and older), and ego integrity vs. despair (60 and older). If our psychosocial development goes through stages, so also do our cognitive (J. Piaget) and moral developments (L. Kohlberg). It is to J. W. Fowler's credit that he attempts a synthesis of these three lines of study as he integrates into them the stages of faith. It is my opinion that Fowler's own theory of pluralistic religious development ultimately guides some of his stages, but he nonetheless remains a pioneer in the study of faith development.

A few observations should make obvious the relevance of Erikson and Fowler for faith development, whether that faith takes place through socialization, a liturgical process, or a decision. Small children may well identify with their parents by expressing faith, but this faith is as much their parents' as their own. The stories of my students confirm this observation many times over. Two things are sure about the faith of a child: (1) it should never ever be discouraged or trivialized, yet (2) because it belongs to a developmental stage, that faith must further develop as the child enters adolescence and adulthood. As a child's faith ought not to be minimized, neither should it be congratulated as a complete or final expression of faith. The personal-decision orientation has a tendency of failing to recognize the development of faith in each stage of life. Flannery O'Connor, who was unafraid to pop sacred balloons, once said, "Stories of pious children tend to be false."[19]

Furthermore, those who do not develop a basic trust as small children will have an immensely difficult time trusting others later on in life—including God, with the latter expression of mistrust directly related to the former. Faith is learned at the hands of a mother and father; it is transferred in time to God. That transfer process can begin at a young age as a child exhibits and identifies with the faith of his or her parents. Faith must also go through a stage of individuation and is not in complete form until the person is an adult and mature.[20] Each of the orientations needs to meet the fact of faith development by constructing strategies for the ongoing development of faith.[21] In accordance with the general observation that faith and conversion develop, we might contend that conversion as a mature and full experience cannot happen until a person has a formed her or his identity. If conversion is about shaping the self's identity around

Jesus, then conversion doesn't maturely take place until that person has individuated—and this means the age will fluctuate from person to person. If this leads us to see the critical age for such development in conversion during adolescence and beyond, it should not lead us to obliterate the real and important development of faith in children. We need merely to put it in developmental context.

It is a particularly noticeable fact that many who go through the process of a decision conversion do so as adolescents or young adults, when they are undergoing crises connected with identity, fidelity, and roles—and this makes sense because it is the season of identity formation. Long ago, William James made this observation: "Conversion is in its essence a normal adolescent phenomenon, incidental to the passage from the child's small universe to the wider intellectual and spiritual life of maturity."[22] This stage in life deserves special treatment and unconditional respect, for "it is in adolescence that the fully formed adult self begins to emerge, and if a person has been fortunate, allowed to develop at his or her own pace, this self is a liberating force, and it is virgin . . . cognizant of oneself as valuable, unique, and undiminishable at core."[23]

I am aware that the stories of my students are particularly illustrative of conversion because of the stage of their own life development. But so aware am I of it that I feel it is unfair to minimize or trivialize it. Adolescence and young adulthood are the stages in life when humans individuate by separating from parents to shape a personal identity. This phase is noted by a delicate balance of both attachment to parents and separation from them. It is not unusual for teenagers to "rebel" against parental authority though some do so with more turmoil than others. A certain amount of friction is the healthy expression of individuation. Few have expressed this process more eloquently than Brian Doyle, an editor and writer in the Pacific Northwest:

> Like most children, I loved my parents without qualification until I was a teenager, when I began to hate them for the boundaries they placed about me; and then when I woke up from those years, at about age nineteen, I began again to love them without qualification but also with a deepening sense of the thousand ways in which they had given lives for me, to me.[24]

In the process of individuation, the adolescent-becoming-adult will often exhibit a more mature level of individual faith of which the parent may be completely unaware (who would tell their parents at this age?!). The story of Sophie presented in chapter 3 tells a particularly emotional tale of both detachment and attachment. Her feelings about her parents were at least normal and understandable.

Most importantly, what is happening in this phase is complex: faith development is cognitive, spiritual, moral, and psychosocial individuation, an assumption of religious responsibility for oneself. Each dimension of life is involved and the helter-skelter of it all is often confusing. The development of trust, autonomy, and industry in the context of shaping identity all converge to permit someone at this age to make a more mature religious commitment. This is the way God made us: we learn faith through the environment in which we are reared, and faith emerges (or doesn't emerge) in the stages we undergo. The faith commitment in the lives of many adolescents and young adults expresses loyalty and fidelity to the "symbolic universe" in which they were nurtured. But because they are individuating, their faith is absorbed freshly and individually. Sometimes they sense they are the first to find it!

I was nurtured into faith in a church environment that did not understand the complexities of the adolescent and young adult experience. I learned from that experience that forcing adolescents into religious conformity does more damage to faith development than good. Adolescents must be treated with care; it is a difficult time in human development. Faith development is all rolled up into this swirling evolution of the person. Accordingly, parents must purge from themselves their sense of "peer approval" with respect to the faith of their children, for if they do not, they will let the desire for approval in the church have too much power, and it will lead them to force their children into conformity. If an adolescent is forced into faith development before he or she is ready, that adolescent may cave in, leading to premature religious development that will never grow as it should and could, or the adolescent may rebel—and this rebellion is justified. I have seen numerous college students recover their faith when they learned that their parents meant no harm, regardless of what their motivations seemed to have been. They then see that their rebellion was really an expression of individuation, an expression of the need to be treated with respect and integrity and self-identity. They see that their rebellion was normal and healthy. When college students see that this was at the root of rebellion, they can also learn that God was not in that forceful attempt to conform. God is elsewhere—and he gives the person respect to join the circle at the proper time.

On the other hand, some adolescents and young adults will convert here as a form of compensation for the lack of development of trust, autonomy, and industry at a younger age. In other words, some conversions at this age are driven as much by what social scientists call "attachment theory," the finding in God of what is lacking in personal family relationships and personal identity. Since I believe God has made us to be relationally satisfied, I find no problem in finding compensation for our pasts as a motivating factor for conversion. (It was probably one of Zacchaeus's biggest motivations.) It also makes sense to think that some conversions at this age are motivated by the desire for intimacy and love, that is, in finding in a church what one needs in personal development. In my judgment, this too is healthy and good: God wants us to find in him and in his people a safe haven, a place of love, fellowship, and intimacy.

When midlife sets in, we find other correlations of life development and faith development. It may be that fewer conversions are found at the ages of thirty-five and older because the patterns of life have been established: people can be too happy as they are to need conversion. Or, because basic trust (or other fundamental features of life development) has fallen off the tracks, the person may be given to isolation and despair too much to be vulnerable to faith in God. It may also be that at this age the despair resulting from previous phases of development drives the person to find some form of happiness in God and in the religious community. In fact, for thirty years some scholars have maintained that midlife is a crucial time for faith development—one either moves forward or one regresses in faith.[25] James Fowler sees three crucial dimensions/stages of faith that can be involved at this age of development: synthetic-conventional (where faith is a personal absorption of one's inherited faith), individuative-reflective (where faith becomes more radically individuated), and conjunctive (where faith becomes more dialogical with the wider realities of the world). Some in midlife years do not move beyond the synthetic-conventional; others can find peace at the individuative-reflective, while fewer press on to a "faith within the cosmos." What Fowler should not do, however, is to judge the faith of others on some ideological scale of evolution.

A marvelous example of faith in midlife crises is the recent vulnerable autobiography of Parker Palmer, a well-known educator and spiritual writer. In his "confession," Palmer shows the interpenetration of spiritual yearning and personal identity formation. For Palmer, learning who he was, learning to what vocation he had been called, was the result of looking within to see what God had made him to be. It was discovering the true self—not the vain, egocentric self constructed to make a big impression in one's world. The following words aptly summarize his quest and show a proper sensitivity in handling spiritual/sacred matters with the same hands that touch on psychosocial matters:[26]

> By surviving passages of doubt and depression on the vocational journey, I have become clear about at least one thing: self-care is never a selfish act—it is simply good stewardship of the only gift I have, the gift I was put on earth to offer to others. Anytime we can listen to the true self and give it the care it requires, we do so not only for ourselves but for the many others whose lives we touch.

Palmer's spiritual and vocational quest was a discovery of the self. Conversion, though it may involve the pain of depression or the anxiety of fear, also is a self-awakening, the revival of the self God has made us to be.

These amateur remarks about the development of faith are not intended to do anything but show the interlocking nature of human development and faith development. Others may come along and fill in the picture more completely. This study is about conversion, and conversion is about the development of faith in the lives and hearts of many kinds of people. If we give proper heed to our sociological and psychological contexts today, we will find that Jesus led his followers into a conversion that was sensitive to such issues. His message about conversion was full of respect for the special integrity of each person he encountered. He called people into the kingdom of God, but each person had to hear that message, ponder it, and come to Jesus as a person with a history and a future. Conversion is complex, as each person is complex. Our theories of conversion ought to reflect this complexity, and in so reflecting it, we can become sensitive to the integrity of others and learn to appreciate each of the stories we see written on the tapestries of our neighbors.

Notes

Introduction

1. William James, America's first major scholar of the psychology of religion as well as an eccentric genius, offers the following definition: ". . . the process, gradual or sudden, by which a self hitherto divided, and consciously wrong inferior and unhappy, becomes unified and consciously right superior and happy, in consequence of its firmer hold upon religious realities" (*The Varieties of Religious Experience*; intro. R. Niebuhr; New York: Simon & Schuster [Touchstone], 1997), 160. Originally published in 1902. James admits to the limits of our knowledge of conversion through psychology (165).

2. I recommend the following for a survey of options: H. Newton Malony and S. Southard, eds., *Handbook of Religious Conversion* (Birmingham, Ala.: Religious Education Press, 1992).

3. *Speak, Memory: An Autobiography Revisited* (intro. B. Boyd; New York: Alfred A. Knopf [Everyman], 1999), 12.

4. A recent collection of stories of converts to Rome can be found in P. Madrid, ed., *Surprised by Truth: Eleven Converts Give the Biblical and Historical Reasons for Becoming Catholic* (New Berlin, Wis.: Basilica, 1995).

5. See her "Parker's Back," in *Everything That Rises Must Converge* (New York: Farrar, Straus & Giroux, 1965).

6. Joseph Epstein, *The Middle of My Tether: Familiar Essays* (New York and London: Norton, 1987), 112. Epstein, however, is speaking of a childhood so happy he had little reason to hide in some corner to read books. I echo his language proudly.

7. On this, cf. D. W. Hudson, "The Catholic View of Conversion," in H. Newton Malony and S. Southard, *Handbook of Religious Conversion*, 117–119.

8. *Collected Works* (New York: Library of America, 1988), 949 (letter on 28 August 1955 to "A.", for "Anonymous," who was later discovered to be Betty Hester). See also her letter to "A." on 30 October 1955.

9. The most widely read study is that of James Fowler, *Stages of Faith: The Psychology of Human Development and the Quest for Meaning* (San Francisco: HarperSanFrancisco, 1995); see also his *Becoming Adult, Becoming Christian: Adult Development and Christian Faith* (rev. ed.; San Francisco: Jossey-Bass, 2000). His proposal, however, occasionally becomes far too culturally and ideologically shaped. See also B. Munsey, ed., *Moral Development, Moral Education, and Kohlberg: Basic Issues in Philosophy, Psychology, Religion, and Education* (Birmingham, Ala.: Religious Education Press, 1980); L. Aden, D. G. Benner, J. H. Ellens, eds., *Christian Perspectives on Human Development* (Grand Rapids: Baker Book House, 1992).

10. Old Tappan, N.J.: Chosen Books, 1976.
11. An incisive critique of his can be seen in J. D. Hunter, *American Evangelicalism: Conservative Religion and the Quandary of Modernity* (New Brunswick, N.J.: Rutgers University Press, 1983), 73–101. Self-critique within evangelicalism can also be seen in J. F. Engel, "The Road to Conversion: The Latest Research Insights," *Evangelical Missions Quarterly* 26 (1990): 84–95.
12. See J. W. Fowler, *Stages of Faith*, 3–36.
13. C. S. Lewis, *The Letters of C. S. Lewis* (ed. W. H. Lewis; rev. by Walter Hooper; New York: Harcourt Brace Jovanovich, 1988), 446.
14. E. W. Gritsch, *Born Againism: Perspectives on a Movement* (Philadelphia: Fortress Press, 1982).
15. K. A. Olsson, *Passion* (New York: Harper & Row, 1963), 72.
16. Jim Wallis, *Faith Works: Lessons from the Life of an Activist Preacher* (New York: Random House, 2000), xxvii–xxviii.
17. "Writing as a Means of Grace," in W. Zinsser, ed., *Going on Faith: Writing as a Spiritual Quest* (rev. ed.; New York: Marlowe & Co., 1999), 127.
18. *Faith Works*, xxvii.
19. Robert Frost, *The Poetry of Robert Frost* (ed. E. C. Lathem; New York: Holt, Rinehart & Winston, 1969), "Mending Wall," 33–34 (I quote lines 32–36, 43–45).
20. Acts 9:1–19; 22:3–21; 26:1–23; from Paul's own hand: Gal. 1:11–17; 1 Cor. 9:1; 15:8–10; 2 Cor. 4:6; 5:18–10; Phil. 3:4–11.
21. For important studies on Paul's conversion, see B. R. Gaventa, *From Darkness to Light: Aspects of Conversion in the New Testament* (OBT 20; Philadelphia: Fortress Press, 1986), 17–51; A. F. Segal, *Paul the Convert: The Apostolate and Apostasy of Saul the Pharisee* (New Haven, Conn.: Yale University Press, 1990).
22. See S. A. Sharkey, "Peter's Call to Conversion," *TBT* 30 (1992): 84–89.
23. The most recent study of conversion contends precisely that Paul's conversion is a paradigm for Christian conversion, and he reduces that conversion pattern to insight (about self and Christ), turning (from and turning to), and transformation (baptism, joining the Christian movement, obedience to his calling). This pattern is then held up as the model into which the Gospel of Mark's theology of conversion must fit. The conversion of the Twelve, according to the author, is central to the purposes of Mark, and he discovers that the Twelve are not fully converted until they return to Galilee to follow Jesus. See R. V. Peace, *Conversion in the New Testament: Paul and the Twelve* (Grand Rapids: Wm. B. Eerdmans Publishing Co., 1999). In what follows I will challenge this proposal regarding the paradigmatic nature of Paul's conversion. I would ask if Peter's conversion story in Luke 5:1–11 does not contain all his elements of conversion, and if it does, what that conclusion might say for his theory.
24. On Nicodemus, see R. D. Witherup, *Conversion in the New Testament* (Zacchaeus Studies: New Testament; Collegeville, Minn.: Liturgical Press [Michael Glazier], 1994, 78–81.
25. *Conversion in the New Testament*, 106.
26. See Kathleen Norris, *Amazing Grace: A Vocabulary of Faith* (New York: Riverhead Books, 1998), 128–138; Roberta Bondi, *Memories of God: Theological Reflections on a Life* (Nashville: Abingdon Press, 1995).
27. *The Varieties of Religious Experience*, 194.
28. *The Education of Henry Adams: An Autobiography* (intro. E. Morris; New York: The

Modern Library, 1999), 34, 232. Adams concluded after his sister died a slow, painful death, that "God might be, as the Church said, a Substance, but He could not be a Person" (289). See the similar story of L. Kriegel, "Synagogues: On Being a Believing Nonbeliever," *American Scholar* 69 (2000): 61–75.

29. "The Force of Spirit," in A. Lightman, with R. Atwan, *The Best American Essays 2000* (Boston: Houghton Mifflin Co., 2000), 124.

30. The best popular study of conversion in the New Testament is R. D. Witherup, *Conversion in the New Testament*, 1994. He gently tacks fifteen theses to the door on pp. 107–110. See also B. R. Gaventa, *From Darkness to Light.*

31. For an insightful, if not always laudable, example of personal context and problems in conversion, see Nancy Mairs, *Ordinary Time: Cycles in Marriage, Faith, and Renewal* (Boston: Beacon Press, 1993). At a broader level, cf. J. Martin, ed., *How Can I Find God? The Famous and the Not-So-Famous Consider the Quintessential Question* (Liguori, Mo.: Triumph Books, 1997).

32. The literature that could be cited on this is immense; I mention only the following: P. Berger and T. Luckmann, *The Social Construction of Reality: A Treatise in the Sociology of Knowledge* (New York: Doubleday, 1989); R. N. Bellah, et al., *Habits of the Heart: Individualism and Commitment in American Life* (New York: Harper & Row, 1986); C. Lasch, *The Minimal Self: Psychic Survival in Troubled Times* (New York: W. W. Norton, 1984); for a brief examination of this problem for understanding biblical texts, cf. B. J. Malina, *The New Testament World: Insights from Cultural Anthropology* (rev. ed.; Louisville, Ky.: Westminster John Knox Press, 1993), 63–89; also, *The Social World of Jesus and the Gospels* (New York: Routledge & Kegan Paul, 1996), 35–96. If Malina, at times, overdoes the differences between ancients and moderns in self-identity, he struggles with the evidence enough to show that we need to be aware of the issues.

33. This is the point of William James's classic, *The Varieties of Religious Experience*, 160–210.

34. This is a virtue of R. D. Witherup's study, *Conversion in the New Testament*. His concluding chapter is as solid a summary of the biblical evidence as I have seen (107–113).

35. On this, see my study "The Hermeneutics of Confessing Jesus as Lord," *ExAud* 14 (1998): 1–17.

36. S. McKnight, *A Light Among the Gentiles: Jewish Missionary Activity in the Second Temple Period* (Minneapolis: Fortress Press, 1991).

37. For a survey of other theories of conversion, see L. R. Rambo, "Theories of Conversion," *Social Compass* 46 (1999): 259–271, where he examines globalization, postcolonial, feminist, crosscultural, religious/spiritual, intellectualist, narrative, identity, ritual, psychoanalytic, archetypal, attribution, attachment, and process and Islamization theories. For my first study of this evidence, cf. S. McKnight, *A New Vision for Israel: The Teaching of Jesus in National Context* (Grand Rapids: Wm. B. Eerdmans Publishing Co., 1999), 156–176.

38. For a shorter, exploratory article on conversion in the early church using an older model, that of Snow and Machalek, see N. H. Taylor, "The Social Nature of Conversion in the Early Christian World," in *Modelling Early Christianity: Social-Scientific Studies of the New Testament in its Context* (ed. P. F. Esler; New York: Routledge & Kegan Paul, 1995), 128–136.

39. *From Darkness to Light.*

40. Finn's study reveals the profound changes in our awareness of not only the ancient

world but the value of sociological study of conversion for assessing evidence about the ancient world. Thus, one may profitably compare the changes by reading the classical study of A. D. Nock, *Conversion: The Old and the New in Religion from Alexander the Great to Augustine of Hippo* (Oxford: Oxford University Press, 1933). For further study on conversion in paganism, cf. R. MacMullen, *Paganism in the Roman Empire* (New Haven, Conn.: Yale University Press, 1981), 94–112; for further study on the Christian era, cf. R. MacMullen, *Christianizing the Roman Empire, A.D. 100–400* (New Haven, Conn.: Yale University Press, 1984).

41.   See 239–257.

42.   This is most notable when Finn examines the first century, for in this portion of his book he restricts his interest to the evidence about baptism and ritual; cf. *From Death to Rebirth*, 137–146.

43.   *Collected Works* (New York: Library of America, 1988), 921 (letter to Carl Hartman, 2 March 1954).

44.   *Orthodoxy* (New York: Doubleday, 1990), 96.

45.   I point the reader to one nice textbook that seeks to explain the situation: B. Holmberg, *Sociology and the New Testament: An Appraisal* (Minneapolis: Fortress Press, 1990).

46.   This is a reprint edition of their earlier volume called *Conversions: The Christian Experience* (Grand Rapids: Wm. B. Eerdmans Publishing Co., 1983). Geza Vermes, famous scholar of the Dead Sea Scrolls, has recently written an autobiography in which he goes through perhaps two conversions, one from Judaism to Roman Catholicism, in which church he became a priest and scholar, and then from Roman Catholicism to Judaism—but the reader is given a challenge to figure out much about these conversions, muted as they are. See his *Providential Accidents: An Autobiography* (New York: Rowman & Littlefield, 1998).

Chapter 1

1.   For the names mentioned in this paragraph, see H. T. Kerr, J. M. Mulder, *Famous Conversions: The Christian Experience* (Grand Rapids: Wm. B. Eerdmans Publishing Co., 1994).

2.   C. H. Spurgeon, *The Early Years (1834–1859)* and *The Full Harvest (1860–1892)* (rev. ed.; Edinburgh: Banner of Truth Trust, 1962, 1973).

3.   J. Pollock, *Wilberforce* (London: Constable, 1977).

4.   I follow modern scholarly custom in using "the" before Galilee.

5.   For the message of the prophets, see J. A. Soggin, "*shuv*, to return," in *Theological Lexicon of the Old Testament* (ed. E. Jenni, C. Westermann; trans. M. E. Biddle; Peabody, Mass.: Hendrickson, 1997), 3.1312–1317; R. J. Sklba, "The Call to New Beginnings: A Biblical Theology of Conversion," *BTB* 11 (1981): 67–73; W. Brueggemann, *The Prophetic Imagination* (Minneapolis: Fortress Press, 1978), 44–61; see also J. S. Kselman, "The Social World of the Israelite Prophets: A Review Article," *RSR* 11 (1985): 120–129.

6.   All quotations of the Bible are from the NRSV.

7.   Literature on the prophets is beyond control; the following are two good introductions to the prophetic vocation: A. J. Heschel, *The Prophets* (2 vols.; New York: Harper & Row, 1962); W. Brueggemann, *The Prophetic Imagination* (Minneapolis: Fortress Press, 1978). For a study of scholarship, see J. Blenkinsopp, *A History of Prophecy in Israel* (rev. ed.; Louisville, Ky.: Westminster John Knox Press, 1996).

8. See E. K. Kaplan, S. H. Dresner, *Abraham Joshua Heschel: Prophetic Witness* (New Haven, Conn.: Yale University Press, 1998); and his essays collected by his daughter, Susannah: *Moral Grandeur and Spiritual Audacity: Essays* (New York: Farrar, Straus & Giroux, 1996).

9. "The Superannuated Man," in C. Lamb, *Essays of Elia and Last Essays of Elia* (London: J. M. Dent, 1929), 226–232, here 232.

10. See R. J. Sklba, "The Call to New Beginnings," 70–72.

11. So R. J. Sklba, "The Call to New Beginnings," 71.

12. Recently E. P. Sanders has contested the centrality of repentance in Jesus' mission. This is not the context for a polemical debate, but one can find important responses in B. D. Chilton, "Jesus and the Repentance of E. P. Sanders," *TynBul* 39 (1988): 1–18; D. C. Allison Jr., "Jesus and the Covenant: A Response to E. P. Sanders," *JSNT* 29 (1987): 57–78.

13. See N. T. Wright, *Jesus and the Victory of God* (Minneapolis: Fortress Press, 1996); M. Borg, *Jesus: A New Vision. Spirit, Culture, and the Life of Discipleship* (San Francisco: HarperSanFrancisco, 1988).

14. For a brief nuanced study of this petition, which in some ways differs slightly from my views below, cf. B. D. Chilton, *Jesus' Prayer and Jesus' Eucharistic: His Personal Practice of Spirituality* (Philadelphia: Trinity Press International, 1997), 41–44.

15. Cf. E. P. Sanders, "Jesus and the First Table of the Jewish Law," in *Jews and Christians Speak of Jesus* (ed. A. E. Zannoni; Minneapolis: Fortress Press, 1994), 55–73.

16. On this, cf. my *A New Vision for Israel: The Teachings of Jesus in National Context* (Grand Rapids: Wm. B. Eerdmans Publishing Co., 1999), 229–233.

17. This interpretation contrasts with the standard view that interprets the parable as speaking of the "mixed body" of the church (both Christians and non-Christians mixed together into one body, and the exhortation is to avoid distinguishing within that body). See, e.g., C. S. Keener, *A Commentary on the Gospel of Matthew* (Grand Rapids: Wm. B. Eerdmans Publishing Co., 1999), 389–390.

18. See my *A New Vision for Israel*, 200–206.

19. See my *A New Vision for Israel*, 176–196.

20. A form critic might contest this point: I am speaking here only of direct evidence for "raising children in the faith," for which there is none in the Jesus traditions. I am not suggesting, however, that the Jesus traditions were not used catechetically in the churches.

21. That the "salvation" of one (Zacchaeus) becomes the salvation of many (the household members) is found frequently in Luke–Acts (cf. 10:2; 11:14; 16:15, 31; 18:8; see also 1 Cor. 7:12–14). Such reflects the socialization nature of Jewish faith as well.

Chapter 2

1. L. R. Rambo, *Understanding Religious Conversion* (New Haven, Conn.: Yale University Press, 1993).

2. John Lofland, so noted for his own studies of conversion, blurbs Rambo's book on the back as follows: "This volume is likely the single most comprehensive compendium of the literature on conversion. It is the new 'must read' for anyone who wants to be abreast of the topic."

3. What follows modifies Professor Rambo's model, yet it remains deeply informed by his proposals. I wish also to express my gratitude to him for his continuing work, which he has, in part, shared with me.

4. G. Viswanathan, *Outside the Fold: Conversion, Modernity, and Belief* (Princeton, N.J.: Princeton University Press, 1998).

5. L. R. Rambo, *Understanding Religious Conversion*, 7 (cf. 2–7).

6. See E. V. Gallagher, "Conversion and Community in Late Antiquity," *JR* 73 (1993): 1–15, for a brief explanation of the value of the social dimension for understanding conversion in the ancient world.

7. And what can be said for "conversion" can be said of "deviance" and "apostasy"; on this see the excellent study of J. M. G. Barclay, "Deviance and Apostasy: Some Applications of Deviance Theory to First-Century Judaism and Christianity," in *Modelling Early Christianity: Social-Scientific Studies of the New Testament in Its Context* (ed. P. F. Esler; New York: Routledge & Kegan Paul, 1995), 114–127.

8. J. S. Fowler, *Stages of Faith: The Psychology of Human Development and the Quest for Meaning* (San Francisco: HarperSanFrancisco, 1981), 282 (italics his).

9. J. S. Fowler, *Becoming Adult, Becoming Christian: Adult Development and Christian Faith* (San Francisco: Jossey-Bass, 2000), 115 (italics his).

10. For other definitions, cf. William James, *The Varieties of Religious Experience: A Study in Human Nature* (New York: Modern Library, 1929), 189; A. D. Nock, *Conversion: The Old and New in Religion from Alexander the Great to Augustine of Hippo* (London: Oxford University Press, 1933), 7; S. Happel, J. J. Walter, *Conversion and Discipleship: A Christian Foundation for Ethics and Doctrine* (Philadelphia: Fortress Press, 1986), 7–25.

11. L. R. Rambo, *Understanding Religious Conversion*, 12–14. An earlier study is that of J. Lofland and N. Skonovd, "Conversion Motifs," *JSSR* 20 (1981): 373–385, where they delineate the following motifs: intellectual, mystical, experimental, affectional, revivalist, and coercive. See also B. R. Gaventa, *From Darkness to Light*, 1–16, who proposes three: alternation, conversion, and transformation. Though these categories are useful instruments for examining the impact of a conversion experience on an individual, they do not permit the kind of classification that a more complete model like that of L. R. Rambo permits because his has a more social rather than individualistic emphasis.

12. From a slightly different angle, one can compare the study of "affiliation" and "disaffiliation" with what is here described as "apostasy." See D. G. Bromley and A. Shupe, "Affiliation and Disaffiliation: A Role-Theory Interpretation of Joining and Leaving New Religious Movements," *Thought* 61 (1986): 197–211.

13. *Apologia Pro Vita Sua* (ed. W. Oddie; Rutland, Vt.: Charles E. Tuttle [Everyman's Library], 1993).

14. See P. Cushman, "The Self Besieged: Recruitment-Indoctrination Processes in Restrictive Groups," *Journal for the Theory of Social Behaviour* 16 (1986): 1–32.

15. See J. T. Duke and B. L. Johnson, "The Stages of Religious Transformation: A Study of 200 Nations," *RSR* 30 (1989): 209–224; also "Religious Transformation and Social Conditions: A Macrosociological Analysis," in *Religious Politics in Global and Comparative Perspective* (ed. W. H. Swatos, Jr.; New York: Greenwood, 1989), 75–109. These studies question standard assumptions of the impact of secularization on religious traditions. They find that social factors, most notably political ones, have a greater influence on religious changes.

16. "The Spread of Religions and Macrosocial Relations," *Sociological Analysis* 52 (1991): 37–53.

17. This notion, clearly true, requires sensitive handling: everyone converts to their own

advantage, that is, because conversion is perceived to meet some need. Since "need" is broad and narrow in scope, we should use this hypothesis carefully.

18. P. Klein, et al., *Growing Up Born Again: A Whimsical Look at the Blessings and Tribulations of Growing Up Born Again* (Old Tappan, N.J.: Fleming H. Revell, 1987).

19. *Orthodoxy* (New York: Doubleday, 1990), excerpted from 58, 60, 61.

20. C. S. Lewis, *The Letters of C. S. Lewis* (to Arthur Greeves, October 18, 1931), 288–289.

21. The same may be said of Frederick Buechner. See his "Faith and Fiction," in *Going on Faith: Writing as a Spiritual Quest* (ed. W. Zinsser; rev. ed.; New York: Marlowe, 1999), 45–64, 51: "And that's why I believe that no literary form is better adapted to the subject of faith than the form of fiction." See also N. Mairs, *Ordinary Time*, 69–72.

22. See D. B. Rutman, *American Puritanism: Faith and Practice* (Philadelphia: J. B. Lippincott, 1970), 114–120.

23. A good example, though concerned with political and social "conversion," can be seen in the brilliant American writer Mary McCarthy, "My Confession." Her observation of the major shifts in her life are apposite: "The 'great decisions'—those I can look back on pensively and say, 'That was a turning-point'—have been made without my awareness. Too late to do anything about it, I discover that I have been chosen." Later, after deserting a viewpoint, she said, "This estrangement was not marked by any definite stages; it was a matter of tiny choices. . . . I did not 'give up' these things; they departed from me, as it were, on tiptoe, seeing that my thoughts were elsewhere." See her *On the Contrary: Articles of Belief, 1946–1961* (New York: Farrar, Straus, & Cudahy, 1961), 75–105.

24. C. Ullman, "Psychological Well-Being among Converts in Traditional and Nontraditional Religious Groups," *Psychiatry* 51 (1988): 312–322; W. B. Bankston, C. J. Forsyth, and H. H. Floyd Jr., "Toward a General Model of the Process of Radical Conversion: An Interactionist Perspective on the Transformation of Self-Identity," *Qualitative Sociology* 4 (1981): 179–297.

25. *Understanding Religious Conversion*, 48–55.

26. See esp. P. H. Wiebe, *Visions of Jesus: Direct Encounters from the New Testament to Today* (New York: Oxford University Press, 1997), who sketches and evaluates "Christic apparitions" in the history of the church. For a good survey of the impact of religious experiences, cf. R. V. Peace, *Conversion in the New Testament*, 65–79.

27. This is the special thesis of Walter Conn, *Christian Conversion: A Developmental Interpretation of Autonomy and Surrender* (New York: Paulist Press, 1986); see also R. C. Fuller, *Religion and the Life Cycle* (Philadelphia: Fortress Press, 1988).

28. An alarmingly open description of a protean self can be seen in Seymour Krim, "For My Brothers and Sisters in the Failure Business," who confesses his own self-malleability throughout life. See his *What's This Cat's Story? The Best of Seymour Krim* (New York: Paragon, 1991).

29. On 29 December 1759 Samuel Johnson published a sermon-like essay in *The Idler*, no. 81, on the values of misery, one of which was that it leads to religious impulse. I quote him at length: "In childhood, while our minds are yet unoccupied, religion is impressed upon them, and the first years of almost all who have been well educated are passed in a regular discharge of the duties of piety. But as we advance forward into the crowds of life, innumerable delights solicit our inclinations, and innumerable cares distract our attention; the time of youth is passed in noisy frolics; manhood is led on from hope to hope, and from project to project; the dissoluteness of pleasure, the inebriation of

success, chain down the mind alike to the present scene, nor is it remembered how soon this mist of trifles must be scattered, and the bubbles that float upon the rivulet of life be lost for ever in the gulf of eternity. To this consideration scarce any man is awakened but by some pressing and resistless evil. The death of those from whom he derived his pleasures, or to whom he destined his possessions, some disease which shows him the vanity of all external acquisitions, or the gloom of age, which intercepts his prospects of long enjoyment, forces him to fix his hopes on another state, and when he has contended with the tempests of life till his strength fails him, he flies at last to the shelter of religion." I take this entry from Samuel Johnson, *Selected Writings* (London: Penguin, 1986), 233–234.

30. *Plain and Simple: A Woman's Journey to the Amish* (San Francisco: HarperSanFrancisco, 1989), 4.
31. A survey can be found in J. T. Richardson, "The Active vs. Passive Convert: Paradigm Conflict in Conversion/Recruitment Research," *JSSR* 24 (1985): 163–179.
32. For a discussion of Lewis's debates over excessive fantasizing and love dreaming, see G. Sayer, *Jack: C. S. Lewis and His Times* (San Francisco: Harper & Row, 1988), 123–124.
33. See C. S. Lewis, *Narrative Poems* (ed. W. Hooper; San Francisco: Harcourt Brace Jovanovich, 1979), 1–91; *Surprised by Joy: The Shape of My Early Life* (rev. ed.; San Francisco: Harcourt Brace Jovanovich, 1995).
34. *Apologia Pro Vita Sua*, 176.
35. See, e.g., M. B. McGuire, "Discovering Religious Power," *Sociological Analysis* 44 (1983): 1–10.
36. Portland, Oregon: Multnomah, 1986.
37. Brian Doyle, *Credo* (Winona, Minn.: Saint Mary's Press/Christian Brothers Publications, 1999), 29.
38. *Apologia Pro Vita Sua*; see also G. Viswanathan, *Outside the Fold*.
39. Cf. B. D. Chilton, *Rabbi Jesus: An Intimate Biography* (New York: Doubleday, 2000), xvii–xxii.

Chapter 3

1. Simone Weil, *Simone Weil Reader* (ed. G. A. Panichas; Wakefield, R.I.: Moyer Bell, 1999), 10–26.
2. *Ordinary Time: Cycles in Marriage, Faith, and Renewal* (Boston: Beacon Press, 1993), 81 (cf. also 83–91).
3. I give one example for each: T. Ladd and J. A. Mathisen, *Muscular Christianity: Evangelical Protestants and the Development of American Sport* (Grand Rapids: Baker Books, 1999), for a lucid survey of the mutual relation of sports and evangelical Christians; J. Pelikan, *Christianity and Classical Culture: The Metamorphosis of Natural Theology in the Christian Encounter with Hellenism* (New Haven, Conn.: Yale University Press, 1993); T. Beaudoin, *Virtual Faith: The Irreverent Spiritual Quest of Generation X* (San Francisco: Jossey-Bass, 1998).
4. L. R. Rambo, *Understanding Religious Conversion* (New Haven, Conn.: Yale University Press, 1993), 81, 84, calls this "volitional" and describes it as learning techniques for living. I modify here to "pragmatic."
5. Here L. R. Rambo, *Understanding Religious Conversion*, 84–85, describes how converts are attracted by a personal relationship to a charismatic leader. A fuller statement can

be found in his earlier article "Charisma and Conversion," *Pastoral Psychology* 31 (1982): 96–108. The charismatic leader can be attractive because he or she embodies the faith, is a model, is a teacher, is an affirmer, is a cause of improvement, or can be a source for public relations.

6. See L. Dawson, "Self-Affirmation, Freedom, and Rationality: Theoretically Elaborating 'Active' Conversions," *JSSR* 29 (1990): 141–163. L. R. Rambo, *Understanding Conversion*, 97–101, uses the following terms: for the advocate—tolerance, translation, assimilation, Christianization, acculturation, incorporation; for the potential convert—oscillation, scrutinization, combination, indigenization, retroversion. Each of these is explained as the dialectical strategy used by advocate and potential convert in the encounter.

7. *Apologia*, 231. See also p. 242 for the process of his decision. Newman then came to the view that he would have to work out how doctrine developed. A resolution of that issue, he concluded, would lead him to the Roman Catholic communion (see 263, 269). He had come to a resolution before finishing that work.

8. "Social Cocoons: Encapsulation and Identity Transformation Organizations," *Sociological Inquiry* 54 (1984): 260–278; see also L. R. Rambo, *Understanding Religious Conversion*, 103–108.

9. Both St. Augustine and Martin Luther frequently were alone to work through their struggles; this is self-induced encapsulation.

10. An important study on the affective nature of conversion is J. Lofland and R. Stark, "Becoming a World-Saver: A Theory of Conversion to a Deviant Perspective," *American Sociological Review* 30 (1965): 862–875; later updated by J. Lofland, "'Becoming a World-Saver' Revisited," *American Behavioral Scientist* 20 (1977): 805–819. For an influential study on utopian movements and commitment, cf. R. M. Kanter, *Commitment and Community: Communes and Utopias in Sociological Perspective* (Cambridge, Mass.: Harvard University Press, 1972).

11. On this, see the informative study of C. Ullman, *The Transformed Self: The Psychology of Religious Conversion* (New York: Plenum Press, 1989), 29–106. See also J. Allison, "Adaptive Regression and Intense Religious Experience," *Journal of Nervous and Mental Disease* 145 (1968): 452–463, who studied twenty male seminary students and discovered their conversions to be a beneficial psychological shift. His more complete analysis of one student can be found in "Religious Conversion: Regression and Progression in an Adolescent Experience," *Journal for the Scientific Study of Religion* 8 (1969): 23–28. More recently, L. A. Kirkpatrick builds on the seminal studies of John Bowlby in "An Attachment-Theory Approach to the Psychology of Religion," *International Journal for the Psychology of Religion* 2 (1992): 3–28, and uses the concept of attachment theory (the biosocial need to maintain proximity to the primary caregiver) profitably to explain compensatory aspects of conversion.

12. See esp. D. A. Snow and R. Machalek, "The Convert as Social Type," in *Sociological Theory 1983* (ed. R. Collins; San Francisco: Jossey-Bass, 1983), 259–289, who argue that converts can be distinguished socially on the basis of their rhetoric. See also their broader study, "The Sociology of Conversion," *Annual Review of Sociology* 10 (1984): 167–190. This study was strengthened by C. L. Staples and A. L. Mauss, "Conversion or Commitment? A Reassessment of the Snow and Machalek Approach to the Study of Conversion," *Journal for the Scientific Study of Religion* 26 (1987): 133–147.

13. For an application of attribution theory to religious phenomena, cf. B. Spilka, P.

Shaver, and L. A. Kirkpatrick, "A General Attribution Theory for the Psychology of Religion," *Journal for the Scientific Study of Religion* 24 (1985): 1–20. The narratives of the Old Testament are shaped by such concerns: e.g., Joshua and Judges are notable for their attributional explanations of Israel's course of history.

14. J. S. Fowler, *The Stages of Faith: The Psychology of Human Development and the Quest for Meaning* (San Francisco: HarperSanFrancisco, 1981), 4. This theme is developed insightfully in the chapter called "Faith as Imagination"; cf. 24–31.

15. See P. Berger and T. Luckmann, *The Social Construction of Reality: A Treatise in the Sociology of Knowledge* (New York: Doubleday, 1966), 147–163, here 158–163.

16. *Social Construction of Reality*, 158.

17. *Ordinary Time: Cycles in Marriage, Faith, and Renewal* (Boston: Beacon Press, 1993), 68.

18. A thorough study of rituals as part of the conversion process in the ancient world is T. M. Finn, *From Death to Rebirth: Ritual and Conversion in Antiquity* (New York: Paulist Press, 1997).

19. *Amazing Grace: A Vocabulary of Faith* (New York: Riverhead Books, 1998), 64, 65.

20. So, e.g., P. Cushman, "The Self Besieged," who examines the various features of the process. See also the insightful study of R. Ofshe and M. T. Singer, "Attacks on Peripheral versus Central Elements of Self and the Impact of Thought Reforming Techniques," *The Cultic Studies Journal* 3 (1986): 3–24.

21. See the important criticism of reductionism in conversion studies by Eileen Barker, "The Conversion of Conversion: A Sociological Anti-reductionist Perspective," in *Reductionism in Academic Disciplines* (ed. A. Peacocke; London: Society for Research into Higher Education and NFER-NELSON, 1985), 58–75, who examines false explanations of conversion to the Unification Church.

22. Jim and Brian Doyle, *Two Voices: A Father and Son Discuss Family and Faith* (Liguori, Mo.: Liguroi Publications, 1996), 67.

23. *Memories of God*, 73.

24. *Apologia Pro Vita Sua* (ed. W. Oddie; Rutland, Vt.: C. E. Tuttle [Everyman's], 1993), 239. Later, Newman speaks of the intensely personal nature of his conversion: "My own soul was my first concern, and it seemed an absurdity to my reason to be converted in partnership. I wished to go to my Lord by myself, and in my own way, or rather His way" (256).

25. Anguish and introspection have been associated especially with Puritan conversion experiences; see C. L. Cohen, *God's Caress: The Psychology of Puritan Religious Experience* (New York: Oxford University Press, 1986). A good example may be seen in David Brainerd; cf. H. T. Kerr and J. M. Mulder, *Famous Conversions: The Christian Experience* (Grand Rapids: Wm. B. Eerdmans Publishing Co., 1994), 71–80.

26. Noted long ago by William James, *The Varieties of Religious Experience* (intro. R. Niebuhr; New York: Simon & Schuster, 1997), 173–179.

27. *Understanding Religious Conversion*, 132–137.

28. C. S. Lewis, *The Letters of C. S. Lewis* (to Mrs. Ashton, July 17, 1953), 432.

29. C. S. Lewis, *The Letters of C. S. Lewis* (to Mrs. Sonia Graham, May 15, 1952), 421. Lewis advises: "This is the push to start you off on your first bicycle: you'll be left to [do] lots of dogged pedalling later on."

30. A very good study that shows how the group influences the convert's language is J. A. Beckford, "Accounting for Conversion," *British Journal of Sociology* 29 (1978): 249–262, who examines the reports of those converting to the Jehovah's Witnesses.

31. W. Zinsser, ed., *Going on Faith: Writing as a Spiritual Quest* (rev. ed.; New York: Marlowe & Co., 1999), 10.

32. J. Pelikan, "Writing as a Means of Grace," in W. Zinsser, ed., *Going on Faith*, 131. Nancy Mairs speaks for the writers of spiritual autobiography when she says, "The only way I can find out [about my life of faith] is through language, learning line by line as the words compose me" (*Ordinary Time: Cycles in Marriage, Faith, and Renewal* [Boston: Beacon Press, 1993]), 1 (cf. also 100). The entirety of Kathleen Norris's important book is constructed around coming to terms with Christian vocabulary; cf. her *Amazing Grace: A Vocabulary of Faith* (New York: Riverhead Books, 1998). Notice p. 6: "In many ways, it is my accommodation of and reconciliation with the vocabulary of Christian faith that has been the measure of my conversion, the way in which I have entered and now claim the faith as my own." At times, however, I find she treats some words as if they were a wax nose that can be readjusted to suit the face.

33. *Memories of God: Theological Reflections on a Life* (Nashville: Abingdon Press, 1995), 187.

34. See C. Ullman, *The Transformed Self*.

35. *Essays* (London: J. M. Dent, 1999), 101.

36. For a nice survey of four dimensions of conversion, cf. F. A. Eigo, ed., *The Human Experience of Conversion: Persons and Structures in Transformation* (Villanova, Pa.: Villanova University Press, 1987). Separate essays are written on cognitive, affective, moral, and religious conversion. This final essay is where Gelpi's study can be found. Gelpi contends that Jesuits need to work toward a complete integration of conversion; see his plea and personal pilgrimage in "The Converting Jesuit," *Studies in the Spirituality of Jesuits* 18 (1986): 1–38.

37. See S. McKnight, *A Light Among the Gentiles: Jewish Missionary Activity in the Second Temple Period* (Minneapolis: Fortress Press, 1991); for a different perspective, see L. H. Feldman, *Jew and Gentile in the Ancient World: Attitudes and Interactions from Alexander to Justinian* (Princeton, N.J.: Princeton University Press, 1993); for the later period, see R. MacMullen, *Christianizing the Roman Empire (A.D. 100–400)* (New Haven, Conn.: Yale University Press, 1984).

38. *Orthodoxy*, 79.

39. *Orthodoxy*, 158, 160.

40. *Memories of God: Theological Reflections on a Life* (Nashville: Abingdon Press, 1995), 76.

41. *Amazing Grace*, 251–252.

42. E.g., the words of John Henry Newman, *Apologia*, 273: "I have been in perfect peace and contentment; I have never had one doubt. . . . it was like coming into port after a rough sea; and my happiness on that score remains to this day without interruption." On Newman's reflections in the years immediately after his conversion, see the insightful study of his letters to correspondents by S. L. Jaki, *Newman's Challenge* (Grand Rapids: Wm. B. Eerdmans Publishing Co., 2000), 79–106.

43. *Orthodoxy* (New York: Doubleday, 1990), 11.

44. D. L. Gelpi, "Religious Conversion: A New Way of Being," in *The Human Experience of Conversion: Persons and Structures in Transformation* (ed. F. A. Eigo; Villanova, Pa.: Villanova University Press, 1987), 175–202.

45. G. Viswanathan, *Outside the Fold*, xvi. Italics added.

46. In Jerald C. Brauer's study "Conversion: From Puritanism to Revivalism," *JR* 58 (1978): 227–243, one also explores the sociopolitical and ecclesiastical roles of conversion. See also J. A. Beckford, "The Restoration of 'Power' to the Sociology of Religion,"

Sociological Analysis 44 (1983): 11–32, which explores the return of power to how sociologists understand religion. This study suggests a similar sociopolitical dimension to conversion (though Beckford's study is broader than sociopolitical power).

47.   To understand Newman fully, one needs to read his book over the shoulder: *Apologia Pro Vita Sua*; see also the definitive biography of Ian Ker, *John Henry Newman: A Biography* (New York: Oxford University Press, 1988).

48.   G. Viswanathan, *Outside the Fold*, 44.

49.   Newman on one occasion described the negative side of conversion as follows: "The stars of this lower heaven were one by one going out" (*Apologia*, 155).

50.   Newman constantly threw pointed darts at liberalism; see the important appendix, "Note on Liberalism (1865)," in *Apologia Pro Vita Sua*, 385–395. When speaking of John Keble, a leading voice in the Tractarian movement, Newman utters words eerily like his own approach: "What he [Keble] hated instinctively was heresy, insubordination, resistance to things established, claims of independence, disloyalty, innovation, a critical, censorious spirit" (389). Newman's bedrock need for authority shaped his conversion to Roman Catholicism; the theme is found on nearly every page of his *Apologia Pro Vita Sua* (e.g., 109).

51.   G. Viswanathan, *Outside the Fold*, 48.

52.   Viswanathan, *Outside the Fold*, 50 (italics mine). The rest of the chapter fundamentally explicates this statement, though the concepts of belief and state-versus-nation are developed further.

53.   *Apologia Pro Vita Sua*, 271.

Chapter 4

1.   In using the Gospels' information, I am not claiming that every detail can be authenticated for discussions about the "historical Jesus." Instead, we are concerned here with the information about conversion as reported in the church's Gospels.

2.   Suggestive examples of the value of social-scientific approaches can be found in J. H. Neyrey, ed., *The Social World of Luke–Acts: Models for Interpretation* (Peabody, Mass.: Hendrickson, 1991).

3.   *From Death to Rebirth: Ritual and Conversion in Antiquity* (New York: Paulist Press, 1997), 108 (italics added).

4.   David Wells uses the term "insider" to describe Jewish conversions to Jesus; he offers some sensitive and sane remarks about conversion in his study of the biblical view of conversion. Cf. *Turning to God: Biblical Conversion in the Modern World* (Exeter: Paternoster, 1989), 27–47.

5.   Judas presents a negative example of conversion: (1) he sins; (2) he comes to his senses and "repents" (cf. Matt. 27:3–10); but (3) he fails to come to terms with either God's gracious forgiveness or his sense of being forgiven. A recent study attempts to revive the reputation of Judas by revising the tradition history about Jesus; see W. Klassen, *Judas: Betrayer or Friend of Jesus?* (Minneapolis: Fortress Press, 1996). See the review of R. E. Brown in *JBL* 117 (1998): 134–136. More satisfactory is R. D. Witherup, *Conversion in the New Testament* (Zacchaeus Studies; Collegeville, Minn.: Liturgical Press [Michael Glazier], 1994), 40–42.

6.   Mark 6:3: each is named after a patriarch. "James" is "Jacob/Yakov"; "Joses" is "Joseph/Yosef"; "Judas" is "Judah/Yudah"; and "Simon" is "Simeon/Shimeon."

7.   On the Twelve, cf. S. McKnight, "Jesus and the Twelve," *BBR* (2001): forthcoming.

8. For an introduction, see J. M. Ford, "BTB Readers Guide: Bookshelf on Prostitution," *BTB* 23 (1993): 128–134.

9. See Tal Ilan, *Jewish Women in Greco-Roman Palestine* (Peabody, Mass.: Hendrickson, 1996), 216–220; see also C. S. Keener, "Adultery, Divorce," in *Dictionary of New Testament Background* (ed. C. A. Evans and S. E. Porter; Downers Grove, Ill.: InterVarsity Press, 2000), 11–12 (on prostitution in the ancient Mediterranean basin). For a survey of the evidence in ancient Israel, see I. N. Raskow's study *Taboo or Not Taboo: Sexuality and Family in the Hebrew Bible* (Minneapolis: Fortress Press, 2000), 27–30.

10. See here K. E. Corley, *Private Women, Public Meals: Social Conflict in the Synoptic Tradition* (Peabody, Mass.: Hendrickson, 1993).

11. See here J. D. G. Dunn, "Pharisees, Sinners, and Jesus," in *Jesus, Paul, and the Law: Studies in Mark and Galatians* (Louisville, Ky.: Westminster John Knox Press, 1990), 61–88. For example, Pharisees might call the followers of Jesus "sinners," Sadducees might call the Pharisees "sinners," and the Essenes might call the Sadducees "sinners"—and not mean by that anything but "you violate the Torah as we interpret it." In other words, "sinners" might not be the "wicked."

12. See E. P. Sanders, *Judaism: Practice and Belief, 63 BCE– 66 CE* (Philadelphia: Trinity Press International, 1992), 280–289. Luke's "called 'zealot'" could mean either "was zealous" or "was a Zealot." The concrete evidence for the party "Zealots," however, relates to a period more than thirty years later.

13. On "Godfearers," see pp. 172–73.

14. See, for example, the fine study of C. D. Gartrell and Z. K. Shannon, "Contacts, Cognitions, and Conversion: A Rational Choice Approach," *RRelRes* 27 (1985): 32–48.

15. On the Galilee, cf. the raging discussion among G. Vermes, *Jesus the Jew: An Historian's Reading of the Gospels* (London: Collins, 1973), 42–57; S. Freyne, *Galilee from Alexander the Great to Hadrian 323 B.C.E. to 135 C.E.: A Study of Second Temple Judaism* (Edinburgh: T. & T. Clark, 1998); R. A. Horsley, *Galilee: History, Politics, People* (Valley Forge, Pa.: Trinity Press International, 1995); *Archaeology, History, and Society in Galilee: The Social Context of Jesus and the Rabbis* (Valley Forge, Pa.: Trinity Press International, 1996).

16. Scholarship debates the ethnic makeup of the Galilee, but it seems most likely that the villagers were mostly Jewish. Gentiles lived in places like Sepphoris, Tiberias, and the Decapolis. In places like these one also finds more urbanization and Hellenization.

17. R. A. Horsley, *Archaeology, History, and Society in Galilee*, 178.

18. *Jesus the Jew*, 57.

19. For a re-creation of a family's worship in Jerusalem, with some *élan*, see E. P. Sanders, *Judaism: Practice and Belief 63 BCE–66 CE* (Philadelphia: Trinity Press International, 1992), 112–116. For a more imaginative but historically justifiable re-creation (except the decision to give Jesus older brothers), see P. Fredriksen, *Jesus of Nazareth, King of the Jews* (New York: A. Knopf, 1999), 42–50.

20. A recent, wide-ranging study of the history of the movement can be found in M. O. Wise, *The First Messiah: Investigating the Savior Before Jesus* (San Francisco: Harper-SanFrancisco, 1999).

21. Scholars differ on the percent Jews paid for taxes. E. P. Sanders estimates only 15.2 percent while others as much as 30 percent. See his *Judaism: Practice and Belief*, 146–169.

22. For a nice study, see E. M. Meyers, E. Netzer, and C. L. Meyers, *Sepphoris* (Winona Lake, Ind.: Eisenbrauns, 1992).

23. For my attempt, see *A New Vision for Israel: The Teachings of Jesus in National Context* (Grand Rapids: Wm. B. Eerdmans Publishing Co., 1999), 70–155.

24. This insight is at the bottom of J. Riches's book *Jesus and the Transformation of Judaism* (London: DLT, 1980).

25. The crisis brought on by a protean selfhood is a peculiarly modern phenomenon and will play no part in our discussion.

26. See here the balanced studies of J. P. Meier, *A Marginal Jew: Rethinking the Historical Jesus* (Anchor Bible Reference Library; New York: Doubleday, 1994), 2.773–837; G. H. Twelftree, *Jesus the Miracle Worker: A Historical and Theological Study* (Downers Grove, Ill.: InterVarsity Press, 1999), 304–310.

27. The "protean selfhood" describes a modern human complex, so we have left it out. I suggest it is possible that some ancients followed Jesus because they had a highly adaptable "self."

28. The most important study of Jesus from a psychological angle is that of J. W. Miller, *Jesus at Thirty: A Psychological and Historical Portrait* (Minneapolis: Fortress Press, 1997), which contains a very helpful survey of scholarship (103–119).

29. For discussions here, cf. B. Chilton, *Jesus' Baptism and Jesus' Healing: His Personal Practice of Spirituality* (Harrisburg, Pa.: Trinity Press International, 1998), 58–97; at a more technical level, see S. McKnight, "A Parting within the Way: Jesus and James on Israel and Purity," in B. Chilton and C. A. Evans, *James the Just and Christian Origins* (SupplNovTest XCVIII; Leiden: E. J. Brill, 1999), 83–129.

30. For a scholarly defense of this view, see S. Mason, *Flavius Josephus on the Pharisees: A Composition-Critical Study* (StPB 39; Leiden: E. J. Brill, 1991), 342–356.

31. For more, see my *A New Vision for Israel*, 70–155; for a more intense study, see D. C. Allison, *Jesus of Nazareth: Millenarian Prophet* (Minneapolis: Fortress Press, 1998); in broader context, see B. Witherington III, *Jesus the Seer: The Progress of Prophecy* (Peabody, Mass.: Hendrickson, 1999).

32. *The Social Construction of Reality: A Treatise in the Sociology of Knowledge* (New York: Doubleday, 1966).

33. See McKnight, *A New Vision for Israel*, 179–187. For the broader discussion, cf. H. Moxnes, ed., *Constructing Early Christian Families: Family as Social Reality and Metaphor* (New York: Routledge & Kegan Paul, 1997); C. Osiek and D. L. Balch, *Families in the New Testament World: Households and House Churches* (The Family, Religion, and Culture; Louisville, Ky.: Westminster John Knox Press, 1997).

34. Subtitled *Spirit, Culture, and the Life of Discipleship* (San Francisco: Harper & Row, 1988).

Chapter 5

1. Actually, when scholars contend Jesus was unlike rabbis in that he initiated the call, all they are saying is (1) Jesus is not a rabbi, and (2) usually, Jesus is better than Jewish rabbis. However, if Jesus is not a rabbi but a prophet-like figure, he would differ in that prophets are given to calling people to follow their message and themselves. Thus, what the statement of many says is more accurately this: Jesus calls people like prophets while rabbis teach students who come to them. Both are acting appropriate to their calling. Comparisons, then, are useless, or silly, or both.

2. See S. McKnight, "Jesus and Prophetic Actions," *BBR* 10 (2000): 197–232.

3. For instance, N. T. Wright, *Jesus and the Victory of God* (Minneapolis: Fortress Press,

1996); S. McKnight, *A New Vision for Israel* (Grand Rapids: Wm. B. Eerdmans Publishing Co., 1999); B. Witherington III, *Jesus the Seer: The Progress of Prophecy* (Peabody, Mass.: Hendrickson, 1999).

4. W. Brueggemann, *The Prophetic Imagination* (Philadelphia: Fortress Press, 1978), 82.
5. See S. McKnight, *A New Vision for Israel*, 197–237.
6. See R. Bauckham, "James and the Jerusalem Church," in *The Book of Acts in Its Palestinian Setting* (The Book of Acts in Its First Century Setting 4; ed. R. Bauckham; Grand Rapids: Wm. B. Eerdmans Publishing Co., 1995), 415–480, here 452–462.
7. See S. McKnight, "Jesus and the Twelve," *BBR* 11 (2001): forthcoming.
8. Brian Doyle, *Credo* (Winona, Minn.: Saint Mary's Press/Christian Brothers Publications, 1999), 47.
9. *A New Vision for Israel*, 233. I borrow in this section from 233–236.
10. The term "must" (*dei*) has an important place in Luke's Gospel; including dinner with Zacchaeus lifts the event from the norm. Cf. 2:49; 4:43; 9:22; 13:33; 17:25; 18:1; 21:9; 22:37; 24:7, 26, 44.
11. On this passage see esp. J. B. Green, *The Gospel of Luke* (New International Commentary on the New Testament; Grand Rapids: Wm. B. Eerdmans Publishing Co., 1997), 666–673.
12. We may never know just exactly what the ruler asked. Mark has "Good Teacher, what must I do to inherit eternal life?" (10:17); Matthew: "Teacher, what good deed must I do to have eternal life?" (19:16). Matthew's use of "good" with "deed" appears to be his own redactional reworking.
13. G. Viswanathan, *Outside the Fold: Conversion, Modernity, and Belief* (Princeton, N.J.: Princeton University Press, 1998).
14. For an example from Plutarch's life of Cicero: "When Crassus was about to set out for Syria, wishing that Cicero should be a friend rather than an enemy, he said to him in a friendly manner that he wished to dine with him; and Cicero readily received him into his house" (*Cicero* 26.1).
15. A convenient summary can be seen in *Jesus' Prayer and Jesus' Eucharist: His Personal Practice of Spirituality* (Valley Forge, Pa.: Trinity Press International, 1997), 52–58.
16. *The Social Construction of Reality: A Treatise in the Sociology of Knowledge* (New York: Doubleday, 1966); I use their terms from 129–183.
17. Ground-breaking application of P. Berger and T. Luckmann can be found in the technical studies of P. F. Esler, *Community and Gospel in Luke–Acts: The Social and Political Motivation of Lucan Theology* (SNTSMS 57; Cambridge: Cambridge University Press, 1987); J. A. Overman, *Matthew's Gospel and Formative Judaism: The Social World of the Matthean Community* (Minneapolis: Fortress Press, 1990).
18. I discuss the kingdom teaching of Jesus more completely on pp. 130–31.
19. See C. Brown, "What Was John the Baptist Doing?" *BBR* 7 (1997): 37–50; S. McKnight, "Jesus' New Vision within Judaism," in *Who Was Jesus? A Jewish-Christian Dialogue* (ed. P. Copan and C. A. Evans; Louisville, Ky.: Westminster John Knox Press, 2001), 73–76.
20. *Understanding Religious Conversion* (New Haven, Conn.: Yale University Press, 1993), 120.
21. The same role is given to 70/72 others in the Q tradition; cf. Luke 10:1–16.
22. *A New Vision for Israel*, 166–176.
23. On this, cf. T. M. Finn, *From Death to Rebirth: Ritual and Conversion in Antiquity* (New York: Paulist Press, 1997).

24.   I analyzed this under the category of "internal repentance" and the cost of "self-denial" in *A New Vision for Israel*, 194–196.

25.   *Jesus* (trans. J. R. Lord; ed. J. Reumann; Philadelphia: Fortress Press, 1973), 61.

26.   *A New Vision for Israel*, 194.

27.   B. J. Malina, *The Social World of Jesus and the Gospels* (New York: Routledge & Kegan Paul, 1996), 67–96.

28.   See C. L. Staples and A. L. Mauss, "Conversion or Commitment? A Reassessment of the Snow and Machalek Approach to the Study of Conversion," *JSSR* 26 (1987): 133–147.

29.   *Outside the Fold: Conversion, Modernity, and Belief* (Princeton, N.J.: Princeton University Press, 1998).

30.   See the helpful survey of conversion from a social angle in H. C. Kee, *Christian Origins in Sociological Perspective* (Philadelphia: Westminster Press, 1980), 74–98.

31.   For the text, cf. J. Reynolds and R. F. Tannenbaum, *Jews and Godfearers at Aphrodisias: Greek Inscriptions with Commentary* (Cambridge: Cambridge Philosophical Society, 1987).

32.   Cf. S. McKnight, *A Light Among the Gentiles: Jewish Missionary Activity in the Second Temple Period* (Minneapolis: Fortress Press, 1991), 110–13.

33.   This is a complex discussion. I recommend the following as places to begin: B. D. Chilton, *A Galilean Rabbi and His Bible: Jesus' Use of the Interpreted Scripture of His Time* (Good New Studies 8; Wilmington, Del.: Michael Glazier, 1984); C. A. Evans, "Old Testament in the Gospels," in *Dictionary of Jesus and the Gospels* (ed. J. B. Green, S. McKnight, and I. H. Marshall; Downers Grove, Ill.: InterVarsity Press, 1992), 579–590; C. H. Dodd, *According to Scriptures: The Sub-Structure of New Testament Theology* (London: James Nisbet, 1952).

34.   The most important book on Jesus as a religious person is M. Borg, *Jesus: A New Vision. Spirit, Culture, and the Life of Discipleship* (San Francisco: Harper & Row, 1987).

Conclusion

1.   *The Catholic Church and Conversion* (New York: Macmillan & Co., 1950), 30.

2.   "An Only Child," in *A Frank O'Connor Reader* (ed. M. Steinman; Syracuse, N.Y.: Syracuse University Press, 1994), 282.

3.   *Understanding Religious Conversion* (New Haven, Conn.: Yale University Press, 1993), 1–19.

4.   This was also the conclusion of Thomas M. Finn, *From Death to Rebirth: Ritual and Conversion in Antiquity* (New York: Paulist Press, 1997); cf. esp. 239–260.

5.   *New Testament Theology: The Proclamation of Jesus* (trans. J. Bowden; New York: Charles Scribner's Sons, 1971), 230.

6.   For an important modern statement of the inherent corporate dimension of the Christian faith, cf. R. Bellah, et al., *Habits of the Heart: Individualism and Commitment in American Life* (Berkeley: University of California Press, 1985); for the relationship of individualism and conversion, see D. L. Gelpi, "Conversion: Beyond the Impasses of Individualism," in *Beyond Individualism* (ed. D. L. Gelpi; South Bend, Ind.: University of Notre Dame Press, 1987), 1–30, who begins with Jonathan Edwards.

7.   *Amazing Grace: A Vocabulary of Faith* (New York: Riverhead Books, 1998), 42.

8.   For an example, see Brian Doyle's journey with Jesus in his essay "The Gaunt Man," in Jim and Brian Doyle, *Two Voices: A Father and Son Discuss Family and Faith* (Liguori,

Mo.: Liguori Publications, 1996), 128–130.

9. An older study repays reading: R. N. Flew, *Jesus and His Church: A Study of the Idea of the Ecclesia in the New Testament* (2d ed.; London: Epworth Press, 1943).

10. *Amazing Grace*, 82, 83.

11. *Slouching towards Bethlehem* (New York: Farrar, Straus, & Giroux, 1999), 139.

12. *Seeing Mary Plain: A Life of Mary McCarthy* (New York: W. W. Norton & Co., 2000).

13. New York: Harcourt, Brace, & Co., 1957.

14. *Memories of a Catholic Girlhood*, 19, 27 (the entire chapter is in italics as a prefatory note to the reader). Her painful death, endured with characteristic stoical fortitude, is recorded in F. Kiernan, *Seeing Mary Plain*, 704–742. She apparently kept her promise to the end, though she did write, in "A Believing Atheist," *Vassar Views* (November 1992), ". . . when I die I hope that some kindly Protestant pastor will say last rites over me even though I am outside his Church. At least I am baptized, which will help [. . .] I do not believe in God or an afterlife or in the divinity of Christ. . . ." She also said that through various sources she had "regained bit by bit the underlying Christian doctrine which I accept today as being part of me, whether I like it or not." See F. Kiernan, *Seeing Mary Plain*, 735, 52. Pages 51–52 record what others thought of Mary's faith. For Mary's own account of an early denial of faith, cf. *Memories of a Catholic Girlhood*, 111–126.

15. *Collected Works* (New York: Library of America, 1988), 913 (letter to Robie Macauley, 13 October 1953).

16. See their study *Conversion and Discipleship: A Christian Foundation for Ethics and Doctrine* (Philadelphia: Fortress Press, 1986), 53–82.

17. Walter Conn, *Christian Conversion: A Developmental Interpretation of Autonomy and Surrender* (New York: Paulist Press, 1986); L. Aden, "Faith and the Developmental Cycle," in *Christian Perspectives on Human Development* (ed. L. Aden, D. G. Benner, and J. H. Ellens; Grand Rapids: Baker Book House, 1992), 19–33.

18. See E. H. Erikson, *Childhood and Society* (New York: W. W. Norton, 1985).

19. See her essay "Introduction to A Memoir of Mary Ann," *Collected Works* (New York: Library of America, 1988), 822.

20. See Kathleen Norris, *Amazing Grace*, 24–25.

21. For a brief study, see W. Conn, "Adult Conversions," *Pastoral Psychology* 34 (1986): 225–236.

22. William James, *The Varieties of Religious Experience* (intro. R. Niebuhr; New York: Simon & Schuster, 1997), 167.

23. Kathleen Norris, *Amazing Grace*, 75.

24. Jim Doyle and Brian Doyle, *Two Voices*, xiv. Their book illustrates the point I am making. Here we find a father's faith and love being passed on to his son who, in adjusted form, passes the faith on to his three children.

25. This view is especially articulated by Seward Hiltner, "Toward a Theology of Conversion in the Light of Psychology," *Pastoral Psychology* 17 (1966): 35–42.

26. Parker Palmer, *Let Your Life Speak: Listening for the Voice of Vocation* (San Francisco: Jossey-Bass, 2000), 30–31.

Index of Ancient Sources

Index of Subjects